HOW TO MAKE MOVIES WITH YOUR HOME VIDEO CAMERA

First published in 1986 in Canada by B. Mitchell
Canadian edition ISBN 0-999-92209-2

A TEMPLAR BOOK

Devised and produced by Templar Publishing Ltd
Old King's Head Court, Dorking, Surrey, England

Library of Congress Cataloging-in-Publication Data

Dollin, Stuart.
        How to make movies with your home video camera.

        1. Video tape recorders and recording—Amateurs'
manuals.   2. Television—Production and direction—
Amateurs' manuals.   3. Home video systems—Amateurs'
manuals.   I. Title.
TK9961.D65   1986   778.59'9   86-12287
ISBN 0-399-51283-7

Editor: Nicholas Bellenberg
Designer: Mike Jolley
Illustrator: Trevor Wooldridge, The Design Shop
Production: Sandra Bennigsen
Typesetting: Templar Type
Origination: Anglia Reproductions Ltd, Witham, Essex, England
Printed and bound in Italy by Motta, Milan

2 3 4 5 6 7 8 9 10

THE HOME
VIDEO
DIRECTOR'S
HANDBOOK

BY STUART DOLLIN

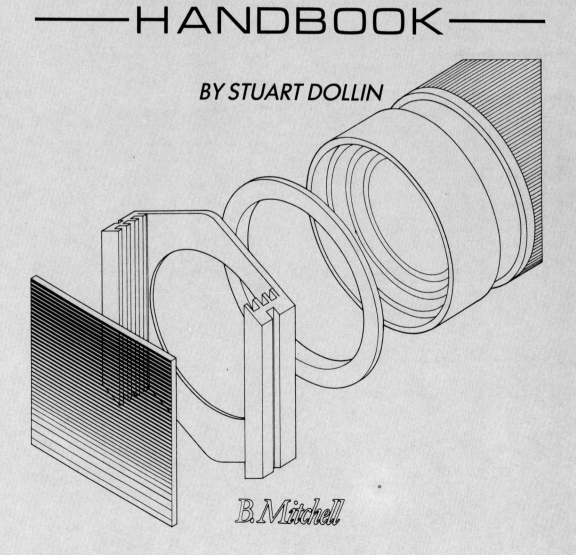

B. Mitchell

CONTENTS

INTRODUCTION

THE RISE OF TELEVISION

No one person can be credited with the invention of TV because many different discoveries came together to make it possible. The story probably started in 1873 when two scientists, Louis May and Willoughby Smith, discovered the **photoelectric effect** – the ability of certain materials to convert light energy into electrical energy. Electricity could, of course, be sent over long distances by wire, and so the idea of sending pictures over long distances – **television** – was born.

In 1880 two Englishmen, Ayrton and Perry, devised a system called **electric vision**. With this an image could be focused on an array of photocells which would each produce an electrical signal, the strength of the signal depending on the strength of the light falling on the photocell. Each of these photocells would be individually connected to a lamp in a similar array which would then glow with a brightness corresponding to the strength of the electrical current produced by its corresponding photocell. The system didn't work, however, simply because the photocells couldn't produce enough power to light the lamps.

In 1884 German scientist Paul Nipkow devised the technique called **scanning**. This allowed you to send all the information required to build up a picture down just one pair of wires. In Nipkow's system the image was focused onto a revolving perforated disc. The holes were arranged so that each one passed across the image a little lower than the previous one. The effect was to allow light from the object to pass through to the photocell as a series of strips across the object. In this way a signal, not too dissimilar to a modern TV signal, came out of the photocell. At the other end, a lamp was connected to the output of the photocell, and this was viewed through a similar spinnning disc. Because the two discs were identical, and were spinning at identical speeds, an image of the original object could be built up. As both discs were spinning very fast, the eye appeared to see the whole picture, and not just a series of lines. In fact, if the human eye and brain did not react in this way – if **persistence of vision**, as it is called, did not exist – even modern television and cinema would not be possible. In the end Nipkow's system didn't work for the same reason as Ayrton and Perry's electric vision – the photocell simply didn't produce enough current to light the lamp sufficiently.

It took the early 20th-century invention of amplifying valves and the ingenuity of John Logie Baird to make Nipkow's mechanical ideas work in practice. But by now the writing was on the wall. Mechanical systems were very limited in their scope for development and a new system based on electron beams looked much more promising. Electrons are electrically charged particles which, in a **cathode ray tube**, are emitted from a cathode (negatively charged plate). Cathode rays had been discovered as long ago as 1878 but the significant breakthrough came in 1923 when Russian scientist Vladimir Zworykin invented a special cathode ray tube for use in a camera. Here the image was focused onto a sensitive plate. This was scanned by an

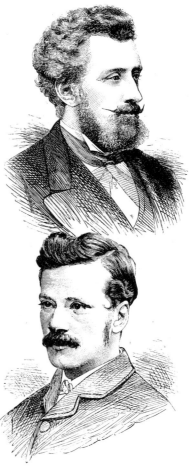
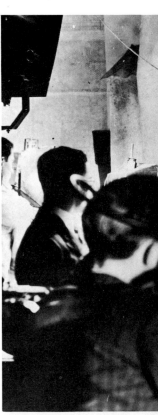
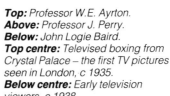
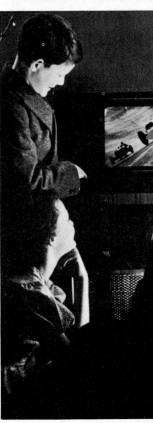

Top: Professor W.E. Ayrton.
Above: Professor J. Perry.
Below: John Logie Baird.
Top centre: Televised boxing from Crystal Palace – the first TV pictures seen in London, c 1935.
Below centre: Early television viewers, c 1938.

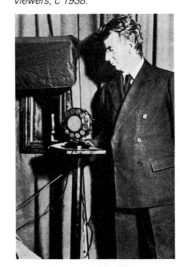

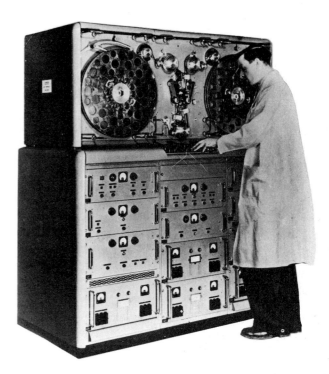

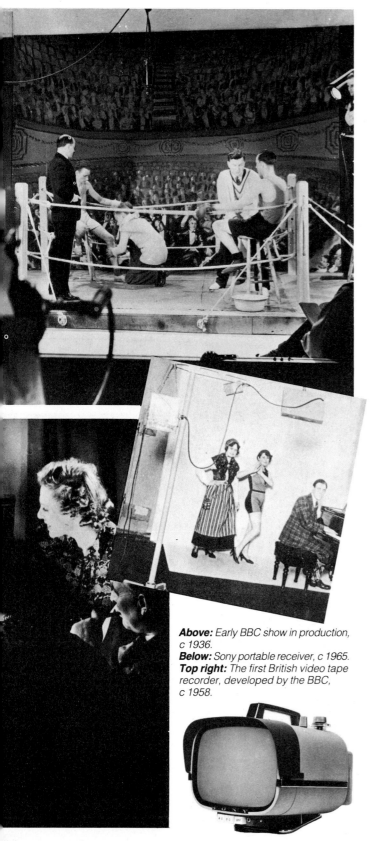

Above: Early BBC show in production, c 1936.
Below: Sony portable receiver, c 1965.
Top right: The first British video tape recorder, developed by the BBC, c 1958.

electron beam and a varying electrical signal came out the other end. There were no moving parts to wear out and there was great scope for further development. Zworykin's other development was the cathode ray picture tube, on which the camera tube's output could be displayed.

Although the British Broadcasting Corporation (BBC) experimented with the mechanical Baird system, they soon chose an electronic system for regular broadcasts and these started in 1936, just in time to capture the coronation of King George VI. TV broadcasting started in the USA in 1939 but both services were suspended during the war.

During this period and particularly after the war, work was pushing ahead to develop a color TV system. The US started the first regular color service in 1951. There were technical drawbacks associated with the NTSC system adopted in the US, and the UK and West Germany opted for the PAL system when they began color broadcasting. Although this took longer to develop, it is regarded by many as technically superior. Regular color broadcasts started in the UK in 1967.

Other postwar developments included the development and widespread use of satellites for long-distance transmissions. The very first transatlantic satellite link via Telstar was quite an occasion. Nowadays we take for granted the fact that we can see live TV pictures from anywhere in the world.

Video recorders are another recent invention. Until the early 60s virtually all television programs were live or made on film. There was no way of recording live broadcast material except by pointing a film camera at the screen and actually filming it, which was expensive and not particularly satisfactory in terms of picture quality when rebroadcast. In the 1950s both Ampex (audio tape recorder manufacturers) in the USA and the

BBC in the UK were keen to develop a workable video recorder. The invention of the helical scan concept (mounting the heads on a revolving head drum to drastically increase head-to-tape speed, see page 28) made broadcast and, later on, domestic video recorders possible. The first viable professional video recorder was demonstrated by Ampex in 1956, and the machine quickly became a broadcast standard. The Dutch company Philips launched the first domestic video recorder in 1971. Japan, however, came to take over the market with the Beta format (launched in 1974) and later the VHS format (launched in 1976) which has now become the world leader.

Video discs followed in the early 80s and with the latest format, 8mm video, it is hoped that at last the world will be able to use a single compatible video tape format, in the same way that we have one audio cassette format.

How TV works

The whole idea of television is that visual images – pictures – are converted into electrical signals, which are then turned into radio waves and transmitted over the air. These radio waves are picked up by the TV receiver and reconverted into electrical signals which are then displayed as images by the TV's picture tube. The accompanying sound is processed in a similar way.

Right: *The first home video cassette recorder, launched by Philips in 1971.*
Below: *The latest in TV and home video technology, from Sony.*

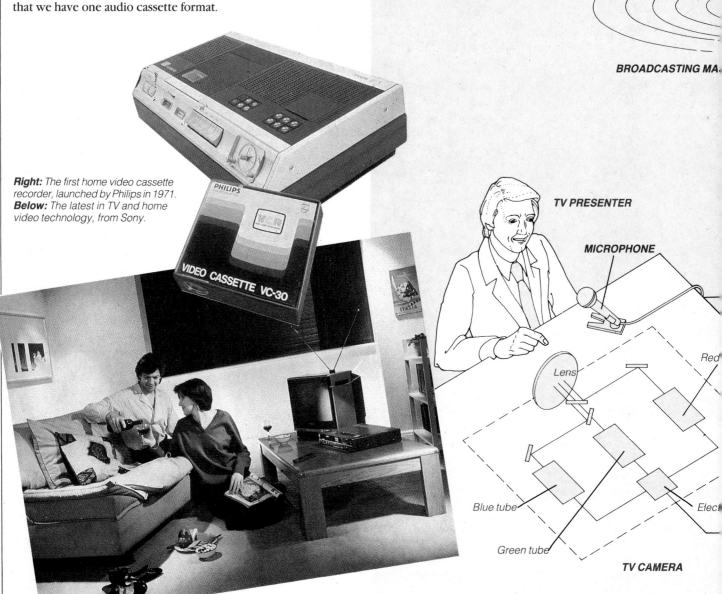

PHILIPS

VCR

VIDEO CASSETTE VC-30

BROADCASTING MA

TV PRESENTER

MICROPHONE

Lens

Red

Blue tube

Elec

Green tube

TV CAMERA

But how does this all work in practice? We shan't go into all the technicalities of television transmission here, but a simple explanation will help in understanding the basics of TV and video.

If we assume that a TV program is being broadcast 'live', then the first link in the picture chain is the camera in the studio. The image that the camera 'sees' is focused on its pick-up tube, the surface of which is light sensitive. This light-sensitive surface is scanned by a cathode ray 60 times a second, to give as output an electrical signal. This, in turn, is used to make up two interlocking field scans – one made up of the odd numbered lines, and the other of the even numbered lines. These two field scans are used to reduce picture flicker as much as possible. In the US the television picture is made up of 525 lines of information altogether. That gives 30 full picture 'frames' of information per second.

Picture constituents

In color television, the image on which the camera is focused is split up into its primary constituents – blue, green and red – which, depending on the system in use, may or may not have their own separate pick-up tubes. In order to convey all the picture information about a color scene successfully, the camera actually has to give as output a signal which contains brightness (**luminance**), hue (**chrominance**) and **synchronization** information.

The luminance information tells whatever receives this video signal how bright the scene would be if viewed as a simple black and white picture. The chrominance signal contains the color information – breaking the scene down into the three primary colors, red, blue and green – while the synchronization parts of the combined signal tell the equipment when each scanned line begins and when each field scan starts. All of this video signal information is combined with the sound, which has been processed separately. It is then all modulated with a radio frequency signal and broadcast.

The TV set

At the other end of the chain is your television aerial. This picks up the broadcast signal and feeds it to your TV set. Inside the television, the video and sound signals are unscrambled from the radio frequency 'carrier' signal. The sound is processed and sent as output to the loudspeaker, while the video information is used to drive the cathode ray picture tube. In the cathode ray tube are three electron guns – one each for the three color signals (red, blue and green). The output from these (cathode rays) is varied according to the chrominance and luminance information and guided across the screen in interlacing field scans by circuitry that is controlled by the broadcast synchronization signals. Each color's cathode ray beam hits a particular type of phosphor dot on the front of the TV screen. These phosphor dots are arranged in patterns of three – one for each color. When they are hit by the cathode rays they glow, the brightness of the glow being controlled by the strength of the cathode ray hitting them. The end result of this instantaneous process is, of course, the color picture taken by the camera live in the television studio hundreds of miles away.

Video recording

Sometimes – quite frequently in fact – the signals from the TV camera are recorded onto a video recorder rather than going directly to the transmitter. When the appropriate time comes, these signals are replayed from the recorder and broadcast to be turned back into pictures by the TV set. Your home video recorder does exactly the same job.

RECEIVING AERIAL

ELECTRONICS

LOUDSPEAKER

Red, green and blue cathode ray tubes

Scanning pattern

ELECTRONICS

TV SCREEN

Red

Blue   Green

PHOSPHOR DOTS

EQUIPMENT

THE CAMERA

The obvious starting point in video film-making is the camera. Despite the 'high-tech' appearance of some sophisticated models, the video camera is fundamentally a very simple machine. This is particularly true for modern cameras, as most of the setting up procedures – focusing, setting the light, and so on – have now been automated. The video camera is made up of two distinct elements – the **optics** and the **electronics**.

The **optics** section of the camera collects the light from the scene being photographed and focuses it into a clear image – just like any camera does. The **electronics** turn that image into electrical signals which can be recorded onto magnetic tape.

We have to use a **lens** to focus the light, and virtually all video cameras use a **zoom** lens. This enables you to record many shots – from a wide panoramic view to a tight close-up – without having to change the lens. The light passes through an **iris** – a hole that automatically alters in size to ensure that the brightness of the image is correct. In other words, it makes sure the picture is not over- or underexposed. Some cameras offer a manual iris override for special effects. Bringing the picture into sharp focus can either be done manually or, as in the more sophisticated cameras, automatically. The final image is projected onto the camera pick-up tube. This is where the **electronics** start.

The pick-up tube is the **interface** (transition point) between the optics and the electronics. It is the video equivalent of the film in a still or cine camera, and turns the image into electrical signals. Instead of using different types of film for different lighting conditions – indoors and outdoors – the electronics adjust the picture accordingly, making sure that colors are recorded accurately.

Like any other camera, a video camera has a **viewfinder**. In this case it is usually a miniature black and white TV screen with colored lights or other indicators at its sides to relay additional information. Occasionally optical viewfinders are used. These allow you to see what the camera lens is seeing – like an SLR camera does – but cannot let you replay and view your recordings as with the electronic type.

Video cameras are also fitted with a **microphone** (mic) to record sound. This may be built-in, hand-held or mounted on a telescopic **boom**.

All the electrical signals which go to and from the camera are carried on a multi-way cable to the recorder. The signals are video (pictures) and audio (sound) from the camera; video and audio back from the recorder (if the camera has an electronic viewfinder); remote stop/start (so you can stop and start the recorder from the camera); and power.

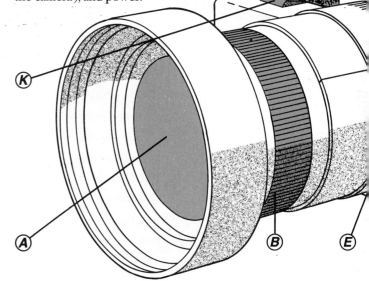

(A) The lens: A complex array of specially shaped pieces of glass focuses light from the scene being photographed into a sharp image. Usually the lens is a zoom lens which allows selection of a wide variety of shots, from wide-angle to close-up.

(B) Focusing ring: The focusing ring is the ribbed part of the lens barrel which is turned to bring the image into focus. In many cameras this is automated.

(C) Auto-focus pick-up: The focus setting of a lens depends on the distance between the lens and the subject. An **auto-focus** mechanism works by transmitting an infra-red beam which is reflected by the subject. The camera measures the time the infra-red signal takes to return and calculates how far away the subject is. The focusing ring is then adjusted by an electric motor.

(D) Auto-focus one-shot button and on/off switch: Sometimes auto-focus mechanisms do not work particularly well. Then you can put the camera in **manual focus** mode. Pressing the 'one-shot' button causes the camera to focus on one particular part of the scene, and that focus setting is locked.

(E) Manual zoom lever: This allows you to change the focal length of the lens and so move from close-up to wide-angle or vice versa. The process of moving from one focal length to another is called **zooming**.

(F) Iris control: The **iris** is the device that controls the amount of light passing from the lens onto the image pick-up tube. In virtually all video cameras this is automatic. Some cameras have a manual override which is usually used only in difficult lighting conditions or for special effects.

(G) Backlight and sensitivity switches: A subject in front of a brightly lit background presents a difficult exposure situation. The automatic system sets the camera's sensitivity for the background so the subject will be in silhouette. The backlight control compensates for this by opening up the aperture above the optimum setting. The extra sensitivity settings are for low light conditions.

(H) Automatic white balance button: Different forms of light can make the color white appear to be either blue or yellow. To compensate·for this, the camera's electronics can be adjusted by selecting the appropriate **filter**, pointing the camera at a white object and pressing the **auto white balance** button.

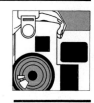

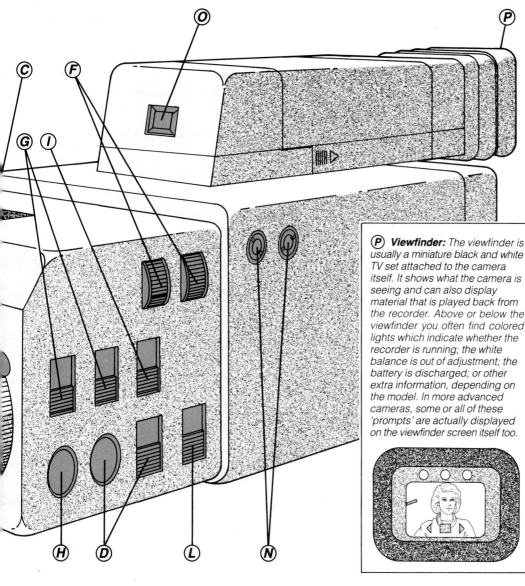

Connectors and cables

Multi-way: This cable carries the video and audio signals in and out of the camera, the DC power supply, and remote control lines. Not all cameras and their multi-way cables and connectors are compatible with all portable recorders.

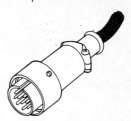

Earphone: Usually this plugs into a 3.5mm jack socket. The earphone allows you to hear what the microphone picks up – very useful when recording in difficult conditions.

Microphone: Again, usually a 3.5mm jack socket. This allows you to use a different microphone from the one fitted to the camera – very useful if you want to get the microphone close to the subject.

(P) Viewfinder: *The viewfinder is usually a miniature black and white TV set attached to the camera itself. It shows what the camera is seeing and can also display material that is played back from the recorder. Above or below the viewfinder you often find colored lights which indicate whether the recorder is running; the white balance is out of adjustment; the battery is discharged; or other extra information, depending on the model. In more advanced cameras, some or all of these 'prompts' are actually displayed on the viewfinder screen itself too.*

TYPICAL HOME VIDEO CAMERA SHOWING MAIN OPERATING FEATURES

(I) Filter setting: *This usually has two positions – daylight or indoor light. The filter is used in conjunction with the white balance system to match the camera's electronics to the light source used.*

(J) Remote stop/start button: *This is simply a trigger or thumb-operated switch which stops and starts the recorder when connected to the camera.*

(K) Power zoom button: *Virtually all video cameras have a motorized zoom lens. To go from close-up to telephoto and vice versa you press a button and an electric motor changes the focal length of the lens smoothly and evenly. Occasionally cameras have a facility to alter the rate of zoom.*

(L) On/off/standby switch: *On/off is straightforward enough. The standby position reduces power consumption. The pick-up tube is like an old-fashioned radio valve – it needs time to warm up. Switching from off to on means waiting several seconds for this to happen. The solution is to have a standby position which keeps the tube warm for instant pictures but shuts off all the rest of the electronics to conserve power.*

(M) Microphone: *This picks up the sound from the scene being recorded. It may be a very simple device that can pick up sound from all around the camera or it may be directional, picking up sound from within a narrow band. In some cases microphones can be interchanged according to the application.*

(N) Microphone and earphone sockets: *These external sockets allow you to connect up an alternative mic. The earphone socket allows the user to connect up an earphone and listen to what is actually being recorded.*

(O) Tally light: *A lamp on the front of the camera tells the subject that the recorder is running and that the camera is 'live'.*

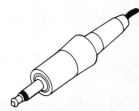

Power: The power connection can be made in a wide variety of configurations. Basically it allows you to power up the camera independently of the recorder – for example from an AC power supply, a battery or a car battery.

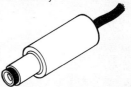

THE LENS – WHY HAVE ONE?

Focal length

When parallel rays of light pass through a lens they are bent and meet (focus) at a point some distance behind the lens. This is called the **focal point**.

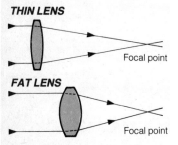

THIN LENS

Focal point

FAT LENS

Focal point

The distance between it and the lens is called the **focal length**. In a video camera, the focal point has to be the face of the pick-up tube. A fat lens has a short focal length, a thin one a longer focal length. In practice, light rays become parallel when they come from an object more than about 30 feet away from the lens, so objects more than this distance away are always going to be in focus. When you get closer, the lens has to be moved nearer to the screen to keep the object in focus. There is also a minimum focal distance, inside which you cannot focus at all.

Focal length is also related to the area of the scene that is registered on the screen – called the **field of view**. Generally the shorter the focal length, the wider the field of view. Video cameras only have one lens, but because you can change its focal length (by zooming) you can change the field of view. Both fixed and zoom lenses are usually described by their focal length. A 28mm lens is a wide-angle, 135mm a telephoto, a 50mm more or less normal (in SLR camera terms) and a 10–60mm is a zoom that goes from 10mm wide angle to 60mm close-up.

Before a video camera can begin to record a scene in front of it, it has to turn that scene into an image on the front of the pick-up tube. It does this with the help of a lens.

Light can be thought of as an infinite number of rays which either emanate or are reflected from every point of an object. Because they travel in all directions they will not form a coherent image without something to 'coordinate' them. This is exactly what the lens does.

When light passes into glass (or any other transparent medium), it is bent or refracted. You can see this effect for yourself simply by putting a pencil into a glass of water. It will appear to bend at the point at which it enters the water because light rays bouncing from it

are refracted differently by the liquid. The amount by which the light is bent in a lens depends on the angle at which the light hits the surface of the glass. Because a lens is curved, some light rays are bent more than others and can be brought together to form an image.

In practical terms, a simple lens has many drawbacks. White light is built up of a spectrum of colors and a single lens bends each component color by a slightly different amount. The resulting image will have red and blue fringes around each object. The answer to this problem is to assemble several single lenses to make these defects cancel each other out. This is called a **compound lens** and is a basic component of every video camera.

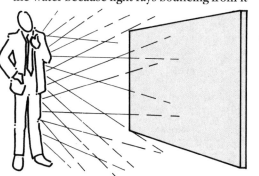

Without a lens: *Rays of light are reflected in all directions from every point on the object. No image is formed on the screen because all the rays overlap, cross over and are randomly organized.*

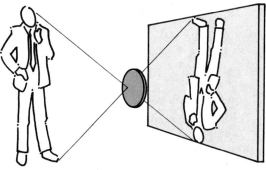

With a lens: *Only light rays traveling in the same direction from each point on the object are allowed to reach the screen. The lens focuses the light rays.*

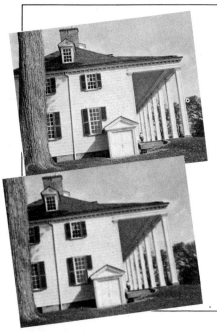

Focusing

To give a sharp and clear image, the rays of light coming from the object must converge (focus) at a point on the image pick-up tube behind the lens. Focusing involves moving the lens backwards and forwards until the rays of light do indeed converge. It is usually pretty easy to see when an object is in focus in your video camera, and setting focus involves no more than twisting the lens focus ring until the image is clear and sharp in the viewfinder. Some cameras have an auto-focus system to do this for you.

You can expect to have to refocus if you change the scene you are viewing – just as you have to refocus a still camera for different pictures. You also have to expect to refocus if you change the focal length of the lens – if you zoom in and out of an object. But if you focus the lens at the maximum focal length for the scene you want to shoot and then zoom out to a smaller focal length, the object will remain in focus. You still have to adjust the focus if you move the camera position, and this is where auto-focus becomes particularly useful.

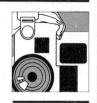

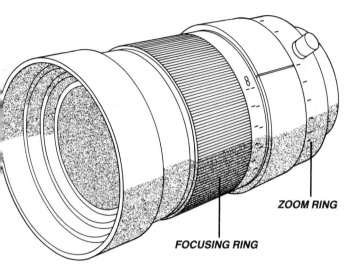

ZOOM RING

FOCUSING RING

THE ZOOM LENS

Virtually all video cameras are fitted with a zoom lens, which allows you to shoot a wide variety of different shots without having to change lenses. The lens is described by its minimum and maximum focal lengths and often as a ratio between those numbers. A typical description might be 12–72mm lens, 6X or 6:1 zoom ratio.

The focal length can be changed manually by twisting the zoom ring. Marked around the outside of the zoom ring will be a set of numbers that indicate the lens' setting. Most video cameras have a **power zoom** system. This is an electric motor which twists the ring at an even, steady rate.

Another ring is used to focus the lens. This is usually calibrated in both feet and meters and indicates how far away the object should be to remain in focus. There may also be a depth of field scale which tells you the range of distances at which objects will be in focus at different apertures.

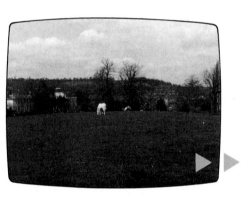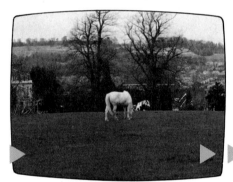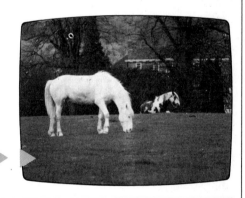

Focusing a zoom lens

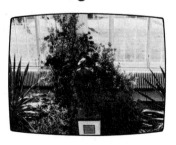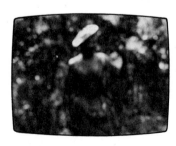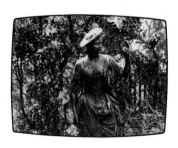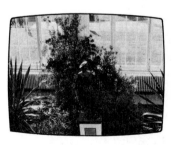

1 This is the scene you want to shoot. Think about how much you are going to zoom in (increase focal length) and zoom out, and decide on the maximum zoom point.

2 Zoom into that object – it will, no doubt, go out of focus.

3 Bring it back into focus. Any vertical lines in the object should make it easy to see when you've achieved the best focus. If your camera has auto-focus, it may be as well to turn it off if the object is a significant distance away.

4 Zoom back to your original scene and check the focus again. This is known as the **back focus**. All parts of the shot between the wide-angle and the maximum zoom will now stay in focus.

APERTURE AND EXPOSURE

The lens' aperture refers to the size of the hole in the iris through which the light passes. This varies according to the brightness of the scene being photographed. The brighter the light, the smaller the aperture. This happens automatically to match the brightness to the image pick-up tube's range of sensitivity. Light entering the camera can vary infinitely in brightness but the pick-up tube will only give proper results within a small range of light intensity. Sometimes a manual override is provided, although this is rarely calibrated.

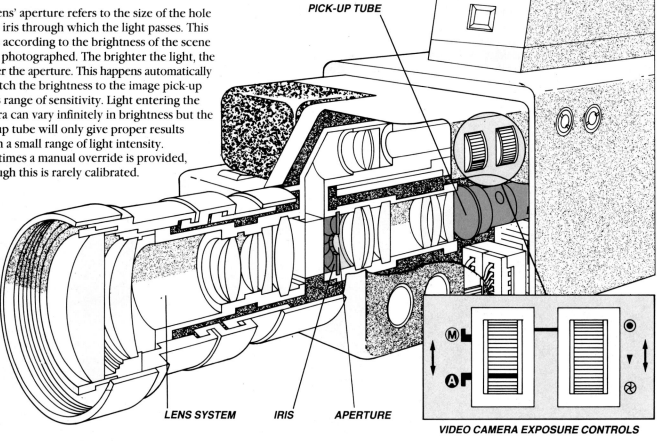

PICK-UP TUBE

LENS SYSTEM   **IRIS**   **APERTURE**

VIDEO CAMERA EXPOSURE CONTROLS

Getting it right

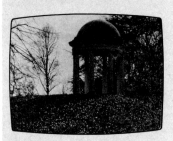

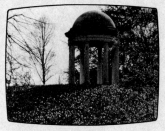

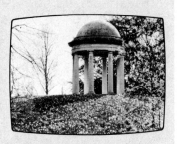

Inset drawing above, shows the video camera exposure controls in detail. The control on the left switches exposure between automatic and manual operation. When in manual mode, the control on the right is used to vary the aperture according to the user's needs.

Underexposed: *The scene is too dark. Light objects are nearly as dark as the dark ones and there is little contrast overall. Colors will be very murky with a great tendency to muddy green and brown. Bright reds and blues are completely lost.*

Correctly exposed: *The correct balance of light and shade. The colors will be as close to natural as the technology allows. Contrast is clear without fuzziness.*

Overexposed: *This scene is completely bleached out. Highlights are completely white with color fringing (known as solarization) while the dark areas are very dark. Intermediate tones have disappeared and the contrast is heightened.*

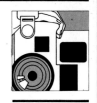

APERTURE AND DEPTH OF FIELD

Apart from governing the amount of light reaching the pick-up tube, the aperture also affects the amount of the image that is actually in focus. Imagine you've focused the camera on a subject 15 feet away. There will be a range of distances that are in focus in front and behind that object. At one aperture setting it may be that objects 3 feet in front and behind the object will remain in focus, but at another setting the focus range could be as little as 1 foot either way. This range is known as **depth of field**. Generally speaking the smaller the aperture, the greater the depth of field.

Unless you want to use a limited depth of field for a visual effect, the general rule is to light your subject as brightly as possible so that the aperture closes right down – thus giving you the maximum depth of field. **This is especially important at the top (telephoto) end of the lens' focal length range, where focusing becomes extremely crucial.**

Macro

This refers to a lens facility which allows focusing a very small distance from the lens – typically as small as 5mm. Without macro, the usual minimum distance at which objects can be focused is around 18 inches. With proper lighting, macro allows objects to be recorded in extreme close-up and can be very useful for shooting illustrations, insects and other small objects.

Pulling out a small button on the top of the zoom lever usually puts the camera into macro mode. Once in macro mode, focusing is achieved by moving the zoom control or simply by varying the distance between subject and camera. Cameras without this facility can take extreme close-ups by using an extra screw-on lens.

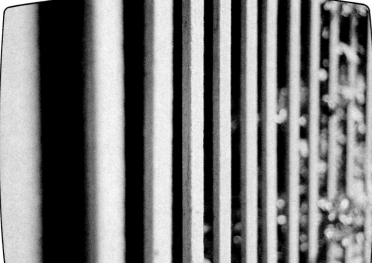

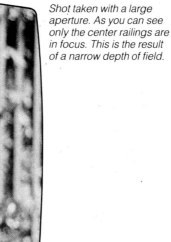

Shot taken with a large aperture. As you can see only the center railings are in focus. This is the result of a narrow depth of field.

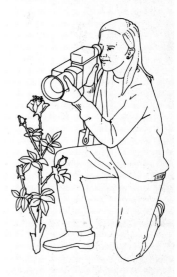

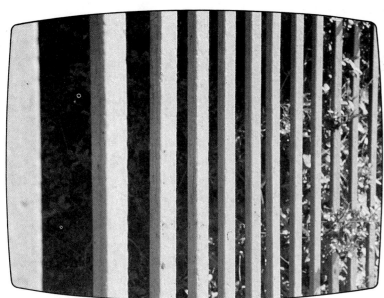

Shot taken with a small aperture, giving an increased depth of field. Railings in foreground and background are now much sharper.

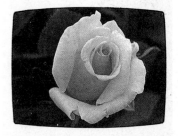

The CCD

The biggest drawback of the camera tube centers around the fact that it is a form of radio valve or vacuum tube. As such, it is relatively heavy, fragile, consumes a large amount of power and takes time to warm up. Recent developments in photo-electronics have led to a solid state image device – the CCD (Charge Coupled Device) which is used in more and more modern video cameras. These CCDs consist of an array of photo-electric devices arranged in rows on an integrated circuit (IC). They are connected in threes – to take care of the three primary colors – and each individual device is connected to a switching circuit which generates the same type of output that you get from a conventional pick-up tube.

The CCD's advantages of low power consumption, instant switch on and light weight are immediately obvious. Others such as lack of image lag and better low light performance are only just becoming apparent.

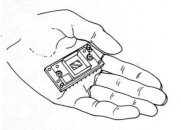

INSIDE THE CAMERA

The main function of a video camera is to convert a pattern of light – the image – into an electrical signal that can be recorded onto magnetic tape. The various features of the optical system allow you to select the image, but the electronics enable the recording process to take place.

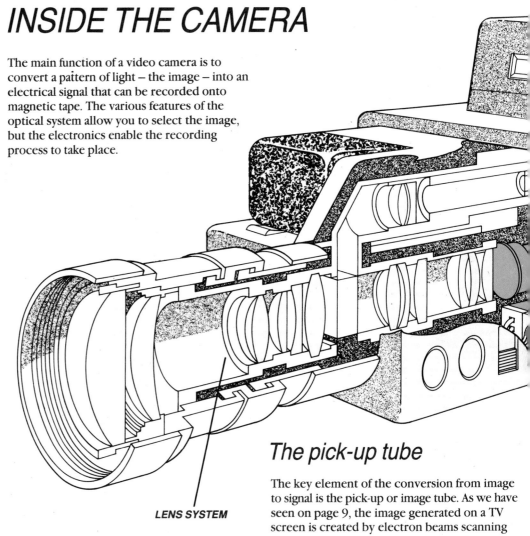

LENS SYSTEM

The pick-up tube

The key element of the conversion from image to signal is the pick-up or image tube. As we have seen on page 9, the image generated on a TV screen is created by electron beams scanning

As we have seen on page 9

Light and electronics

The important thing to remember about the electronics of video, is that the camera is only a device that converts light into electrical signals – in the same way that a microphone is a device which turns sound into electrical signals. So terms like **noise**, when applied to video, mean unwanted signal or interference. Similarly a very bright source of light becomes a very large signal and a dim light, a small one.

The more brightly lit the object you are shooting, the

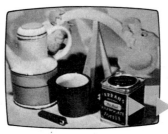

better results you get. Your 'wanted' signal is many times bigger than the 'unwanted' or **noise** signal. (Noise in picture terms looks like the 'snow' you can see on a badly tuned TV

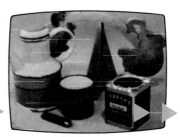

picture.) As the illumination gets dimmer, the camera's electronics increase in sensitivity to make the best of the reduced picture signal. Unfortunately this gives a

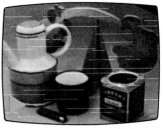

noisier picture and the color quality also suffers. This sequence of photographs shows how the video camera's picture deteriorates with diminishing light.

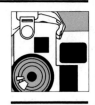

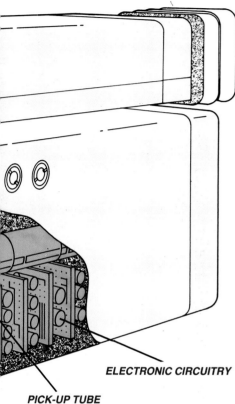

ELECTRONIC CIRCUITRY

PICK-UP TUBE

SINGLE TUBE CAMERA SYSTEM

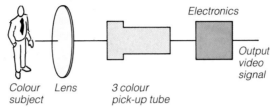

Electronics

Output video signal

Colour subject | Lens | 3 colour pick-up tube

THREE TUBE CAMERA SYSTEM

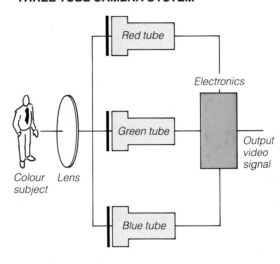

Red tube

Electronics

Green tube

Output video signal

Colour subject | Lens

Blue tube

Understanding specifications *video cameras*

Horizontal resolution: *This is measured in lines shot from a special test pattern. It allows the user to judge the sharpness of the picture. A good figure for a domestic camera would be 350 lines – an average one, 300. A broadcast quality camera would give around 600 lines resolution.*

Video signal-to-noise ratio: *A signal-to-noise (s/n) ratio tells you how much bigger the wanted signal is in relation to the unwanted or noise signal. This is measured in decibels (dB) and the higher the figure the better. A good domestic camera will have a video s/n figure of 45dB, a broadcast quality camera around 55dB.*

Minimum illumination: *This tells you the minimum light level needed for acceptable pictures and is measured in lux. As an indication, bright candlelight is about 15 lux, a conventionally lit living room around 50 lux and daylight starts at 1000 lux.*

Audio signal-to-noise ratio: *The problems for sound are hum and hiss. The higher the audio s/n figure, the better the camera. Low performance here is usually down to the relatively poor quality microphones fitted to many video cameras.*

Power consumption: *Like all things electrical, a video camera consumes electrical power which is measured in watts (W). The bigger the camera, the more power it consumes.*

across the back of the TV's glass screen which is coated with phosphors that glow when the beam strikes them. The patterns of light and dark that make up the image are recreated on screen by varying the beam strength. Colors are created from the three primaries of light – red, blue and green – by using three electron beams to strike phosphors which emit these primary colors.

The image being photographed – which is usually of varying light intensity over its area – is focused on the pick-up tube's screen. This screen is made of glass, coated with a photoconductive substance. This enables it to conduct electricity in varying degrees, according to the level of light it is exposed to. When a picture image is focused on the end of the tube, the screen's ability to conduct electricity (called its resistance) will vary over its surface, according to the areas of light, dark and intermediate shades that make up the image.

To reproduce that image, the photoconductive screen's resistance at all the points of the image has to be measured and recorded, and this is where the electron beam comes in. The electron beam in the camera tube scans over the photoconductive screen in just the same way as the beam in a TV receiver's picture tube.

When the electrons meet the photoconductive screen they complete an electrical circuit. The strength of the electrical signal is determined by the resistance of the screen at that point, which in turn is determined by the level of light falling upon it, and the circuitry ensures that the output of the pick-up tube can be re-synchronized to make up the picture. So, very simply, we can begin to understand the basic principle behind the creation of a video picture.

Dealing with color complicates this simple explanation. The simplest but most expensive method is to use three pick-up tubes, one for each primary color. The incoming image is split up into the three primary colors by splitting the image into three identical beams which are passed through colored filters before reaching three identical pick-up tubes.

Single tube color cameras use a tube coating of three different materials, each sensitive to one of the three primaries. So the electron beam is able to pick up a pattern of primary color responses – red, blue, green; red, blue green; etc. The composite output video signal containing the brightness (called luminance) and color (known as chrominance) information is then fed into the rest of the camera electronics (see page 9).

Recorder remote control

It is becoming increasingly widespread to duplicate the video recorder controls on the camera. When used with a compatible recorder it is possible to control some or all of the functions entirely from the camera – including picture search, freeze frame, as well as stop and start.

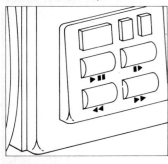

THE CHARACTER GENERATOR

Character generators are now found on more and more video cameras – either as an 'add-on' box, as shown here, or as an integral part of the camera. They are essentially small computers which store the alphabet numbers and some symbols as electronic graphics. These can be called up on the screen in various combinations, sizes and colors – the variation depending on the model.

They can even be superimposed over the scene itself while the camera is recording, and quite complex title sequences can be constructed. Most generators also contain a built-in calendar (which will display day, month and year) and a stop-watch function. These too can be superimposed over live action.

Unfortunately, you cannot use the generator to superimpose titles at a later stage in recording, although some add-on units do allow this.

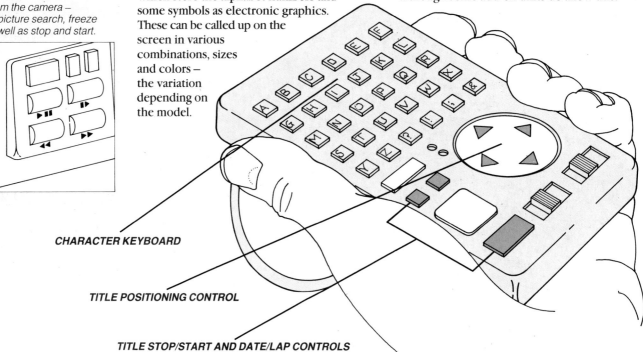

CHARACTER KEYBOARD

TITLE POSITIONING CONTROL

TITLE STOP/START AND DATE/LAP CONTROLS

Automatic fade in and out

Without proper professional editing equipment it has previously been almost impossible to fade video images in or out to black or white. However, some cameras now have a fade out/fade in feature that will do just this as shots are recorded. Use is simple – you just select the facility, start the shot running and at the right time press the fade button which will fade the scene out to black before stopping the recorder. The opposite can also be achieved. By selecting the facility before shooting, pressing the start button will bring the scene up from black instead of abruptly starting the recorder. The audio system may also be linked to this fade in/out system and may fade up and down in sympathy. This is useful for titles and specific shots that might close a section in a film.

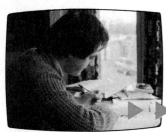 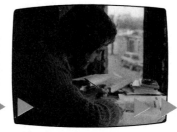 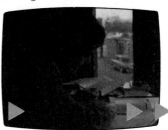 

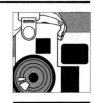

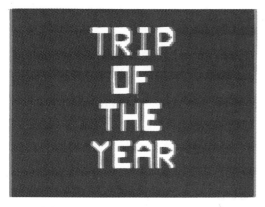

This is an example of a typical title put at the start of a video production. It's big, can be moved to any part of the screen and would usually be shown in any one of up to seven colors:

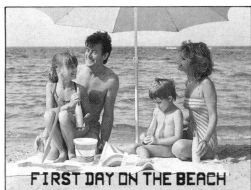

Another title, this time a quarter of the size. This is more manageable for subsidiary titles or even little reminders. These can even be used for a cast list, perhaps superimposed over a picture of the cast member.

Image reversal

This is a typical picture taken with a video camera. It uses a full range of tones.

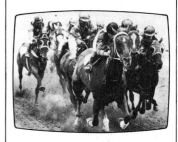

This picture is a negative image of the one above. It was produced by simply flicking over the image reversal switch that is a feature of some cameras.

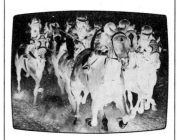

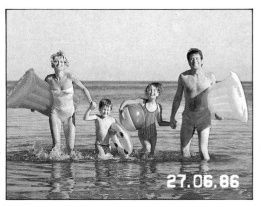

This time it's the date. Most cameras will have dates for up to 20 years stored in the memory.

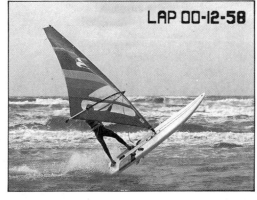

The stop-watch function. This is accurate up to a tenth of a second and can be useful for adding information and a sense of drama to sporting events.

This image is a negative picture like a photograph negative. The facility is very useful for seeing what color prints will look like from negatives, and for special effects.

  The quality of the image, however, depends on illumination. If it is necessary to turn a black on white image into a white on black one, beware. Unless the white is really white it won't reverse out as black, but as a dark grey. The quality of color images that are reversed in this way can also be adversely affected by insufficient illumination.

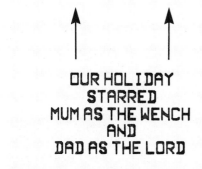

Scrolling titles from the top or bottom of the screen gives a useful moving effect.

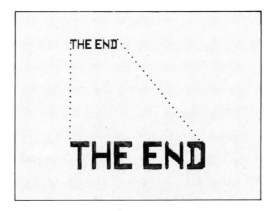

Zooming titles in and out, either from the corner or the centre of the screen, adds another dynamic effect to your capabilities. Next time you watch a film or TV programme, study the way the title sequences are made.

THE RECORDER

FEATURES

Although there are certain differences between the various models of video recorders, they all share a great many things in common. A portable recorder will record video signals either from a camera or another video source (such as another video recorder) via its direct audio and video connections. It runs from batteries which are also used to power the camera. Running the recorder from an AC supply involves using either a compact power adaptor (which slips ino the recorder's battery compartment), or a separate tuner/timer or battery charger power unit.

Like AC machines, portable recorders are available in all the major formats – VHS, VHS-C, Beta and 8mm. Some notable non-standard features available are: multiple recording speeds which allow you to double or treble the recording time on the cassette; stereo sound; Dolby noise reduction for better sound performance; and hi-fi (depth multiplex) sound. What's called a 'flying erase head' can also be a feature. This means that you are able to get interference-free joins between successive 'takes'.

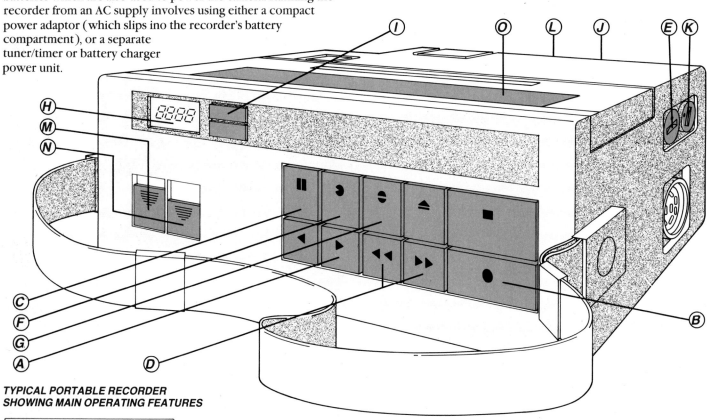

**TYPICAL PORTABLE RECORDER
SHOWING MAIN OPERATING FEATURES**

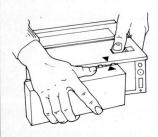

Battery: All portable recorders run on batteries. The usual types are rechargeable nickel-cadmium cells. They are usually made in special packs which slot into the recorder as shown here. Compact power adaptors are also available which slot into the battery compartment, enabling the recorder to run from AC.

(A) Play: Puts the recorder into playback mode. Several seconds will elapse between pushing the button and getting a picture as the recorder has to **lace up** the tape, and the tape speed has to stabilize.

(B) Record: Press this together with 'play' and the recorder goes into record mode. Again several seconds elapse before the machine actually starts recording.

(C) Pause: Stops the tape running through the recorder although it is still in contact with the recording heads. In playback mode you get a still picture. 'Pause' lets you go straight into playback or record without waiting for the tape to lace up and run up to speed.

(D) Rewind/fast forward/picture search: 'Rewind' and 'fast forward' simply move the tape along at high speed in one of two directions. You get no picture and there is a certain delay between 'play/record' and the wind functions. 'Picture search' is the visual equivalent of 'fast forward' or 'rewind'. With it you can scan through a tape at high speed with an on-screen picture at up to 10 times normal speed. 'Picture search' usually shares the 'rewind' and 'fast forward' buttons and is engaged by first switching the machine to 'play'.

(E) Slow motion: Runs the picture at less than normal speed. It can be a variable or fixed speed depending on the recorder.

(F) Audio dub: Allows you to record a new sound track for existing pictures. The old sound track is erased but the pictures aren't. On some stereo models it is possible to retain the old sound track on one channel and put a new or complementary one on the other channel.

(G) Insert edit: Very important tor editing, as you can see in Section Four. Allows you to insert a portion of video material into the middle of another recording, with no picture break up.

(H) Counter: Literally a four-digit indicator that gives you some idea of the whereabouts of particular segments on the tape.

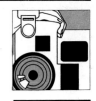

Connecting up to your TV

One of the greatest advantages of video is that you can see what you are shooting on a TV screen as you shoot it. The best way to connect your recorder to a TV or monitor is via the direct video and audio outputs. However, not all TVs have video and audio inputs so the connection is usually made via the aerial input.

To do this, turn on the recorder's test signal generator (see your handbook) or play back a tape with some material on it. Connect the recorder's RF (radio frequency) out socket to the TV's aerial socket with the cable provided. Select the AV channel on the TV (or a spare one if there isn't a specific AV channel) and start tuning that channel as you would if you were trying to pick up a broadcast signal.

Eventually you'll find the output of the recorder. Adjust the tuning until the picture is free from interference, and the sound is also clear with no background noise – and that's it! · To the TV, the recorder's output is just like that of a TV station and is tuned in exactly the same way.

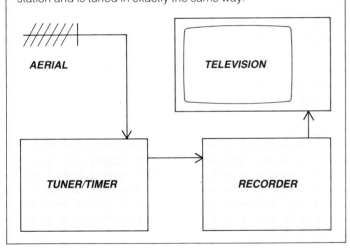

AERIAL

TELEVISION

TUNER/TIMER

RECORDER

Ⓘ **Memory rewind:** *Press this and when the tape is wound back or forth it will stop when the counter reaches 0000. Used in conjunction with the zero reset button, it allows you quickly to find any point on the tape.*

Ⓙ **Remote input:** *Some models have a remote control unit which is connected to the recorder by using this socket. (At back.)*

Ⓚ **Tracking:** *Used to match recordings made on other machines to your recorder, by compensating for minute mechanical differences between machines.*

Ⓛ **Speed:** *Multi-speed options are becoming common on portables. By changing the tape speed it is possible to get more time on any particular length of tape. (Control at back.)*

Ⓜ **Camera/recorder switch:** *Switches control of the recorder between the buttons on its front panel and a duplicated set of controls on the camera.*

Ⓝ **Dolby noise reduction:** *Improves sound quality and works in the same way as the Dolby system found on standard audio cassette recorders.*

Ⓞ **Tape compartment:** *Holds the video cassette that the machine is using.*

Connectors

RF or aerial: *Usually called co-axial or co-ax for short. They carry signals at radio frequencies. This is the sort of connection you find on the back of the TV for the aerial input and is also used when direct video and audio links are not available.*

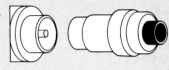

Multi-way tuner/timer plug: *These are rarely standard, but vary from machine to machine. They carry signals from a companion tuner/timer unit – video and audio in/out; power in; and some remote control functions. This socket is also used when connecting up an AC power unit/battery charger.*

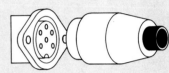

Multi-way camera socket: *Connects the camera to recorder and carries all the necessary electrical signals. These include video and audio in/out; power, remote control and other information lines.*

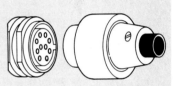

BNC connector: *The standard connector for video signals. It has a centre pin and an outside collar with a twist lock fitting to ensure a secure, interference free connection between plug and socket.*

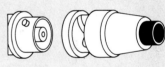

Phono connector: *Also called a 'cinch' or RCA connector, this is the standard connection for most audio lines. Unlike the BNC connector it does not lock onto the socket. There are some recorders which have phono sockets for video use.*

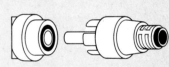

3.5mm jack: *A miniature jack socket used for a variety of different applications. Most usual are microphone inputs and earphone outputs. It is also used for remote control inputs.*

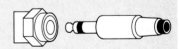

Power connector: *A variety of sizes and designs exist, all used to feed the correct DC voltage into the recorder – either from a car battery adaptor or a non-standard power adaptor. They are also found on cameras.*

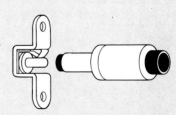

5-pin DIN: *Usually used as an audio connector. It has a standard connection configuration for audio in/out on video and audio recorders. Useful when you want to connect your video recorder into a hi-fi system for sound dubbing or re-recording.*

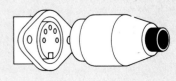

Video signal-to-noise ratio:
Tells you how much greater the wanted picture signal is in relation to the unwanted noise. This is measured in dB (decibels). The higher the figure, the better the performance.

Horizontal resolution: *Indicates how much detail the recorder can record. This is measured in lines as for cameras (see page 17). The higher the figure the better the performance.*

Audio signal-to-noise ratio:
Shows how much greater the wanted audio signal is relative to the unwanted hiss and other noise. Measured in dB. The higher the figure the better. A figure of 40dB is quite common but can be improved with Dolby noise reduction. Some newer recorders have hi-fi sound giving a figure of 80dB.

Audio frequency response: *The frequency range of sound which the recorder can reproduce. A typical range goes from 80Hz to 10kHz. This can be improved by Dolby noise reduction. If the recorder has hi-fi sound the response is in the range of 20Hz-20kHz.*

Power consumption: *Measured in watts (W). The higher this figure is, the shorter the time the batteries will last between charges.*

Weight: *A small consideration until you think how long you're going to have to carry the recorder and its batteries around. Because lighter alloys and plastics are now being used for recorder chassis, along with developments in head technology, standard size recorders are getting lighter. The use of smaller cassettes (such as VHS-C and 8mm) means that everything can be half its usual size and weight. A typical VHS recorder might weigh 8lb, a VHS-C or 8mm as little as 4lb.*

INSIDE THE RECORDER

The head drum assembly is an important and delicate part of the video recorder. The record/playback and erase heads are mounted on the drum which is driven by a precision electric motor. This must revolve at exactly the right speed or the heads won't pick up the video information. The linear tape speed must be precisely controlled for the same reasons. Speed control is carried out by an electronic feedback system. When a video recording is made, a series of **control pulses** is laid down on the tape. These are an electronic equivalent to the sprocket holes in a piece of film. When the tape is replayed, the control circuit reads these signals and compares them to a built-in reference signal. If there is a difference between the reference and control signals the circuit adjusts the motor until the speed is synchronized

Stopping and starting the recorder to make a

new recording disturbs the control track, which is why you get interference between successive recordings. When you make an insert edit recording, the control track is *not* disturbed. Putting the machine into pause does not disturb the track either.

Apart from the precision mechanics of the head drum, video recorders also have to have a system to extract the tape from the cassette and wrap it around the drum. Different formats use different arrangements but the principle is still the same. The tape is wrapped around as much of the drum's circumference as possible, in a diagonal fashion (called **helical wrap**).

The video heads are extremely small and delicate because of the job they have to do, and can easily be permanently damaged by careless handling. If you do 'get inside' a video recorder, never touch the heads. There has been debate over whether video heads need cleaning or not. The action of the video recorder has been thought to be self-cleaning but there are circumstances where this may not be enough. In this case consult your instruction manual.

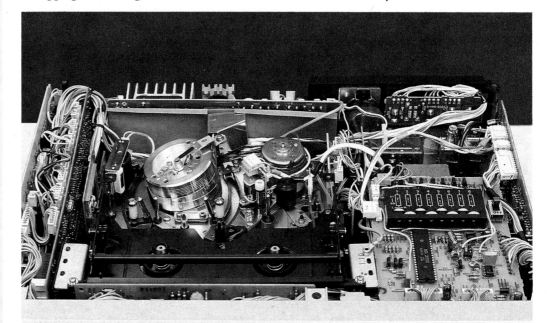

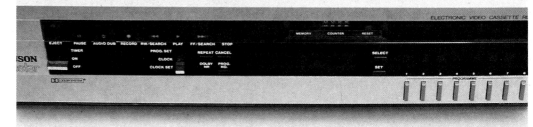

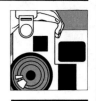

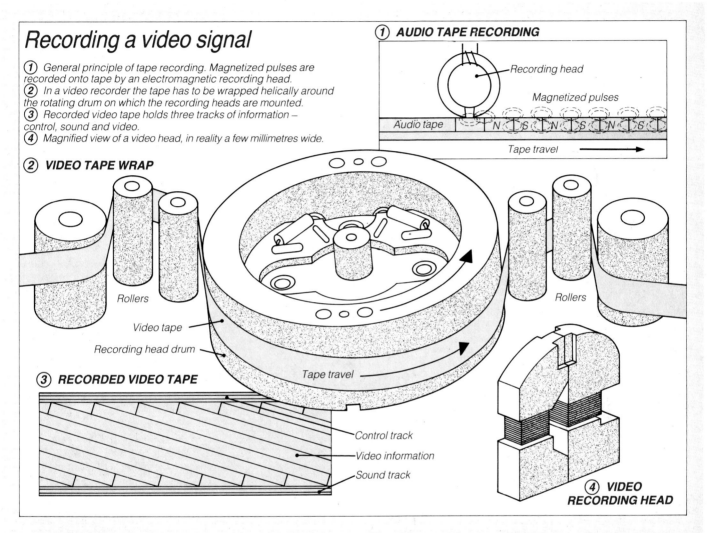

Recording a video signal

(1) General principle of tape recording. Magnetized pulses are recorded onto tape by an electromagnetic recording head.
(2) In a video recorder the tape has to be wrapped helically around the rotating drum on which the recording heads are mounted.
(3) Recorded video tape holds three tracks of information – control, sound and video.
(4) Magnified view of a video head, in reality a few millimetres wide.

(1) AUDIO TAPE RECORDING

Recording head
Magnetized pulses
Audio tape
Tape travel

(2) VIDEO TAPE WRAP

Rollers
Video tape
Recording head drum
Rollers
Tape travel

(3) RECORDED VIDEO TAPE

Control track
Video information
Sound track

(4) VIDEO RECORDING HEAD

Recording an electrical signal onto magnetic tape is not, in itself, a difficult task. In the case of an audio recorder, the electrical signals which represent the sound are turned into varying magnetic pulses by a **recording head**. The magnetic tape is moved over the recording head at a constant speed, and the varying magnetic pulses record magnetic fields on the tape. These magnetic fields correspond to the strength and frequency of the original signals.

Replaying the tape is essentially the same process put into reverse. Then the magnetic fields recorded on the tape induce corresponding electrical signals in the playback head, which are amplified and turned back into sound through a loudspeaker.

Recording and replaying video signals works on the same principles but, of course, with a few differences. Video signals have much higher frequencies than sound and this means that the tape used to record them has to move past the heads at a higher speed. It also has to have a wider 'contact' area in which to store the greater amount of electrical information.

The video recorders used by television companies are very large machines, some using tape that is up to 2 inches wide. Tape of this size is obviously impractical for domestic machines, so in home recorders – and lightweight portable professional machines – the problem of tape speed is overcome by mounting the heads on a rotating drum and recording the information in a series of diagonal strips across the tape. This effectively makes the relative speed between the tape and the head much faster – 486 centimeters per second is common – even though the tape itself is moving at a **linear tape speed** of only 2.34 centimeters per second.

Except in the newer hi-fi video cassette recorders (see page 27), the sound heads are not mounted on the rotating drum. The sound reproduction relies on fixed heads which record the sound in a linear strip at the edge of the tape. The tape speed at which the sound is recorded is therefore very low, which is why the usual sound quality is not very high.

THE CAMCORDER

TWO IN ONE

The camcorder is simply a combined camera and recorder – the answer to home recording's biggest drawback of having to cart around two separate pieces of equipment. The all-in-one unit's shortcomings have been the size of the cassette and the video head assembly, plus its power requirements which influence both weight and bulk.

Sony was the first company to use a full size Beta cassette, in an all-in-one unit, by drastically reducing the size of the head drum and its associated hardware to make the **Betamovie**. The snag here was that you couldn't play back from the camera but had to insert the Beta cassette into a VCR to see your recording.

JVC went one better with the VHS-C cassette, a cigarette pack sized case with 30 minutes of VHS tape inside. These were first seen as the basis for a number of small, light, separate portable recorders. Their true value is demonstrated in their current range of camcorders.

8mm is a recent development, created as a format for the camcorder market, and so has certain advantages over the others. For example, hi-fi sound has been a design feature from the start, and twin speed recording means that up to 3 hours' time is available per cassette. Not to be outdone, Panasonic has also recently launched a camcorder but it uses the full-size VHS cassette, cutting out the need for adaptors.

Whatever the make or format, all camcorders have features in common. Basically, you have nothing more than a camera and recorder in one package, so the camcorder has most of the features listed for recorders and cameras. The location of the controls obviously varies from model to model, but those for the camera section are located at the front of the unit. The recorder controls can be in any number of places – every manufacturer seems to choose somewhere different. When you compare different camcorders, the specifications that we looked at for separate cameras and recorders still apply (see pages 17 and 22).

All camcorders have a system of standby switches so that the parts of the camera that aren't being used are not powered – saving the batteries. So, if you're viewing material that has been shot previously, the camera section will be turned off. Conversely if you're using the camera just to set up a shot then the recorder part will not be on.

Camcorder pros and cons

Advantages
- Just one unit to contend with; no trailing cables or wires.
- Price lower than a camera/ recorder combination of the same specification.
- Available in all standard formats.
- Useful as a playback unit when editing.

Disadvantages
- Performance not as good as could be obtained with the best domestic equipment.
- Small physical size may not be as convenient to keep steady as a larger camera.
- Cannot be easily used as a 'first' home recorder (with one or two exceptions).

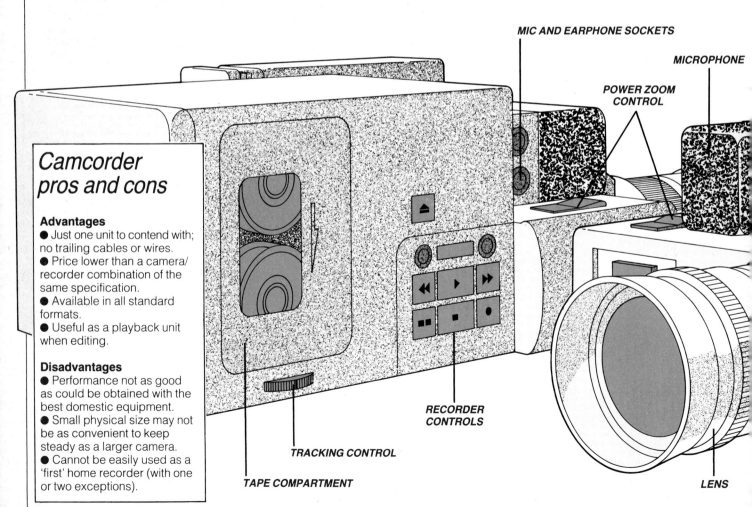

MIC AND EARPHONE SOCKETS

MICROPHONE

POWER ZOOM CONTROL

RECORDER CONTROLS

TRACKING CONTROL

TAPE COMPARTMENT

LENS

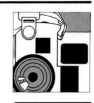

The cradle

One disadvantage of the camcorder is the fact that it is very inconvenient to use the recorder section on its own. Recording off-air programs, for example, might be difficult, if not impossible. The stand-alone portable on the other hand can be linked to a companion tuner/timer. Together the pair function as an AC machine with all the features that such a machine offers.

Some of the manufacturers of 8mm equipment have recognized these problems and supply a 'cradle' which contains a tuner/timer, as well as all the bits and pieces necessary to power the camcorder from AC and charge its batteries. The recorder controls on the camcorder are presented in the most convenient position, and the linking cables are kept out of the way. Another feature offered is infra-red remote control.

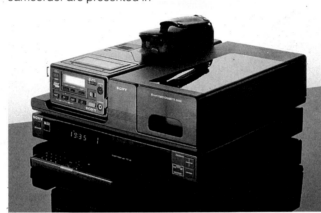

Format by format

Betamax: The Sony Betamovie, now in its latest incarnation complete with auto-focus and CCD image pick-up.

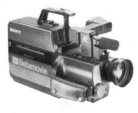

VHS: The Panasonic camcorder – this uses full-size VHS cassettes, but still has auto-focus.

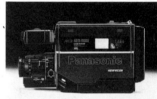

VHS-C: The first camcorder. This one features auto-focus and has an optional add-on character generator.

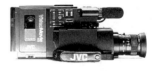

8mm: The latest format. As well as auto-focus, it features hi-fi sound and twin recording/playback speed as standard. An optional plug-in character generator is also available.

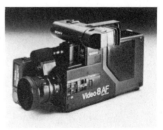

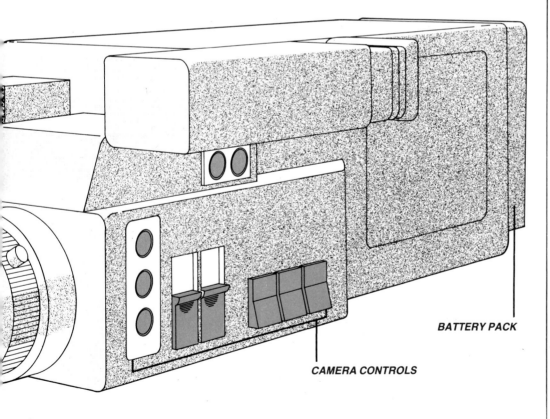

BATTERY PACK

CAMERA CONTROLS

TYPICAL CAMCORDER SHOWING MAIN OPERATING FEATURES

RECORDER FORMATS

Although the problems of video recorder design are universal, different companies decided to solve them in different ways when they went into video. Philips was the first company to launch a video cassette recorder in Europe, based on the VCR format, while in Japan JVC and Sony were working on their own domestic cassette systems. Sony devised the U-Matic cassette format, still in use professionally, which uses ¾ inch tape. The Betamax format was developed from this. JVC in the meantime had created and launched VHS, which now dominates the world market. From VHS came VHS-C – the 'C' standing for compact. This was developed for use with video cameras – in portable recorders and especially the all-in-one camcorder. It utilizes standard VHS tape in a smaller package, but can be played in a standard VHS recorder with an adaptor.

With an eye on the same portable market, Sony and Philips produced an entirely new cassette format – 8mm – so called because the tape is 8mm wide . Its initial use was in the camcorder market which, it was hoped, would take over from 8mm cine equipment. At the same time, by getting virtually every other video manufacturer to sign a common standards agreement (although, significantly, JVC did not), it was hoped that 8mm would replace everything else and establish a common format. Using tape cassettes smaller than audio cassettes and equipment designed to record with digital hi-fi sound, it is an exciting prospect.

The cassette

A video cassette is in itself a complex piece of engineering, and has many moving parts hidden inside its plastic casing. The tape itself is the result of many years of research and development. It is no more than 20 microns thick and has to stand up to winding on the tape spools at high speed, as well as being dragged in and out of the cassette shell and wrapped around the head drum thousands of times during its

life. The actual information recorded on video tape has a far higher spread of frequencies than that recorded onto standard audio tape, so the magnetic coating has to be that much more special, too.

Looking inside the cassette, you can see that the tape is wound onto plastic spools fitted with toothed wheels. These prevent the spools turning when they aren't in the recorder.

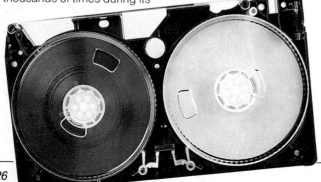

Cassettes for courses

VHS: *Launched by JVC in 1976, the VHS format is now the market leader in many parts of the world. The cassette size is around 7 by 4 inches and the maximum playing time available is 4 hours at standard speed. The actual linear tape speed is 2.34cm/sec and the writing speed 486cm/sec (see page 23). VHS has the edge over Beta in terms of sound quality, although picture quality is marginally worse because of the lower writing speed.*

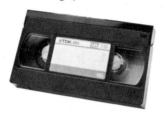

Beta: *Developed by Sony. In areas where Beta was heavily marketed, notably the USA and Japan, it long remained a favorite. Elsewhere it bowed to VHS. Beta cassettes measure 6 by 4 inches and, because of its higher writing speed (583cm/sec), the system has long been noted for its technical excellence. Sound quality suffers from the lower linear tape speed of 1.9cm/sec.*

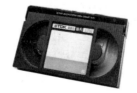

VHS-C: *Short for compact, the VHS-C cassette is about the size of a packet of cigarettes and contains enough standard size VHS tape to last for 30 minutes. Technical standards are as for standard VHS and by placing the VHS-C cassette in a special adaptor, it can be used in any ordinary VHS recorder.*

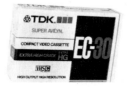

8mm: *The chief advantage of this system is its size – the cassettes are only 3½ by 2¼ inches. The tape is only 8mm wide and the reduction in size has been made possible by the development of a superior tape formulation and better head design. All this is achieved with a lower writing speed (310cm/sec) and linear tape speed of 2cm/sec. Other differences include depth multiplex recording for the sound as standard and a more advanced form of tracking. Maximum tape playing time is presently 90 minutes at standard speed.*

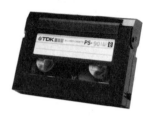

The others: *The only other format currently active on the market is V2000. This was the second format to be developed and launched by Philips. It applied the lessons learnt from both Beta and VHS. It can, for example, be turned over and played on both sides. Twin track sound was designed into it – stereo on VHS and Beta was an afterthought and a compromise at that. The recorders also have a feature called* **dynamic track following** *which means that there is never any picture interference on 'trick frame' functions like picture search and slow motion. It was never particularly successful, despite its technical advantages. Although some machines are still being sold in Europe, the bulk of Philips' machines are now VHS format.*

The CVC format made a brief appearance in the early 80s. It was very similar to 8mm in many ways – including cassette size – but didn't get the backing it needed to succeed.

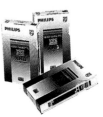

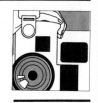

THE SOUND TRACKS

When faced with the problem of developing a home video recorder, high quality sound reproduction was not uppermost in the design engineers' minds. The problems of recording the pictures were far more formidable, and the average TV set's sound reproduction was pretty miserable, even as little as five years ago. So the sound track was tacked on more or less as an afterthought.

Leaving hi-fi recorders aside for a moment, sound is recorded onto a video tape in the same way it is recorded onto an audio cassette – the tape passes over a stationary recording head. Unfortunately the tape passes across that head very slowly – at a linear tape speed of around 2cm/sec. Also the portion of tape allocated to the sound track is very narrow – less than 1mm for mono or half that for each stereo track. This is around a third of the speed of an audio cassette recorder, and runs on an effective tape width which is also a third of an audio cassette's. The result is limited frequency response – and very poor noise figures.

The solution to this problem is ingenious but had to wait for market demand, as well as the perfection of the technical details, before it could be introduced. This is **depth multiplex recording**, and is explained below.

To maintain compatibility with other recorders not fitted with this feature, the linear sound track is retained. Even the 8mm format (which has depth multiplex recording as standard) has a linear audio track. You can use all the tracks to great advantage when dubbing sound (page 130).

Hi-fi sound – the advantages

Extended frequency response: 20Hz to 20kHz with little or no drop-off at either end. This compares to a maximum of 80Hz to 10kHz with the standard sound tracks.

Improved signal-to-noise ratio: Typically 80dB – about double that of the standard spec.

Improved dynamic range: The dynamic range is the difference between the quietest and loudest noises that can be recorded without them either being buried in tape noise or distorted. This is measured in dB and standard tape gives you a figure of around 40dB. With the hi-fi system it doubles to around 80dB.

How it works

The only effective way to better the linear sound quality of a video tape is to increase the writing speed of the audio heads. But you can't increase the linear tape speed without completely changing the specification, and there is no room on the tape to increase the width of the audio track.

The solution lies instead in a characteristic of magnetic tape recording called **azimuth**. The azimuth angle is that at which the tape head is positioned on the recording tape. The angle must be the same for both recording and playback. If you make a recording on one recorder and try and play it back on another in which the heads are set at a different angle, then you won't get anything off the tape.

In depth multiplex recording the audio heads are mounted on the same head drum as the video heads. This increases the writing speed to the same as that for the video signal. For VHS this is 486cm/sec – 207 times better! The audio head records the sound signal at high power deep into the surface of the tape. An erase head close behind then erases that signal from the topmost layer of the tape. Why? So that the video signal can be recorded on top of the audio signal. Because the video and audio are recorded with a vastly different azimuth angle they don't interfere and can be picked up quite separately.

The sound is, in fact, modulated onto an FM carrier signal – it is turned into an FM radio wave – so that the head design can be similar to that used for the video heads, and the sound signal can be dropped into a convenient 'slot' in the video output signal.

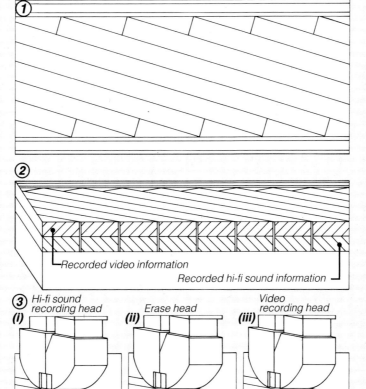

① *The layout of signals recorded onto video tape. Hi-fi sound is recorded under the video signals.* ② *A cross-section through the recorded tape shows the sound signal under the video signal.* ③ *(i) The hi-fi sound is recorded onto the tape first. (ii) Next the top layer of the sound is erased by an erase head. (iii) Finally the video signal is recorded on the top half of the magnetic coating at a different azimuth angle to the sound information.*

ANCILLARY EQUIPMENT

A TUNER/TIMER

A tuner/timer adds to a portable recorder the features and functions that are found on a standard AC recorder. The two together – portable and tuner/timer – function in the same way as a mains VCR. The tuner/timer unit will also recharge the portable's battery – an essential function.

Tuner

As the name implies, this part of the unit tunes into broadcast TV stations and turns them into video and audio signals compatible with the recorder.

Although early models employed manual tuning – they had a separate knob or thumbwheel which was adjusted for each station – virtually all up-to-date tuners are electronic. To tune in each station, you simply press a **search** button. The internal electronics scan the frequency band until they find a strong signal. The user can then assign that station to a particular channel by pressing another button to tell the tuner to keep on looking for the right channel.

Timer

This is the section of the unit that allows the recorder to tape programs off-air unattended. You have to program the day needed, start time and stop time into the machine's memory before selecting the timer record function – just as with a normal VCR.

Remote control

Obviously the tuner/timer must have some control link to the recorder. This is extended on many machines to allow full infra-red remote control over the recorder when it is connected to the tuner/timer.

AC portable

Some manufacturers sell the whole tuner/timer set up as one package. The AC-based tuner/timer actually forms part of a cradle into which the recorder can be locked when not being used in the field. Fixed, multi-way connectors automatically make contact when the two units are linked together and the combined system is, to all intents and purposes, a normal VCR.

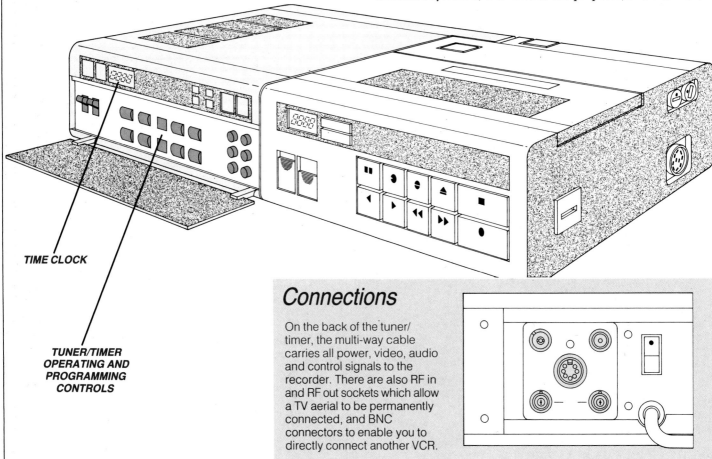

TIME CLOCK

TUNER/TIMER OPERATING AND PROGRAMMING CONTROLS

Connections

On the back of the tuner/timer, the multi-way cable carries all power, video, audio and control signals to the recorder. There are also RF in and RF out sockets which allow a TV aerial to be permanently connected, and BNC connectors to enable you to directly connect another VCR.

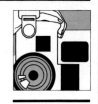

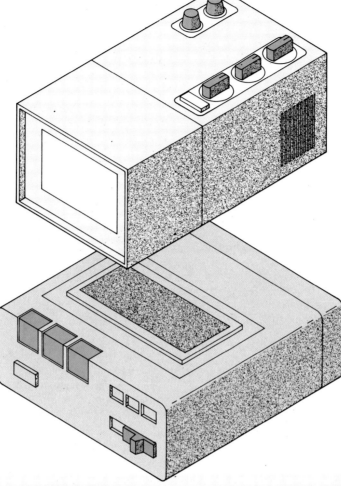

Portable monitor: *A portable monitor TV is invaluable when recording. It enables you to judge color balance and replays recorded footage better than the camera's monochrome viewfinder.*

Tape rewinder: *For the home video director who has everything! This device simply winds tape at high speed. Practically, it saves undue wear on your recorder's batteries.*

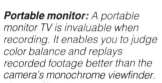

Batteries and battery chargers

The primary power source for a portable recorder is the rechargeable nickel-cadmium (Ni-Cad) battery. Although these have been developed and refined in much the same way as recorders and cameras, they still remain one of the main sources of weight in any recorder or camcorder system. This is almost entirely due to the power requirements of a typical recording system, which are made even greater if the camera used is fitted with autofocus and a motorized zoom mechanism. Batteries which deliver high amounts of power are generally large and relatively heavy, even though recent developments are now coming up with more compact, longer-lasting battery packs. Battery life between charges can now range from 30 to 90 minutes, depending on size and the equipment's power demands.

Tuner/timer units will recharge the recorder's battery while the two are linked together. Camcorder owners usually have to use a special charger. Separate battery chargers are also available for most of the separate recorder ranges. These allow you to charge up both the battery in the recorder as well as a spare. These units also give a power supply to run the recorder or camcorder from the AC supply either while charging takes place or to leave out the battery entirely for indoor work.

It is important to use only a compatible charger for Ni-Cad batteries. They tend to be quite delicate items and any misuse can cause them to lose their ability to store electrical charge.

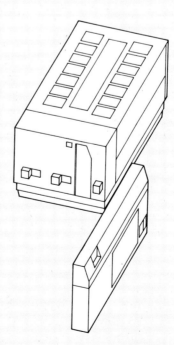

The camera control unit

Occasionally you might want to use a particular video camera with a recorder that doesn't have a compatible camera socket – or maybe doesn't have one at all. In either case, a camera control unit (CCU) is needed. This allows all the various input and output lines in the multiway connecting cable to be terminated separately, as well as providing a power source for the camera.

On the front of the CCU there is usually a multi-way socket compatible with the camera being used. On the back there will be video in/out and audio in/out sockets as well as a remote input. These can then be connected to the appropriate video and audio sockets on the recorder. If there is no camera remote socket then the recorder has to be stopped and started manually.

The connections that have to be made are: CCU video out to recorder video in; CCU audio out to recorder audio in; CCU video in to recorder video out; CCU audio in to recorder audio out; and finally CCU remote in to recorder camera pause (or remote) out.

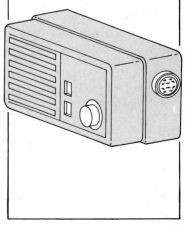

TRIPODS, TRACKS AND DOLLIES

A vital aspect of video production, whether amateur or professional, but one which can be overlooked in the excitement of buying a camera, is the ironmongery that is used to support the camera. There is nothing worse than a video in which the camera wobbles all over the place – it is distracting and looks so off-putting that prolonged viewing is more or less impossible. It is true that professional news crews rarely use tripods, but their cameras are big, heavy and well balanced – which makes them a lot easier to keep steady.

Functions

The ideal video camera support will allow absolutely smooth movements up and down and from side to side. It will also allow you to raise and lower the camera, and to move the whole stand around the floor with perfect smoothness. A movement in any direction should start without a jerk and stop in precisely the right position, again without jerking.

Realization of these ideals involves much in the way of compromise. The most difficult things for a camera support to achieve are jerk-free stops and starts of movement. The most sophisticated method of achieving jerk-free **pan** (side to side) and **tilt** (up and down) motions involves using a tripod that has a **fluid head**. This uses hydraulic damping to absorb and smooth the energy of a movement when it is stopped, allowing the camera to stop more or less instantaneously. Unfortunately, a fluid head is a very expensive piece of equipment and out of the price range of most amateurs. However, a **friction head** tripod is most likely to be affordable. While not as effective, it nevertheless offers a reasonable compromise at a reasonable price.

Achieving jerk-free movement of the whole camera support (what's called dollying) is rather more difficult. Putting wheels on the bottom of the camera support is the usual method of moving it around, but the floor surface has to be extremely smooth.

Outside the TV studio, professional crews either refrain from moving the camera support at all, or lay down a set of tracks – like a miniature railway – if they want to move the camera during a shot. Improvisation can come up with a lot of the answers though, and using a car (perhaps being pushed) is one way to overcome the problem.

Choosing a support

The usual camera support will be some sort of tripod, and the first consideration for any buyer will be, is it strong and sturdy enough to support the video camera without falling over? A tripod that would be perfectly adequate for an SLR camera will not be so good for video.

Next, look at the pan and tilt head. Is there any play or looseness in its construction? In other words, if you tighten all the screws that lock the head in position, does the camera platform still move about? Next, look at the damping system. In the amateur price range it will almost certainly be friction damped. Can you start a pan or tilt movement without jerking, and when you stop the movement and take your hand away will the camera stay in precisely the same position without slipping?

Tripods that can be moved up and down while shooting are unusual, but that up and down movement should still be convenient and, most importantly, the camera shouldn't move once the adjustment has been made.

Turning a simple tripod into a dolly usually involves no more than buying a set of wheels. You should again look for something sturdy and well built. The wheels should not be loose in their mountings and, similarly, the wheel mounts should not have any play in them at the attachment points.

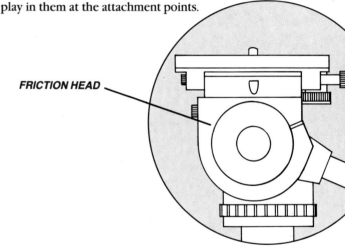

FRICTION HEAD

Monopod: When you're on the move and extreme portability is essential, a **monopod** can be handy. Although it can't stand up on its own, it can give the extra support needed for a steady picture.

Trolley: When not actually shooting, it is much more convenient to load both camera and recorder onto some form of trolley. The trolley also lets you carry a larger number of items around, like spare tapes, batteries, filters and camera supports.

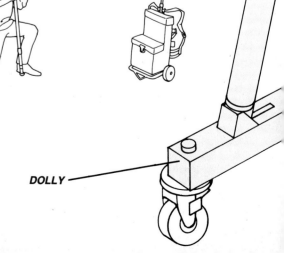

DOLLY

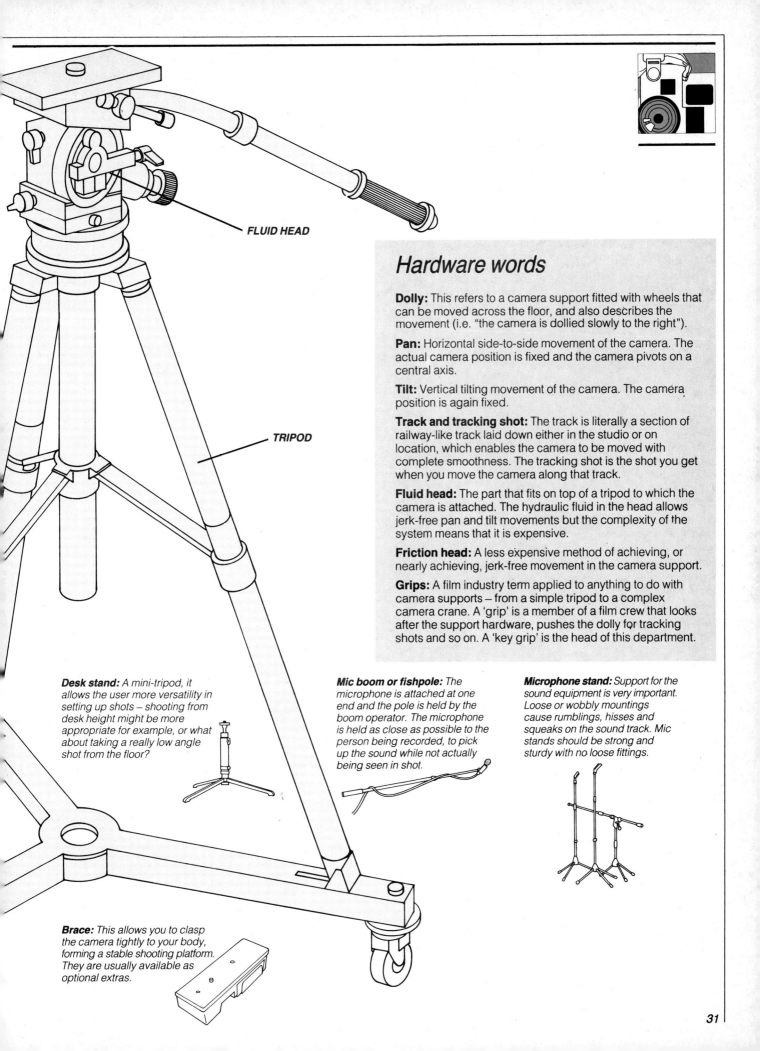

FLUID HEAD

TRIPOD

Hardware words

Dolly: This refers to a camera support fitted with wheels that can be moved across the floor, and also describes the movement (i.e. "the camera is dollied slowly to the right").

Pan: Horizontal side-to-side movement of the camera. The actual camera position is fixed and the camera pivots on a central axis.

Tilt: Vertical tilting movement of the camera. The camera position is again fixed.

Track and tracking shot: The track is literally a section of railway-like track laid down either in the studio or on location, which enables the camera to be moved with complete smoothness. The tracking shot is the shot you get when you move the camera along that track.

Fluid head: The part that fits on top of a tripod to which the camera is attached. The hydraulic fluid in the head allows jerk-free pan and tilt movements but the complexity of the system means that it is expensive.

Friction head: A less expensive method of achieving, or nearly achieving, jerk-free movement in the camera support.

Grips: A film industry term applied to anything to do with camera supports – from a simple tripod to a complex camera crane. A 'grip' is a member of a film crew that looks after the support hardware, pushes the dolly for tracking shots and so on. A 'key grip' is the head of this department.

Desk stand: A mini-tripod, it allows the user more versatility in setting up shots – shooting from desk height might be more appropriate for example, or what about taking a really low angle shot from the floor?

Mic boom or fishpole: The microphone is attached at one end and the pole is held by the boom operator. The microphone is held as close as possible to the person being recorded, to pick up the sound while not actually being seen in shot.

Microphone stand: Support for the sound equipment is very important. Loose or wobbly mountings cause rumblings, hisses and squeaks on the sound track. Mic stands should be strong and sturdy with no loose fittings.

Brace: This allows you to clasp the camera tightly to your body, forming a stable shooting platform. They are usually available as optional extras.

TV STANDARDS

In principle, television is quite a simple thing – an electron beam scans across a TV tube, tracing out a series of lines whose varying brightness builds up a picture. The problems arise when people get down to deciding such aspects as, "how many lines?" and "how many times should the beam make up a complete picture every second?" When the first black and white TV system was introduced by the BBC in 1936, they had decided on the answers to the technical questions and developed the system accordingly. When TV systems were introduced in other countries, some adopted the same system as the BBC. Others, notably the USA, decided to modify it, both to improve on the original and also to comply with such things as different power supplies. The end result is that American transmissions cannot be viewed on UK TV sets, and vice versa.

Color TV was a natural development. Developing a broadcast color TV system involved solving the problem of how to transmit information that would tell the receiver both the brightness of every part of the screen image (luminance) and the color of every part of the screen (chrominance). The Americans were the first to develop a working color TV system. It started broadcasting from New York in 1951.

However, it had its drawbacks. Even during development, the European networks, and in particular the BBC, were not impressed by its technical performance and thought they could do better. This resulted in the development of not one, but two, rival systems. The **PAL** system was created for most of Europe, and **SECAM** for France. Because they had taken longer in development, and had learnt some lessons from the Americans, both these systems were, and still are, superior to the US **NTSC** system.

The countries that came under US influence (such as Japan, continental North America, **Central and South America, and South East Asia**) adopted the NTSC system, while those countries influenced by the UK (notably Australia, India, Pakistan, large parts of the African continent and most of Europe) have adopted the PAL standard. The use of SECAM is rather more patchy, and is not helped by the fact that there are two incompatible SECAM systems. SECAM (V) is used primarily in France and the USSR, but SECAM (H) is common in other French-influenced countries and the Middle East.

TV standards and domestic power supplies around the world

Country	TV standard	Voltage (V)	Frequency (Hz)
Abu Dhabi	PAL B/G	240	50
Australia	PAL B	240	50
Austria	PAL B/G	220	50
Bahamas	NTSC	120/240	60
Bahrain	PAL B	110/220	50/60
Barbados	NTSC	110/220	50
Belgium	PAL B/H	127/220	50
Bermuda	NTSC	120/240	60
Brazil	PAL M	110/220	50/60
Canada	NTSC	120/240	60
Chile	NTSC	220	50
China	PAL	220	50
Colombia	NTSC	110/240	60
Czechoslovakia	SECAM (V)	220	50
Denmark	PAL B/G	220	50
Dubai	PAL B/G	220	50
Egypt	SECAM (V)	220	50
Finland	PAL B/G	220	50
France	SECAM (V)	127/220	50
Germany, East	SECAM (V)	127/220	50
Germany, West	PAL B/G	220	50
Greece	PAL B/G	220	50
Greenland	NTSC	220	50
Hong Kong	PAL I	200	50
Hungary	SECAM (V)	220	50
Iceland	PAL B	220	50
India	PAL B	230/250	50 plus some DC
Indonesia	PAL B	127/220	50
Iran	SECAM (H)	220	50
Iraq	SECAM (H)	220	50
Ireland	PAL I	220	50
Israel	PAL B/G	230	50
Italy	PAL B/G	220	50
Japan	NTSC	100/200	50/60
Kenya	PAL B	240	50

☐ =PAL
☐ =NTSC
▨ =SECAM

Compatibility

Needless to say, TV transmissions in one standard cannot be picked up and displayed as a watchable picture by equipment of another standard. A tape made on an NTSC recorder will not play on a PAL machine for instance – which can cause problems if you intend to make tapes to send abroad.

Compatibility is something to bear in mind if you're taking your video equipment abroad. You will want to plug it in at times – even if only to charge the batteries – and you may even want to connect up a TV to view your results. Whether or not you can do these things depends on the supply voltages your equipment works on (look at the back panel – there may be an adjuster) and the TV system it uses.

Power requirements around the world

When abroad, you'll want to know whether the power supply is going to be suitable for your equipment. So you must consider its voltage and frequency. You can usually assume that the available power supply is AC (alternating current) although in some remote parts of the world you may come across a DC (direct current) system.

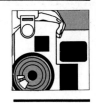

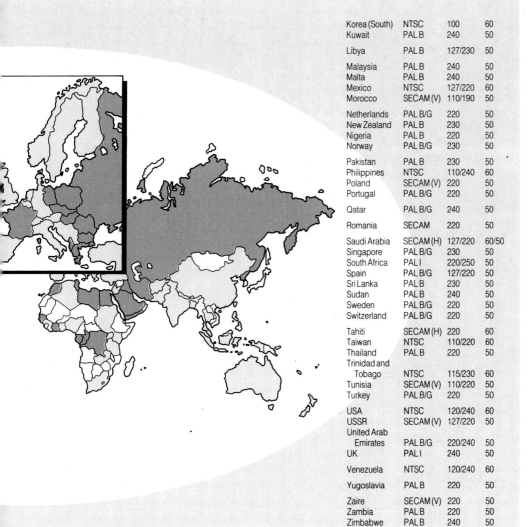

Korea (South)	NTSC	100	60
Kuwait	PAL B	240	50
Libya	PAL B	127/230	50
Malaysia	PAL B	240	50
Malta	PAL B	240	50
Mexico	NTSC	127/220	60
Morocco	SECAM (V)	110/190	50
Netherlands	PAL B/G	220	50
New Zealand	PAL B	230	50
Nigeria	PAL B	220	50
Norway	PAL B/G	230	50
Pakistan	PAL B	230	50
Philippines	NTSC	110/240	60
Poland	SECAM (V)	220	50
Portugal	PAL B/G	220	50
Qatar	PAL B/G	240	50
Romania	SECAM	220	50
Saudi Arabia	SECAM (H)	127/220	60/50
Singapore	PAL B/G	230	50
South Africa	PAL I	220/250	50
Spain	PAL B/G	127/220	50
Sri Lanka	PAL B	230	50
Sudan	PAL B	240	50
Sweden	PAL B/G	220	50
Switzerland	PAL B/G	220	50
Tahiti	SECAM (H)	220	60
Taiwan	NTSC	110/220	60
Thailand	PAL B	220	50
Trinidad and Tobago	NTSC	115/230	60
Tunisia	SECAM (V)	110/220	50
Turkey	PAL B/G	220	50
USA	NTSC	120/240	60
USSR	SECAM (V)	127/220	50
United Arab Emirates	PAL B/G	220/240	50
UK	PAL I	240	50
Venezuela	NTSC	120/240	60
Yugoslavia	PAL B	220	50
Zaire	SECAM (V)	220	50
Zambia	PAL B	220	50
Zimbabwe	PAL B	240	50

Multi-standard recorders and TVs

If you're jetting all over the world and want to collect video tapes from different countries, you can buy video recorders that will play back tapes recorded in different broadcasting standards. The recorder will usually only record in one system (usually the one of the country in which the recorder is being marketed), but will play back tapes made in other standards. But in addition to the multi-standard recorder you also need a multi-standard TV set. Furthermore, the triple standard recorders often sold in the UK play back PAL, SECAM and NTSC. But because they are actually designed primarily for the Middle Eastern market, the SECAM is, in fact, SECAM (H) as used in Saudi Arabia – not the SECAM (V) used in France.

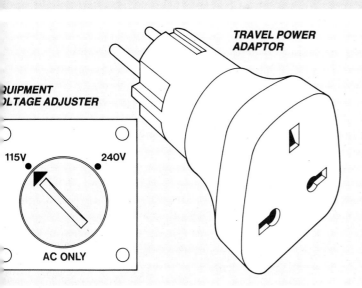

TRAVEL POWER ADAPTOR

EQUIPMENT VOLTAGE ADJUSTER

115V   240V

AC ONLY

Obviously, the correct voltage is important. Connecting 115V equipment to a 240V system could be disastrous!

The correct frequency, measured in hertz (Hz), is important too, though for less obvious reasons. The power frequency is used in TV systems as a reference to which the numbers of picture frames shown per second can be locked.

Items like battery chargers or camera control units can be run from a supply with the 'wrong' frequency, since the AC voltage is converted to a low DC voltage to charge the battery, or run the camera/camcorder.

Generally speaking, you will find that the voltage is either around 240V with a frequency of 50Hz, or around 115V with a frequency of 60Hz. Quite often there is a little adjusting wheel or control on your equipment which allows you to select a voltage closest to the one on offer. It is OK to match to the nearest 10 or 15V, but certainly no more than that.

SOUND

WHAT IS SOUND?

Everyone has heard the words 'sound waves', but what do they actually mean? Quite simply, sound is a series of regular variations in air pressure. It is these variations that are called waves. Imagine a line of dominoes set on end. Knock over the first one and that knocks over the second, which knocks over the third and so on. You can actually see a 'wave' passing along the line of dominoes. The energy put into knocking the first one over has been passed through the line, and a sound wave travels through air in exactly the same way. The only difference is that our metaphorical dominoes stand themselves up again ready for the next wave, so that in reality you can send a number of waves along the line.

The number of waves or cycles per second is called the **frequency** of the sound. The actual unit that stands for cycles per second is Hertz (Hz), named after the nineteenth century German scientist Heinrich Hertz. The size of the 'push' that started the sound wave off is called its **power** and is measured in **watts**.

You may have heard the term watts applied to the power output of an amplifier but you have to be careful here. The power output rating of an amplifier tells you how much electricity it can supply to a loudspeaker, not necessarily how loudly it can play your records. The loudspeaker takes that electrical energy and turns it into sound waves. There is always some loss in that conversion process and the loudness of your sound – the acoustic power – will depend on how good that loudspeaker is at turning electrical energy into sound energy.

If a sound wave meets nothing in its path, it travels on and on until it fades out and dies away. This is because as each atom in the air bangs against its neighbor (the air molecules are our metaphorical dominoes), a little bit of the energy behind them is lost. If the process carries on freely, eventually all the energy is lost.

If the sound wave hits an object it will be partly absorbed and partly reflected. The proportions of the absorption and reflection depend on the material involved. Deep fluffy objects like chairs, curtains and carpets etc, are very good at absorbing the energy of a sound wave so very little is reflected. On the other hand, if the sound wave hits a shiny, hard surface virtually all the energy is reflected and little is absorbed.

You can hear the difference between these situations at home. Just try singing in the bathroom – full of shiny reflective tiles and porcelain – and the living room – full of soft furnishings,

Reverberation and echo

We are all familiar with the difference between what a recording engineer will call a 'live' and a 'dead' sound. Take a cathedral for example. There is a huge amount of space and the walls are hard and reflective to sound. If anyone makes a noise, several seconds may pass before it has spent all its energy. This is an extreme example of a live sound. It causes great problems when recording because one sound won't have died away before the next one comes along.

At the other end of the scale is a room furnished with heavy curtains, thick pile carpets, and deep sofas and chairs. You get the feeling that each sound you make somehow never gets further than your lips. This is very much a dead sound.

Humans are psychologically happiest when sound has a reverberation of around four-fifths of a second.

Those concert halls which have this particular characteristic are regarded as 'good'. In film and TV the ideal reverberation characteristic can be created artificially by adding reverb electronically to the sound track. This is why recorded sound is made deliberately very dead to start off with, so that the engineers can add reverb or any other effect.

It is possible to control the recording environment to achieve acceptable results first time. Choice of microphone can be quite important, but you can also modify the characteristics of rooms to some extent, using reflector boards to add reverb or rugs and blankets to deaden sound.

Echo is often mistakenly thought of as being the same as reverberation. When a sound echoes, it comes back to the listener quite distinctly, but after a period of silence which may be several seconds long. When a sound reverberates, it comes back to the listener after a much shorter time, and keeps on coming back at similarly short intervals, dying quickly away.

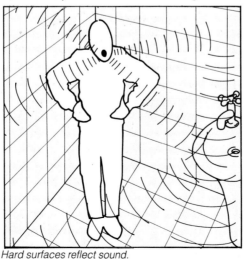
Hard surfaces reflect sound.

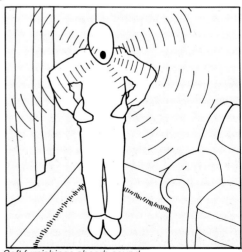
Soft furnishings absorb sound.

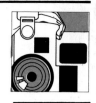

curtains, and carpets.

The other element of sound is its frequency. The human ear can make out sounds ranging from 10Hz up to about 15kHz. This top end perception tends to deteriorate with age and a man of 40 may only be able to hear sounds as high as 12kHz. Strangely, he would still be able to tell if sound frequencies above this figure are missing from recorded material. It is for this reason, as much as any other, that virtually all hi-fi systems have a frequency range of 10Hz to 20kHz.

Another problem is that sounds of different frequencies are absorbed and reflected in different amounts by any material. This can cause headaches when recording music, although speech isn't affected quite as much.

The professional recording engineer has fewer worries now than ten years ago. Recordings can be processed electronically to sound as if they were made in almost any location. Apart from the usual tricks of artificial echo and reverberation, electronics allow the sound itself to be almost infinitely varied. But even without expensive equipment, there are some simple rules that you can follow to ensure that the sound you record is clear and distinct.

Problems

Too much reverb: A room that is too 'live' when you're shooting is relatively easy to correct. The problem is that there are too many flat shiny surfaces bouncing sounds around. The easiest solution is to use blankets, thick curtains or other absorbent materials to cover up those surfaces. Don't forget the floor either – it is quite amazing how much difference just a thick pile rug can make, especially on top of something like parquet flooring. Windows give more problems as glass is probably one of the best reflectors of sound. Simply closing the curtains can work wonders. And if you have to work by the light coming in through the windows, try hanging net curtains.

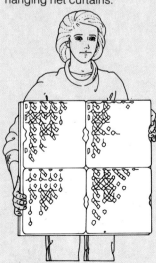

If you can't hang drapes, then making up a few absorbing boards might do the trick. These need be no more than sheets of hardboard with absorbent padding fastened onto one side, and the bigger they are the better. Papier-maché egg cartons are good for absorbing sound, too, and can also be used on absorbing boards.

Sound too dead: This can be both a problem and an advantage. A dead sound is ideal for electronic processing later on. If you can get hold of a reverb unit, then you can make the initial recording with as little natural reverb as possible.

If you don't want to add reverb later, then you'll have to improve the surroundings when recording. Try drawing the curtains back and moving your subject closer to the windows. If you can roll the carpet up to expose a shiny wooden floor, do that; and try moving stuffed or padded furniture as far away from the subject as possible.

If you're in a position where you can't change the room around very much, you will have to use reflector boards. An ideal thing would be a hardboard panel covered with ceramic tiles. Arrange the panels as close to the subject as possible without appearing in shot. You can put the mic

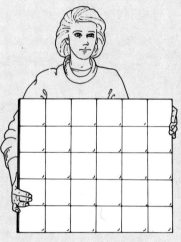

closer to the panels than the subject, so that it picks up more of the reflected sound. You can also use a less directional mic, but be careful not to pick up unwanted sound from behind the camera. This is one of the reasons why it is vital to monitor the sound on a pair of totally enclosed headphones, which let you hear only what's coming from the microphone.

Sound too faint: A tricky problem as you don't have any control over the signal level entering the recorder. Also, if the signal from the mic is low, the recorder turns up the sensitivity to maximum which means that it also boosts all the unwanted background hiss and noise. To overcome this, first get the mic as close to the subject as possible. This may mean using a separate microphone on a boom (and a boom need be no more than a long wooden pole with the mic taped to the end) or a tie-clip mic. Try to deaden the acoustic. Recording sound from a distance in a very live acoustic requires a lot of thinking ahead, especially if it's a situation like a wedding where it may be very difficult to get the mic very close. A shotgun mic (see page 37) can be very useful here.

You should always use headphones to listen to the sound coming into the recorder from the microphone. The only sure way to get the results you want is to experiment, and keep on listening until you get things the way you want them.

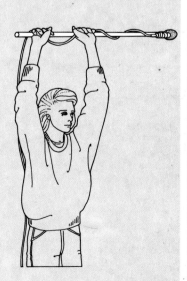

MICROPHONES

In simple terms, a microphone turns sound into electrical signals that can be recorded onto video tape. All home video cameras are fitted with one, but they can often be an afterthought in design terms. The built-in mic is often of quite poor quality, and its mounting position on the camera can sometimes be completely unsuitable for recording sound of an equal quality to that of the picture. Ideally, the microphone should be as close to the subject as possible – without, of course, getting into shot. A microphone mounted on the camera is not going to achieve this, although the boom extensions found on some models go some way to improving the situation.

There are different microphones for different jobs. If you are shooting alone, the shotgun, ultra-directional type is probably the best bet. It will pick up sound from just the subject and not all around. The zoom mic is an interesting variation on this. It can change its pick-up pattern from very directional to being almost omni-directional. This transition is linked into the camera's zoom control. The microphone is at its most directional when the lens is at the telephoto end of its zoom range and vice versa.

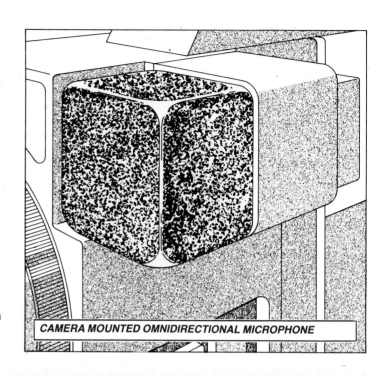

CAMERA MOUNTED OMNIDIRECTIONAL MICROPHONE

How do they work?

There are two types of microphone currently in use with home video equipment – the dynamic microphone and the electret condenser mic.

Dynamic mic: This works in the same way as a loudspeaker – except in reverse. Inside it, the base of a small, domed plastic diaphragm is surrounded by a very fine coil of wire, suspended between the poles of a magnet. Sound waves hitting the cone cause it to move, in turn moving the coil. Moving a coil in a magnetic field causes an electrical current to flow in it (that's how a generator works) and that electrical current is proportional to the size of the sound wave. So you can see how sound waves are converted into a corresponding electrical signal.

Electret condenser mic: The electret condenser microphone consists of two metal plates. The top one is very thin and flexible and carries an electrical charge, supplied by a battery. When a sound wave hits the top plate it moves it fractionally nearer the bottom one. This change in the plate spacing causes what's called the **capacitance** of the circuit to change. In turn this causes an electrical current to flow. Again, you can see how the sound wave causes a mechanical change which in turn makes an electrical current flow.

Which is best? The advantage of the electret condenser mic is that, although more expensive, it is lighter and smaller than the dynamic type. It also gives a more even frequency response and produces a stronger output signal. The chief disadvantage is that if it isn't powered by the camera, it uses a battery which will need replacing.

ELECTRET CONDENSER MICROPHONE

DYNAMIC MICROPHONE

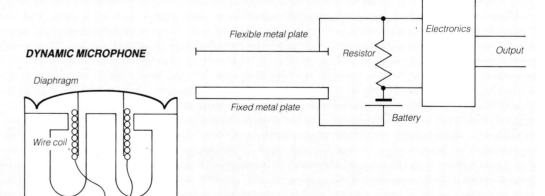

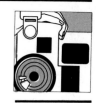

Microphone types

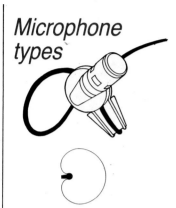

Tie-clip mic: *Very useful if you're shooting an on-screen presenter – even if it is only an introduction to your holiday pics. All the problems of getting a microphone near enough are solved. Not an expensive item and makes any video production look and sound that much more professional.*

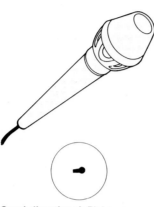

Omni-directional: *Picks up sounds from all around it. Its pick-up pattern is shown above – sometimes referred to as a polar pattern. Most useful for recording ambient sounds, or a group of people sitting around a table. The mic can be suspended out of shot on a boom or hidden in a table ornament.*

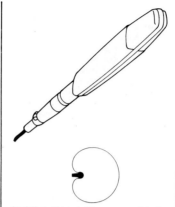

Unidirectional: *Has a one-sided polar pattern, so it picks up sounds from one direction only. The pattern is heart-shaped, so these mics are sometimes called* **cardioid**. *Unidirectional mics are most useful when only one person is speaking, or for hand-held microphone interviews.*

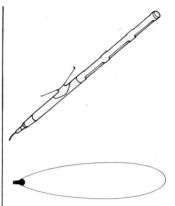

Shotgun or rifle mic: *Designed to be extremely directional – it picks up sounds from one specific direction only, with very little spill at the sides. Useful when you can't get close to the subject. Relatively inexpensive versions are available for the home video market.*

Headphones

Headphones serve one very important purpose when recording sound – either with an audio or video recorder – by letting you hear exactly what is going onto the tape. To do this properly you should not be able to hear any sounds other than those from the headphones. So the headphones you use should have large ear pieces to physically exclude all other sounds. They should also be comfortable – very important if you're shooting for a long time. The flimsy little headphones that are sold with personal stereos are useless for this purpose, as are the hearing aid-type ear pieces supplied by many video manufacturers.

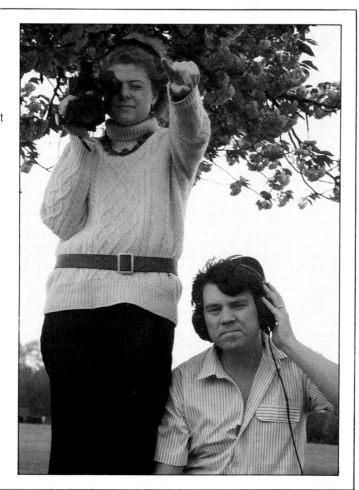

Understanding specifications
microphones

Dynamic mic: *A mic that works on the same principles as a loudspeaker. These give good performance at a reasonable price. They are low impedance which means you can use long cables and connect them to virtually all recorders and mixers.*
Electret condenser mic: *A modified version of the condenser mic. These combine the qualities of a condenser mic without the need to have a separate power source. These are high impedance which means long cable runs are impossible.*
Frequency response: *Like any other part of the audio chain a microphone will have a frequency response. This is a measure of the range of 'notes' a microphone or other sound equipment can successfully turn into signals.*
Impedance: *The electrical resistance of a microphone. The impedance of the mic should match the impedance of the recorder's input. A low impedance mic (no more than 800Ω) will work into a high impedance input but not vice versa. High impedance is typically 25KΩ plus.*

SEPARATE SOUND RECORDING

You might think that there is little point in using a separate sound recorder if you already have a built-in microphone. But if we exclude 8mm video (which uses hi-fi recording) for a moment, it is generally accepted that the quality of video camera sound is not brilliant. So, unless it is absolutely vital to have sound synchronized with pictures, recording the sound separately and transferring it back onto the tape later will give a significant improvement in quality at virtually no extra cost. In the case of 8mm video, hi-fi (AFM) sound is fitted as standard and the actual recorded sound is of high quality.

There is, however, a second reason for recording at least some of your sound track separately. In many cases, the sound that actually fits a certain set of shots may be nonexistent or uninteresting, while other situations may have intrinsically interesting sounds, but are not visually exciting.

So it makes sense to spend some time listening out for suitable sounds to go with your pictures and capturing them on audio tape. Take your holiday video for example. The scenery may have been beautiful and the beach breathtaking, but what about the sound? On the other hand that group of local singers might have been willing to sing for a sound recorder but actually turned out to be very camera shy. The answer? Use an audio recorder to record the singers and dub their sound onto those stunning shots of the beach and the views.

Almost any portable cassette recorder will do the job, as long

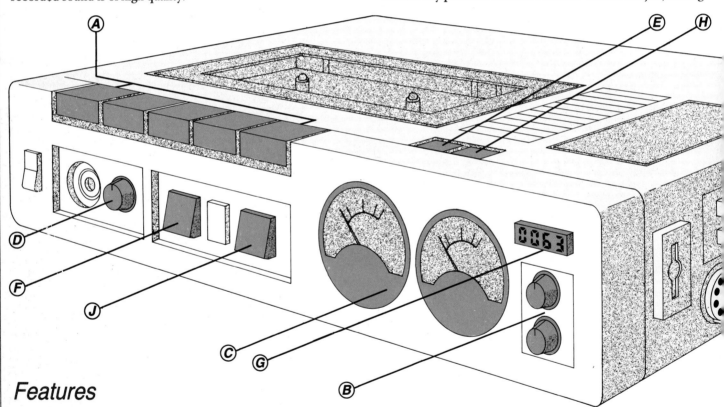

Features

(A) Tape transport controls: Play, record, fast forward, rewind and pause.

(B) Level control: Varies the amount of signal from the microphone actually getting to the tape. The level should be high enough so that the signal does not get lost in tape noise, but not so high that the signal overloads the tape and distorts.

(C) Level meter(s): These indicate what the input level actually is. There may be two if the recorder is stereo, or one if it is mono. The level should be adjusted so that the meter needle or lamp just goes into the 0dB zone on the peaks of the loudest sounds.

(D) Playback volume: Adjusts the volume of sound going into the recorder's speaker when you play back tapes.

(E) Tape type selector: Lets you match the recorder's electronics to the formulation of tape being used.

(F) Noise reduction selection: Portables often feature Dolby noise reduction. This switch allows you to switch the noise reduction system on and off.

(G) Tape counter: Doesn't actually tell you anything about the tape position (like time elapsed or actual tape length) but gives a relative reading of tape used.

(H) Memory rewind: Select this function, and when the recorder rewinds it will stop when the counter gets to 0000. Useful if you want to keep coming back to a certain position on the tape.

(J) Limiter: Stops an overloaded sound getting through to the tape and overloading it, by automatically 'turning down' the input level for the duration of that high-level signal.

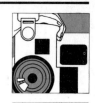

as you can plug in a suitable microphone and earphones. One of the best compromises between quality and portability is a personal stereo that has a recording facility. The unit illustrated below is a larger machine, though, and shows the relevant features and controls. The recorder should of course be able to run from batteries, and compatibility with all tape types would be very useful. One essential feature is a manual level control. This means you are able to adjust the microphone level yourself rather than letting the machine do it for you. Automatic control can result in a sudden upsurge of background noise when the sound you actually want to record goes very quiet. This happens because the automatic circuit then turns the input level up as high as it will go. This is the biggest failing with video recorders' sound recording systems so there's no point in duplicating that fault here. A recorder suitable for capturing sound to add to your videotapes needn't be expensive, but it should have most of the features shown below.

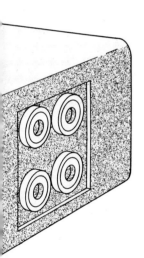

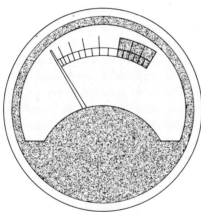

Above: Audio tape recorder level meter. The sound recordist must constantly watch the needle as well as monitoring the sound on headphones. The needle should only peak into the overload region.

Connectors

There are usually two sets of inputs – one for microphones and the other for signal sources such as a hi-fi system or another tape recorder. The mic socket is usually a jack type; the others will generally be phono connectors. The outputs are invariably phono types, or they can be combined with the input in one 5-pin DIN socket. The headphone socket will be a jack, and there may well be a connection for an external power supply. A remote control socket is often provided to connect a mic with a start/stop button.

Types of tape

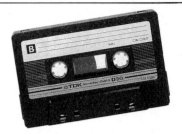

Audio cassettes come in three distinct types of tape formulation. Choice of type depends on what you are going to record.

Type I: The earliest and still most common ferric-type tape. Best used for recording speech and other applications where high performance is not required.

Type II: Chrome and hi-bias tapes. Chrome tape was the first of the 'special' or non-ferrics to come on the market. It offered a better frequency response and brighter treble end. Hi-bias types have superseded these and give the more rounded, ferric-type frequency response with the extended top end of chrome.

Type IV: Metal tape. The tape formulation consists of evaporated metal particles instead of an oxide of metal. This tape offers a wider frequency response and an even performance.

Type III tapes were called ferri-chrome, a hybrid between the ferric and chrome formulations. They were not particularly successful and are no longer sold.

Understanding specifications
audio recorders

Audio frequency response: The range of 'notes' that a piece of audio equipment can reproduce. It is measured in hertz. A hi-fi recorder is capable of a range of 10Hz to 20kHz, while most non-hi-fi recorders will manage 300Hz to 8kHz.

Dolby noise reduction: A patented electronic process that reduces the tape hiss and boosts frequency response in magnetic tape recordings. Dolby B can give a 7 – 10 dB increase in the signal to noise ratio, while Dolby C boosts performance by 15 – 20 dB.

Dynamic range: The range between the quietest and loudest sounds that sound equipment can deal with without distortion. Most hi-fi recorders are around 70dB, although standard video recorders only manage approximately 40dB.

Flutter: Quick variations in the speed of the tape. In video recorders this is usually negligible – less than 0.005%. Flutter should also be negligible in an audio recorder. A good deck would have a flutter figure of around 0.03%. Flutter is audible at around 0.1%.

Signal-to-noise ratio: The proportion of wanted signal-to-noise signal. Signal-to-noise ratios are measured in dB. The higher the figure the better. An audio or hi-fi video deck will give upwards of 60dB, a standard video deck around 45dB.

Wow: Slow variations in tape speed. They sound something like a record with an off-center hole being played. Like flutter, wow figures are expressed as percentages of the variation in speed. The lower the better, of course.

LAMPS AND LIGHTING

WHICH LAMPS TO USE

Good and adequate lighting is very important if you are going to shoot pictures with any authenticity and sparkle. Pictures will be at their brightest and most colorful when shot outside on a bright sunny day. Even on an overcast day, which may seem quite dull in comparison, you will still get far better pictures than you might shooting indoors with ordinary room lighting.

To record indoor scenes with success, you will need extra lighting. You can adapt existing lights or, if you have the opportunity (and cash), bring in a whole host of specialist lamps. What you need depends on the scene you are shooting and how ambitious you want to be. Generally, the more lights you have, the better the results will be, but lighting needs care if you are going to get the best possible shots.

The sun is easy to work with. It gives a bright, even light of a constant color all over the subject. Artificial lights aren't quite as convenient. Different forms of artifical light can have different color temperatures (see page 43) which if mixed can play havoc with the color balance of the video picture. A mixture of colors can be useful for special effects but is not so good if you want an even light. Another problem is that simply pointing a bright light at your subject can light up one side brightly but will amost certainly cast dark shadows somewhere else. Unless you

want to use this specific effect, the usual way around this problem is to employ several lamps – each lighting one side of the subject and filling in the shadows caused by the others.

The easiest and cheapest place to start looking for extra lighting is around the home. It is often possible to turn household lights into quite serviceable movie lamps. Fitting photoflood bulbs into ordinary lamp fittings is a possibility, as is using spot lamps with higher-powered bulbs.

Of specialist lights, the type featured most frequently in video accessory catalogues is the hand-held 1000 watt quartz halogen unit. These give a very powerful spread of light but tend to be rather unsubtle. Although not quite as bright, the standard photoflood lamp is much more useful and no more expensive. The standard QH (quartz halogen) video lamp is used both by amateurs and professionals and is sometimes known as a 'redhead' in the trade. Finally we get to the bigger professional lamps which are used in TV studios. If you are a member of a drama group you

Using domestic lighting

Upgrading household lights can give a remarkable lift in picture quality with very little expenditure. A desk-top spot can be turned into an effective studio light by uprating the bulb, and track lighting can be turned into an effective lighting rig by putting in more powerful spot bulbs. Beware, however, not to exceed the manufacturers' ratings either for power consumption or bulb types. High-power lighting gets very hot so don't overheat anything. Remember the formula 'current = power ÷ voltage', so divide the total wattage of the lamps used by the voltage of your power supply to find out how much current you're drawing. Do not exceed the maximum value for your supply sockets and circuit.

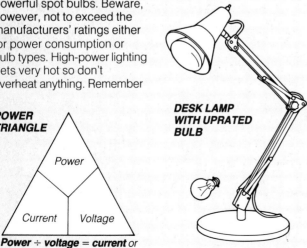

DESK LAMP WITH UPRATED BULB

POWER TRIANGLE

Power

Current | Voltage

Power ÷ voltage = current or
Current × voltage = power

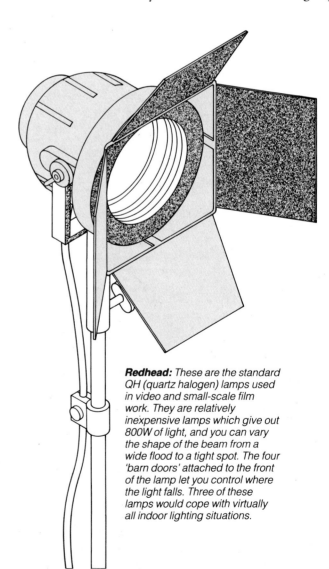

Redhead: *These are the standard QH (quartz halogen) lamps used in video and small-scale film work. They are relatively inexpensive lamps which give out 800W of light, and you can vary the shape of the beam from a wide flood to a tight spot. The four 'barn doors' attached to the front of the lamp let you control where the light falls. Three of these lamps would cope with virtually all indoor lighting situations.*

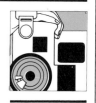

may be able to borrow stage lights. These are just as good as 'proper' video lights and will allow you to experiment with a large variety of settings and ideas.

However, there is more to producing well-lit pictures than just 'throwing' light at the scene. Because TV is a two-dimensional medium, light is used to give an illusion of depth to the pictures. This basically means highlighting some objects while keeping others relatively dim. Other problems set in when your subjects have to move. The perfect lighting set-up for one position may well become wrong when the subject moves to another place, in which case you may have to compromise and light the scene so that everything in it will at least look reasonable. In the end it's what it looks like on the screen that counts. Setting up your shots and lighting with the camera linked into a TV set is always very useful so you can see the end result. Above all don't be afraid to experiment. Video tape is reusable so you can't lose anything by trying novel or unusual ideas.

Handheld video lamps

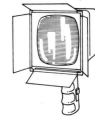

These are high-powered and, depending on the model, can be run from battery or AC. They may or may not have cooling fans, without which it is impossible to run the lamps continuously as the bulb will overheat. These lamps give a flood of very bright light and are useful for simply adding in a wash of extra light. It is not very easy to control the direction of that light, so lighting up specific objects or sections of a scene is very difficult. Outdoors, the battery-powered models can be useful in filling in shadowy areas or highlighting a face on an overcast day, but the lamp has to be color-corrected for daylight with a blue filter.

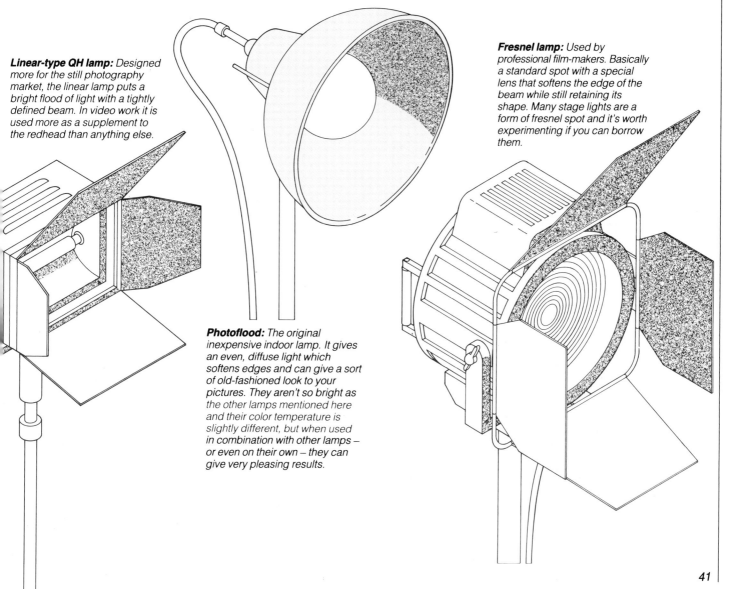

Linear-type QH lamp: *Designed more for the still photography market, the linear lamp puts a bright flood of light with a tightly defined beam. In video work it is used more as a supplement to the redhead than anything else.*

Photoflood: *The original inexpensive indoor lamp. It gives an even, diffuse light which softens edges and can give a sort of old-fashioned look to your pictures. They aren't so bright as the other lamps mentioned here and their color temperature is slightly different, but when used in combination with other lamps – or even on their own – they can give very pleasing results.*

Fresnel lamp: *Used by professional film-makers. Basically a standard spot with a special lens that softens the edge of the beam while still retaining its shape. Many stage lights are a form of fresnel spot and it's worth experimenting if you can borrow them.*

THE NATURE OF LIGHT

The human eye is remarkable – it can compensate not only for a vast range of different brightnesses, but also a huge variety of light sources. In other words a red, white and blue flag which the eye sees in bright sunlight, will still be seen and recognized as the same red, white and blue flag. But try this with a camera (video or other) and the results would be vastly different. If the picture was OK in daylight, it would be a very sorry sight in candlelight – very dim with hardly any, and certainly not the same, colors.

So, to shoot a video picture that looks right, your camera has to be adjusted both for the brightness of the light and the color balance.

Light intensity

The intensity of light is measured in units called **lux**. Candlelight gives around 10 to 15 lux, a fairly average room lit with its own artifical lights measures around 200 lux, inside a room close to a window on a sunny day is about 3,500 lux and outdoors on a clear sunlit afternoon comes in at 35,000 lux. So you can see that light spans quite a range! The minimum light level for decent pictures is quoted in the specification sheet for most video cameras. Some models can record in light as low as 15 lux. However, you will rarely see good pictures that have been taken with light levels much below 500 lux.

Don't forget also that the lower the light intensity, the smaller the depth of field (see page 15). This gets particularly critical when you're working in close-up. Even if the color quality and definition is relatively good in low light levels, the aperture might be wide open, which will give you problems keeping everything in focus.

Very bright light has its snags too. There is the problem of high contrast and reflected light, and the problem of different colors having different 'brightnesses'.

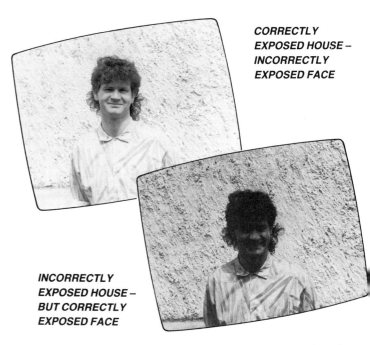

CORRECTLY EXPOSED HOUSE – INCORRECTLY EXPOSED FACE

INCORRECTLY EXPOSED HOUSE – BUT CORRECTLY EXPOSED FACE

Contrast and reflected light: The term 'contrast' describes the range of intensities between the brightest and darkest areas of the scene. Imagine a very bright, sunny day. Just looking around you are aware that areas outside the sunny patches appear to be very dark – especially things like doorways and narrow areas out of direct sunlight. If you look at that scene again in more subdued light, those shadow areas will seem less dark compared to the rest of the scene. The problem becomes more acute the higher in the sky the sun is, and huge expanses of white can make it even worse. This is because the color white reflects most of the light falling on it, so those Mediterranean scenes of white painted villas can cause huge problems if you want to pick up some detail, such as the face of a person standing in front of the building. If you've ever taken snapshots on holiday and wondered why the scene behind photographed perfectly, while the face of the person in the foreground is in deep shadow, that's the reason.

Colour temperature

When you heat an object it will glow – giving out light. That light is a mixture of the different colors of the spectrum. The mix depends on the material and the temperature to which it has been heated. Generally speaking objects glow red at low temperatures, and as the temperature increases their color changes through orange and yellow to blue and finally violet. To make a practical artificial light source (a bulb), a material is chosen (for the filament) that will appear to glow white when heated by making an electric current flow through it. When the eye looks at an object lit by that light source, anything that is apparently white will be seen and perceived as white. If you take that object into sunlight, the eye will still see it as the same white despite the fact that the light is coming from an object glowing at a much higher temperature.

The reality is that the artificial light is giving out light that is predominantly yellow because it has been heated up to a relatively low temperature, while the sunlight is very blue because it is coming from an object – the sun – which is very much hotter. We say that the **color temperature** of the lamp is much lower than that of sunlight. The color temperature is measured in kelvins and the chart opposite gives figures for different light sources and situations.

But where does this leave the video user? Very simply, although the eye and brain can compensate for the fact that whites vary under different illumination, the video camera cannot. This means that every time you move from one light source to another you have to readjust the camera, so that the 'white' produced by that source will actually be white to the camera, and not blue or yellow.

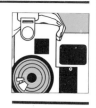

ACTUAL BRIGHTNESS OF COLORS

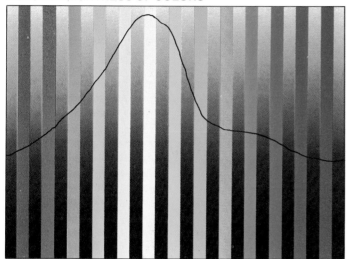

The line indicates the brightness of different colors and their corresponding grey tone values.

Brightness of colors: Peculiarities of the human eye mean that if you set up a series of colored lights of the same intensity (as measured by a light meter), they will not actually **appear** to be of equal brightness. The chart above shows the approximate range of apparent brightnesses of the different colors, from the dimmest (red) to the brightest (yellow). The more brightly lit a scene is, the more accentuated this effect will be.

Shooting a scene with many different colors and shapes – as most will be – causes few problems, but if you are shooting something with huge areas of a single color then difficulties begin, especially if you have a 'dim' color next to a 'bright' one. A shot of someone wearing a red sweater standing in front of a yellow wall is a good example of this. In fact, red is a color to avoid in video work whenever possible. It causes technical problems all along the line and is the most difficult color to reproduce satisfactorily.

What is white light?

In the 18th century, Isaac Newton discovered that white light isn't really white at all, but a mixture of different colors. This range of colors is called a **spectrum**. Looking at the situation the other way around, you can reconstitute white light by mixing the three **primary colors** of light, red, blue and green, as you can see on the right. It is possible or create any color – not just white – by varying the strength of these three primaries (which are different from those of pigments). Without this property of light, color TV and color photography would not 'work' so easily.

The colors that result from a mix of two pure primaries are called **secondary colors**. If you look at the color chart below you can see that there is a secondary opposite each primary. For this reason secondary colors are often called negatives. The negative of blue will be yellow, the negative of red is cyan, and the negative of green is magenta. This is particularly useful to know when you start getting involved in special effects.

MIXING PRIMARY COLORED LIGHT

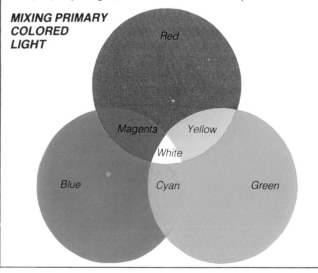

COLOR TEMPERATURE VALUES

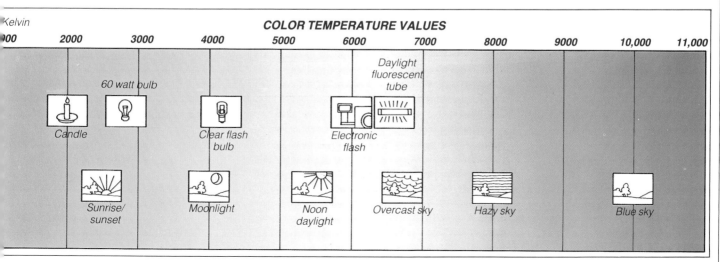

WHITE BALANCE AND COLOR CORRECTION

As we have seen, white light is only truly white when there is an even mix of the three pure primary colors. Most light sources are really either a shade of yellow or blue according to color temperature. Although the eye can compensate for these differences, the camera cannot, and it has to be adjusted so that the 'white' light resulting from any particular form of illumination will actually appear white on the screen.

With earlier models of video camera it was necessary to manually adjust the **white balance** by training the camera on a specially printed chart, while viewing the picture on a TV screen. The camera was then adjusted until the picture matched the chart. Nowadays, white balance is automatic. You point the camera at something white (or even simply switch in a translucent white filter), and press the auto white balance button. The camera will then compare the signal that it is getting from the pick-up tube to a built-in reference and adjust the signal until it matches. Switchable filters are used for the basic color balancing, one for daylight and one for artificial light. These set the camera to be roughly correct leaving the electronics to make the fine adjustments.

In addition to these controls, there may be a manual color correction adjuster. This is supplied so that the operator can make his own adjustments to the electronic setting – either because of peculiar circumstances or for special effects. Usually there is only one control which allows you to either add more red or more blue to the picture. Occasionally there are two controls, one for each color.

Very simple cameras do not offer any form of white-balance adjustment at all, apart from a multi-position switch. If there are four positions, you will have the usual choice between artificial light and daylight, but there may also be a 'candlelight' position at the bottom end meant for extremely low levels of artificial light, and perhaps a bright sunlight setting at the other end of the scale. This is, of course, a compromise between performance and cost, but works well except in more unusual circumstances.

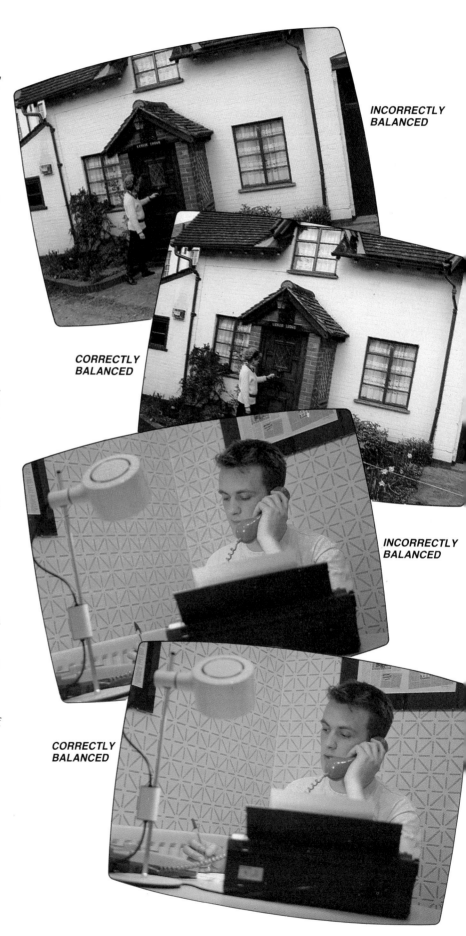

INCORRECTLY BALANCED

CORRECTLY BALANCED

INCORRECTLY BALANCED

CORRECTLY BALANCED

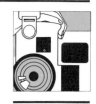

White balance effects

The video camera must, of course, be adjusted properly for accurate color reproduction, but there are certain circumstances where you can use 'wrong' settings to achieve a particular effect.

First of all set up the camera and connect it to a color TV. Look at the picture and adjust the white balance so that it is correct for the type of light (this experiment should be carried out both in artificial light and daylight). Now aim the camera at a collection of brightly colored objects – a red cushion, a yellow flower, a bright blue beach ball, a green jumper and so on. Take a good look at them and their TV image, which should be as close as you can possibly get to the originals.

Now flip over the daylight/ artificial light filter and see how the colors change. If you have everything set up for daylight, switching over to the artifcial light setting will immediately give the whole scene a yellowish tinge, and therefore a 'warmer' feel. Put a person in with your objects and you can soon see the effect on the flesh tones – they begin to glow and the skin loses its pallor (if it's not already tanned and healthy-looking).

Taking the opposite course can be equally revealing. Set up your objects under artificial light and then flip the switch over to daylight. Immediately everything takes on a steely coldness. A blue cast is thrown over the scene and the effect on flesh tones is to turn them almost an eerie blue. This can also be the basis for creating convincing-looking night-time effects.

If your camera is fitted with separate red and blue fine adjusters it becomes easier to vary the range of color settings. Using the red control, for example, allows you to add in just a tinge of warmth,

without altogether losing the basic standard setting.

A further effect worth considering is solarization, but it can only be achieved if you have a manual override on your camera's automatic iris. Very simply, you open the aperture right up until the image is extremely over-exposed. The highlights in the picture bleach out to white and the rest of the background loses much of its detail. By then pushing the white balance massively out of adjustment one way or the other, you can achieve an interesting blue or red tinting effect around the bleached-out sections.

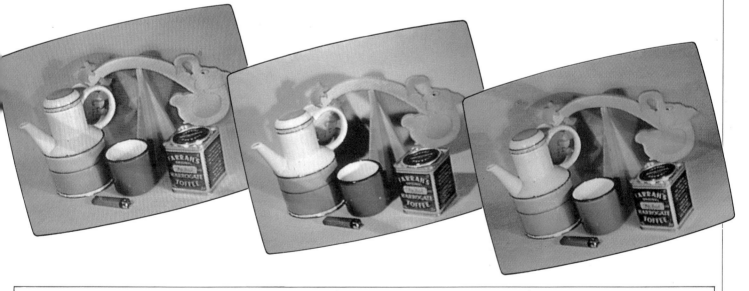

Color cast

Another interesting effect can be gained by the thoughtful placing of your subject. Someone leaning on a red door, for example, will have a strong tint of red about him. Another person sitting close to a TV screen which is showing a green picture, as you might get with a computer display, will be lit a lurid green. Careful positioning can bring all sorts of color casts into play.

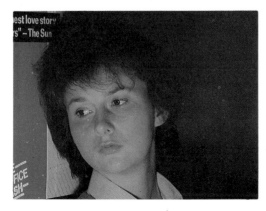

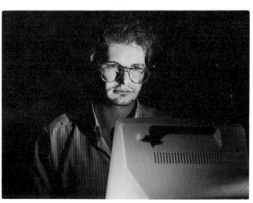

TECHNIQUES

SHOTS

Whenever you set out to record something with any sort of camera, whether you want to take a quick snapshot or a more considered portrait or view, you have to decide how you are going to fill the area of the picture framed by the viewfinder.

In a sense, the stills photographer has things relatively easy. He can only take one picture, one view at a time, usually with only one lens. His options in filling the picture area are therefore limited, which simplifies the choices he has to make.

A video or film cameraman has no such constraints. Because the action is moving, he is being called on continually to think about what he is going to put in the picture area. He has to compose pictures by the score. As the scene changes, so does his composition.

The zoom lens fitted to virtually all video cameras gives him an extra set of options. Not only is he aware of a constant change of objects in his picture area, but he can also change their size and emphasis in relation to that area. The zoom lens enables him to go from a very wide angle shot to a tight close-up. All these choices and decisions are now yours too.

Over to you

Each time you set up a new viewpoint for the camera, you set up a new **shot**. To avoid confusion, a standard set of definitions, based on the portion of a subject that might appear in the viewfinder, has been developed so that different shots can be talked about. (See below and right.) Although these terms have proper definitions, they are not so exact that you can't vary them.

In general, don't use the **medium long shot** (MLS) if you're shooting people. You won't be able to see much of the background, yet your subjects will be too small. A **medium shot**

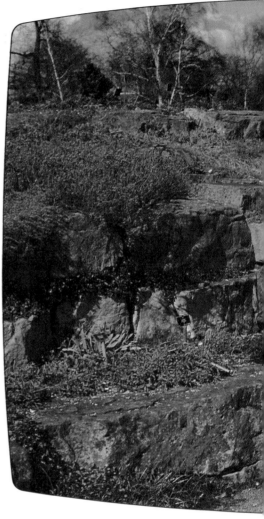

Long shot (LS): *Usually refers to a shot that contains the entire subject from head to foot, but is usually close-up enough to include only a little of the background.*

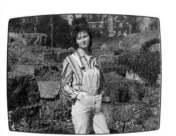

Medium long shot (MLS): *Closer in than the LS, this takes in a person from their knees upwards. This can be useful in certain circumstances but is best avoided with people as they can look too small, while there is not enough background to be useful visually.*

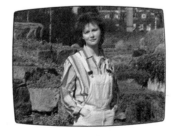

Medium shot (MS): *A favorite of TV news reporters (although it shouldn't be held for too long). An MS takes in the person from the waist upwards. The actual visual interest is in the face – which in an MS is too small to show much detail. A cut to some detail about which the person is talking or perhaps a slow zoom into CU is usually a good follow-up shot.*

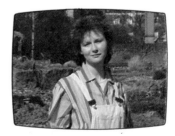

Medium close-up (MCU): *Shows our subject from the chest upwards. Good for someone talking direct to camera if you can't change the shot. Using the zoom lens near the telephoto (long focal length) end of its zoom range and positioning yourself a long distance from the subject will mean that the subject will be focused while the background isn't, thus making the subject stand out.*

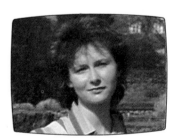

Close-up (CU): *A shot roughly from the shoulders upwards. Shooting from a distance with the zoom at the telephoto end of its range will make the subject stand out.*

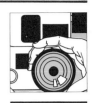

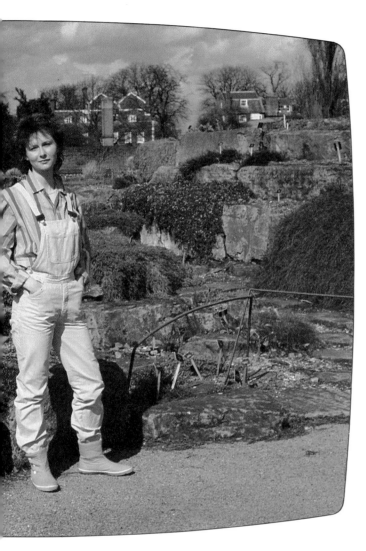

(MS) is fine to start a sequence if you're shooting someone talking to the camera, but the viewer will soon start to get fed up with acres of clothes and it is far better to move in to a **medium close-up** (MCU) after just a few moments.

Then there's the **close-up** (CU). This shot is more intimate, or can be used to give the impression of someone being intimidated if you want to shoot a confrontation. This feeling is heightened with the **big close-up** (BCU).

The large picture opposite shows a typical subject against a general background. This would be called a **very long shot** (VLS) as it contains the subject full length as well as a fair proportion of the background. Once you get past the human scale, most shots are either broad panoramic views or close-ups.

Macro

This is a feature found on most video camera lenses. It allows you to get extremely close to a subject and keep it in focus. Although it is at its most useful for such things as shooting captions, nature close-ups, or recording still pictures and objects, macro also has a use with live action. You can use it to follow eye movements, picking up a reflection of some significant event – a door opening in the eyes is a favorite movie trick – or to follow intricate movements, such as a painter mixing his colors or applying them to a canvas.

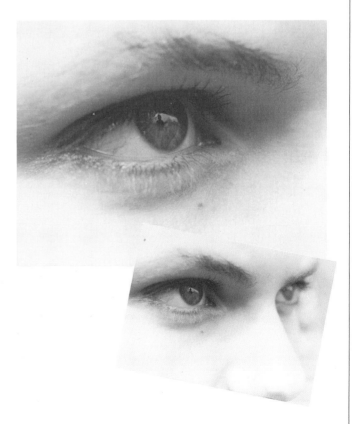

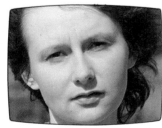

Alternatively, using the lens at a wide angle while getting in really close, can emphasize the menacing aspect of this shot, since the image will be distorted. Be careful of focus, though.

Big close-up (BCU): *Essentially shows chin to forehead. A useful shot, but should be used sparingly unless you want to lessen its effect. Distortions will occur at the wide-angle end of the lens' range.*

PICTURE COMPOSITION

LEARNING TO LOOK

Picture composition is essentially arranging the elements you want to film so that they fill the image area in a pleasing and satisfying way. These picture elements could be people or objects, and you can arrange them by either moving them around or moving the camera around, until they are positioned exactly where you want them.

There are certain 'rights' and 'wrongs' when it comes to picture composition, but in the end what matters is that the final result actually looks pleasing. You should start to train yourself to be aware of absolutely everyting that appears in the viewfinder. The human eye has a wonderful way of ignoring seemingly unimportant things – but video cameras don't. Train yourself to look at every square millimeter of the viewfinder – especially the edges. A camera can flatten the perspective and make some objects appear to be growing out of others – lamp posts from the tops of peoples' heads is one common example. The eye – and brain – tells you they are separate so you perceive them as such. But the camera can't make this distinction, so you must be very aware of how objects appear in relation to each other. Even colors can look different on the screen, so you must be sensitive to this, too. The eye can distinguish between objects that are virtually the same color, but the camera can't, especially at the red end of the spectrum.

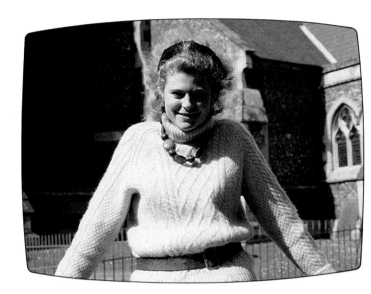

Top: A scene taken in by a camera. The camera lens used has a different focal length from the human eye.
Below: The same scene as viewed by the human eye.

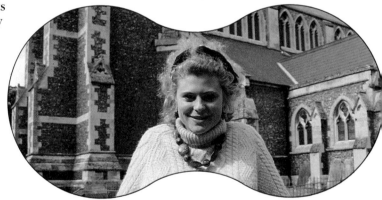

Composition basics

When it comes to photographing faces – and this applies whether you are talking about still, cine or video photography – there are two golden rules to be aware of. Firstly, arrange the face so that the eyes are one third of the distance from the top of the frame. The top of the head should not be touching the top of the screen, nor should the chin be sitting on the bottom of the picture.

The second rule really stems from being aware of everything in the viewfinder image. Make sure that there are no unseemly objects in the background that appear to be growing from the subject's head!

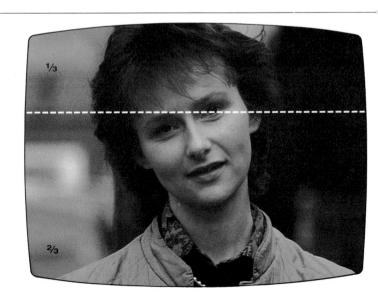

Looking and walking room

Moving on from simple 'front on' shots, if a face is not looking straight ahead but to one side, it should be placed over to one side of the screen to give it '**looking room**' (left). In other words, the face should be looking towards the other 'empty' side of the screen, and not at the very edge of the frame.

Similarly if you are going to shoot someone walking to the right, then keep them over to the left side of the image area (or vice versa). This gives them what's called '**walking room**' (below left).

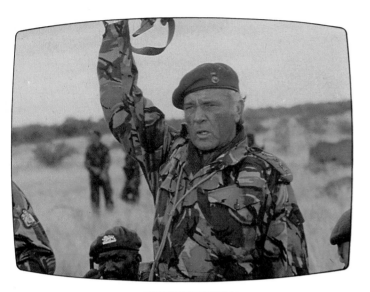

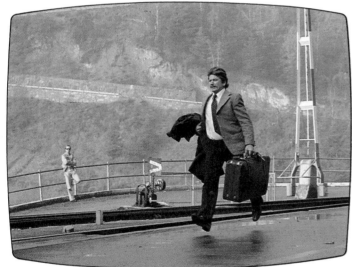

Dividing lines

The **rule of thirds** is almost an extension of looking and walking room. Subjects that are placed bang in the centre of the picture area are, by and large, visually uninteresting. Dividing the frame area into imaginary thirds both horizontally and vertically, and arranging the subject matter along these lines will tend to balance the picture visually and gives a more 'satisfying' image.

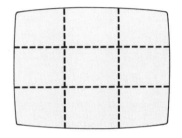

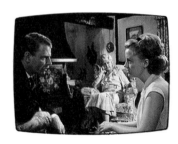

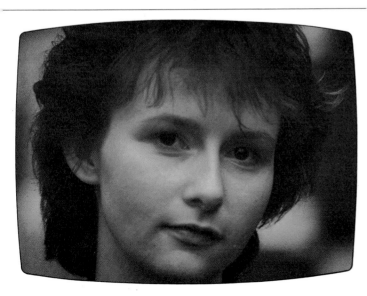

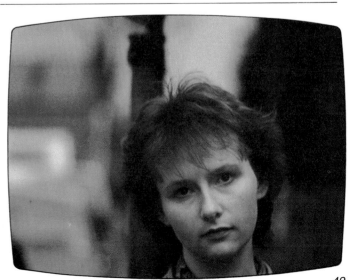

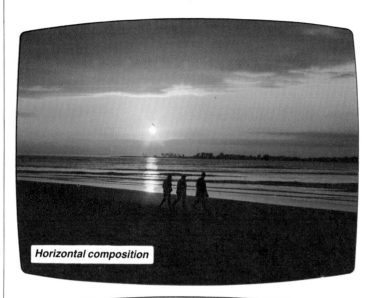

Horizontal composition

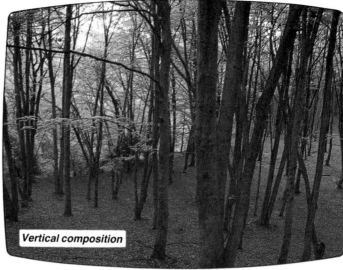

Vertical composition

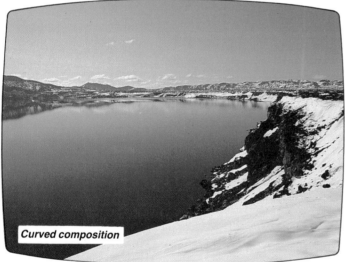

Curved composition

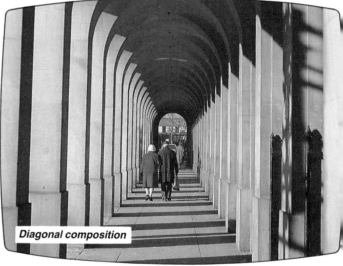

Diagonal composition

Horizontal, vertical, curved and diagonal compositions

These are four of the most basic ways in which pictures can be composed, either by using natural lines, or creating your own by arrangement of people and objects. Different compositions are more effective in certain circumstances than others. For example, horizontal and vertical compositions can be juxtaposed to reinforce a point about contrasts and differences.

Curves generally make quite restful images which can meander through the frame. Composing your picture with strong diagonal shapes – perhaps the arrangement of the heads of the people involved, or using natural lines such as those of a corridor – can guide the viewer's eye and point it at a distant subject, or the main character in a scene.

Visual depth

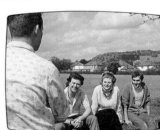

You can give pictures depth by making sure that everyone and everything is not arranged on the same straight line across the screen. Placing a person or an object in the foreground will give the shot depth, as does lighting various parts of the scene differently. Shooting at a distance with the lens at the telephoto end of its range can also add depth by putting the object in focus and keeping the background unfocused.

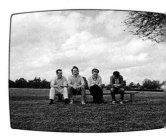

Eye level

A human's average eye level is the height usually used for most TV and film shots. In other words the camera sees the world from roughly the same position that you and I would – around 5 feet from the ground.

There are times when this rule can be broken, however. If you are shooting a person sitting, then it becomes very uncomfortable to watch if the camera is towering over them at 'normal' eye level. The person is put in a position dominated by the camera and looks weak and small. So usually the camera is positioned at the level of someone sitting listening to that person. Children are usually taped better from their own viewpoints too.

When recording a situation in which two people are speaking to each other, you can take the eye-line position of the person who is listening each time, swapping position when the dialogue shifts from one person to the other and back again. This can be done by panning or by shifting the focus between the two people. Alternatively you may want to leave the shot static, but remember that the eyes are important communication contact points in human beings.

The **eye-line rule** can also be broken for special effects, but you should be aware of over-using odd shooting angles. Their dramatic impact will soon be lost if they are repeated too often. The odd worm's eye or bird's eye view can, however, be a very handy addition to your repertoire of shots.

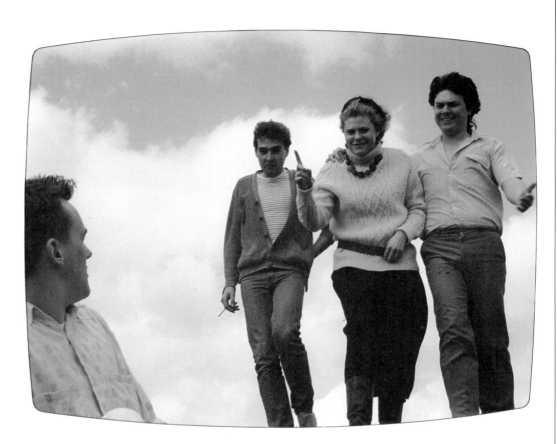

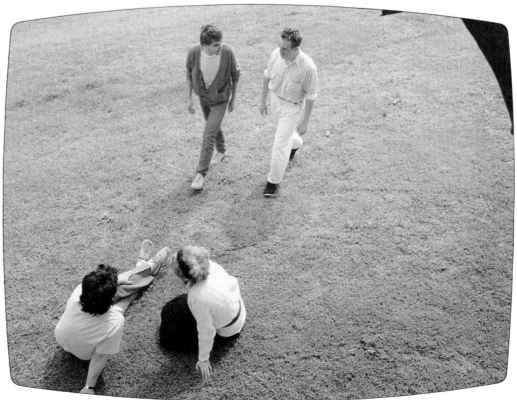

A MISCELLANY OF SHOTS

When a professional video crew sets out to shoot an event, they always take certain types of shots because they know that these will be useful – if not essential – in the final video. These shots have been born out of years of experience. If you follow the same common sense rules, then you'll probably be able to say 'if only I'd thought of that' less often. Try to work out what particular shots do, and how they were constructed, when you watch films or TV. You will then become more aware of the way that you can use different shots to construct the story/narrative structure of your videos.

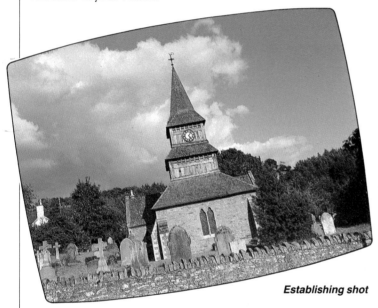

Establishing shot

General view or establisher

As its name suggests, this shot is just a general view of the location you're shooting in. It might be the church if you're shooting a wedding, or a school if you're recording the school sports day or prize-giving. You may not actually use it in the finished tape, but an establishing shot can be very useful in identifying that sequence of shots on the tape, as well as giving you an introduction to that part of the video.

Introductory shot

If you're making a video which includes some form of interview, or even just someone talking to the camera, you should shoot at least one sequence of that person doing something else. If he's a school teacher, you might shoot him in front of his class for example. When added to the final edited video, it makes the person seem much more interesting than just a talking head!

Cutaways

Have you noticed that in TV interviews the interviewer will appear on the screen nodding wisely as the person being interviewed carries on talking? This is a **cutaway** and is there to add visual interest or to hide the fact that something has been cut from the dialogue. In the latter case it is used because although you can chop bits out of the sound track without anyone noticing, you can't do the same with the pictures without the person appearing to move suddenly or jump.

Wallpaper shot

Literally any shot – of a road, cars passing, landscapes, townscapes – that is used to fill the screen while a narrator is talking. Those beautiful beach views, for example, would make good wallpaper shots in your holiday video.

Inserts

Tiny sections of close-up action used to illustrate specific points – like a finger dialing a telephone – which would get lost in a wider view. The pace of action in an insert should be slower than usual, otherwise it can look rather comical.

Jump cuts

Two shots that follow each other but don't follow the logical order of your story, or don't make apparent sense. Take the example of a man shown walking down the street. The next shot might show him sitting in an armchair at home. That sudden jolt is a jump cut and should be avoided in this context. You don't have to show every little detail of his journey, but neither should you shorten it so much that it becomes absurd. On the other hand, jump cuts are often used to take the viewer into another scene or piece of action which might be going on at the same time as your main narrative action.

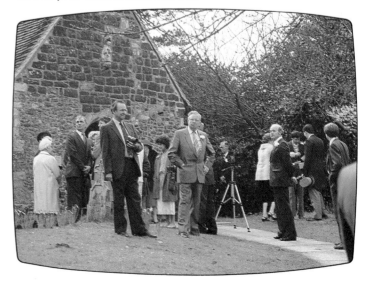

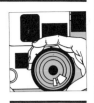

Composition and the moving subject

Although the more usual methods of composition involve moving the camera around to frame your subjects, difficulties arise if the subjects themselves are moving. What about someone coming through a door, or walking down an aisle? The best thing to do here is to arrange your shots so that the moving objects or people end up in a position where the shot's composition is good. Look at an example of a man coming through a door. The shot can be arranged so that he might enter and stop at the corner of a desk or by a chair to his side. It looks perfectly natural and makes a good composition. At the end of his lines he might mop his brow, providing a perfect point at which to cut to another scene.

In the case of a wedding, you obviously can't tell the bride and groom exactly where to stop. However, a little advance research and common sense should give you a good idea of where they will stop. You can then arrange the rest of the shot so that you follow them down the aisle with the camera and end up with the best composition when they stand still.

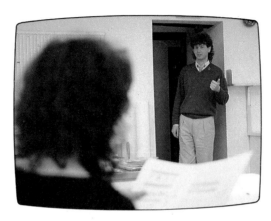

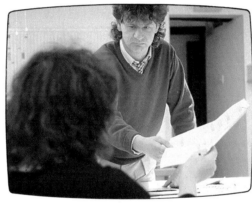

Racking focus

A clever, but effective, movie trick that requires some practice to get right. Suppose you have two people in shot, one is in focus and the other isn't. When you **rack focus**, the first subject is defocused so that the other is brought into focus. Racking focus can be used to catch the reaction of the other person or simply because the dialogue has passed from one to the other.

Using this technique in a shot usually involves two people – one to operate the camera and the other to change the focus. It is most convenient to mark the two focus positions on a piece of tape on the lens' focus ring. The person who operates the focus positions on a piece of tape on the lens' focus ring. The person who operates the circles.

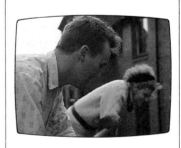

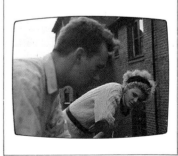

Crossing the line – the 180-degree rule

The diagram to the right shows an imaginary line across the scene that you are shooting. Creating the line creates a continuity problem. It is something which you must positively remember not to do as it is not always obvious. If, for example, you shoot a man walking from left to right across the picture, then in the next shot he must also move from left to right or he will appear to have changed direction. Similarly changing the camera position to the other side of the line, if you're recording two people talking, will make it look as if they have swapped places. You can of course cross the line if you are shooting a continuous shot with a moving camera position, as the moving viewpoint naturally explains what's happening.

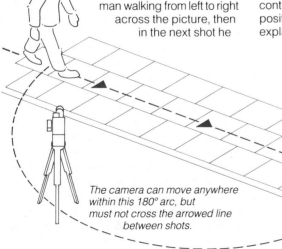

The camera can move anywhere within this 180° arc, but must not cross the arrowed line between shots.

CAMERA MOVEMENT

Although the aim of any cameraman is to get rock steady, jerk-free pictures, more often than not the camera has to be moved in some way – either for effect or to follow the action. Disregarding the handheld camera for a moment, there are only two ways in which the camera can move while mounted on a tripod – from side to side (**panning**) or up and down (**tilting**), with the camera pivoting on a central axis. Of course, these can be combined into diagonal moves with practice. Added to these you can also make the picture move by zooming in and out, as well as tracking the camera on a dolly or rails.

Like any visual effect, camera movement should be used sparingly. Having said that, shots containing camera movement tend to be more dynamic because of the constantly changing viewpoints. A slow tilt upwards gives viewers the feeling that they are carefully examining the subject – suspense and anticipation is built up until there is a feeling of culmination, of something accomplished, as the tilt reaches the top. The buildup can be used to give a feeling of power or even fear. A good example of this technique can be seen towards the end of the film *Planet of the Apes*. Here, a tilt starts on a pile of rocks. As it moves up, it becomes clear that the 'rocks' are the remains of a monument which becomes more and more familiar until the tilt ends on what's actually the upraised arm of the Statue of Liberty.

Pan shots have a similar effect – build up of tension towards a climax. But they have some interesting points on their own. It seems that because we are used to reading and assimilating information from left to right, a pan shot in this direction has a psychological feeling of relaxation. Movement in the opposite direction, right to left, is more disturbing. It is inherently threatening and has a sense of foreboding.

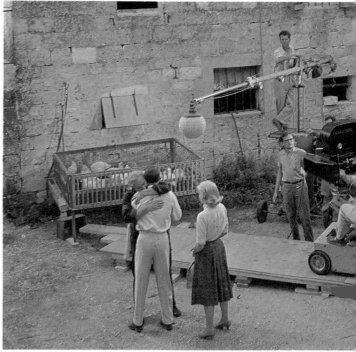

The tracking shot

Something really for the serious amateur or professional studio, as it demands quite a lot of planning. Actually getting hold of and laying rails can be very difficult for the amateur. Using a tripod with wheels is easier, but needs a very smooth surface. Making and adapting trolleys of different sorts is another option. Cars can be used outside, with some helpers to steer and push the vehicle if

The pan

Useful for following someone's eye-line from one object to another or taking in a panoramic view. Before shooting a pan shot, be quite sure where it's going to start and end. Do a few practice swings, paying particular attention to everything seen in the viewfinder, especially at the edges. When shooting landscapes, keep the horizon level throughout.

Keep an eye on the focus. If everything in the pan is roughly at the same distance, then there shouldn't be any problems. Difficulties crop up if you swing from a distant scene to one where there are objects close to the foreground. You have to either re-focus as the nearby object comes into shot – which needs practice, but is effective when you get it right – or re-think the pan shot so that the nearby object is excluded.

A pan should start and finish without jerking. When you are about to begin, start recording, take a deep breath, count to five and begin to pan. At the end of the shot keep very still for a count of five, stop recording, and then let go of the camera. This will help you minimize camera shake and any play or other deficiencies in your tripod head.

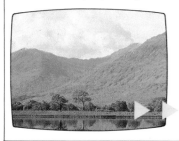
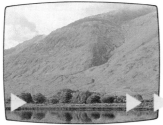
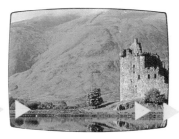
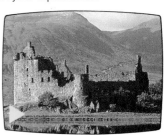

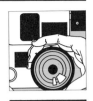

While free use of pan and tilt shots is quite usual, zooming during the middle of a shot is comparatively rare and should be used sparingly. The zoom action is unnatural – no living creature has an optical system that can change its focal length in this way – and so viewing its results looks equally unnatural. It is much better to regard the zoom system as a convenient way of changing the focal length of the lens between shots as well as providing the means for an occasional special effect. The one cardinal rule is not to 'trombone' – that is never zoom in and then out (or vice versa) in the same shot.

If professional crews need to get a shot moving away from an object they will most likely use a tracking shot. These create some problems for the amateur – you are not likely to have tracks to lay, but your tripod can be used with wheels if you have a smooth enough floor to work on. Sometimes a car can be used. The focus may need adjusting during the shot, so a good rehearsal is needed to sort out what to do. The great advantage of the tracking shot is that it isn't unnatural. People do walk towards and away from things all the time so changes in perspective and views do not seem out of the ordinary when seen on screen.

More complex shots can combine any or all of these different camera movements. You may zoom out while tilting upwards, or pan left while tilting down for instance. To combine a tracking shot with a pan or tilt, professionals usually use a *crane*. This is a wheeled trolley with a boom to which the camera is fixed. The actual crane and boom is moved around by several people with the camera and its operator perched on the end. Obviously crane shots are the hardest for the amateur to attempt, but ingenuity can overcome a lot of movement problems. Shooting a sequence in somewhere like a shopping mall, for example, could make good use of the cameraman travelling down an escalator while shooting action on the floor below.

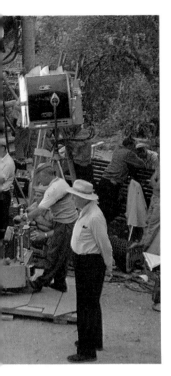

the engine is too noisy. Again, the whole of the shot has to be considered for both composition and focusing, and the 'camera steady' drill detailed for panning should also be followed.

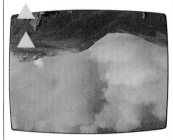
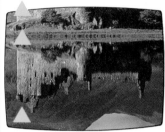
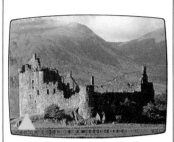

The tilt

This movement can be used to build anticipation and expectation. You must make sure you know where you're going to start and where you're going to end the shot. It is important to check everything seen in the viewfinder in between these points.

Also make sure that everything stays in focus. You may have to adjust focus half way through, which may be a bit tricky, so rehearse the shot a few times before actually shooting.

You can pause during a tilt (or pan) movement and this increases the viewers' feeling of anticipation. Carrying out the tilt employs the same drill as the pan, holding the camera steady while recording a couple of extra seconds at the beginning and end of the shot.

The zoom

A special shot to be used sparingly. The effect of the zoom is to make the subject appear to get bigger and come towards the camera. In a sense this is an unreal shot – it never happens in real life, unlike a pan or tilt. When this impression of external reality is unnecessary, or where the

enhancing effect of magnification is a positive benefit, the zoom is useful and expressive. Practise the zoom a few times, making sure you pay attention to everything that is in the frame, and set the **back focus** as described on page 13. Don't forget that if you move the

camera position then the focus will need re-adjusting.

Zooming in and out from specific points in a scene can be very effective in beginning or ending a shot. You could start with a shot of a row of houses, and zoom into the window of a room where the action is happening.

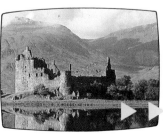
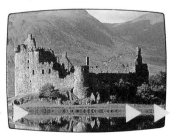
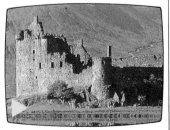

LIGHTING

YOU DON'T SEE WHAT YOU SHOOT

The art of observation and awareness must be extended beyond the composition of elements in the frame to include lighting. Video cameras respond to light in a different way than the human eye (see page 60). The differences are especially noticeable when you consider the lighting in a scene.

Imagine a typical living room, which contains three lamps. To the human eye, these will appear to cast a fairly even spread of light. Through the camera, though, you will see three brilliantly bright objects surrounded by near darkness. Why does this happen? First of all, the camera's automatic iris (see page 14) will set the aperture for the brightest light in the room – the lamps themselves. This, of course, will be far too small a setting for the surrounding illumination. Secondly, even if you manually adjust the iris, you will find that the camera cannot respond to the large range of brightnesses that are present in the room, to give a balanced picture. The human eye and brain are much more sophisticated than a video camera and, between them, compensate for a huge range of illumination.

Shooting outdoors is much easier, mainly because the lighting is much more even, but you can start to get the same sort of problems in very bright sunlight. So wherever you're filming, the general rule is to make sure that the whole image area is as evenly lit as possible. Always check your shot on a color TV, or monitor, wherever possible. This is particularly important if you want to use lighting to create a mood or special effect. Although you will eventually be able to tell by experience whether a particular lighting set-up is adequate or not, there's no substitute for a final visual check. Professionals do it as a matter of course.

Filling in the shadows

When you're lighting a single subject, follow this simple set of rules and you can be sure that your subject will be evenly lit, while still maintaining an impression of depth. This is the **three-point method** which, surprisingly enough, uses three lights.

The first is the **key** light, and is positioned to one side of your subject. This provides a bright source of directional light, a little like the sun would do, and picks out the highlights on one side of the face. However, you can soon see that the other side of the face is left in deep shadow. The contrast between the highlights and the black shadows on the two sides of the face will be too pronounced for most practical purposes, although great for effects.

To overcome this, you need the **fill** light. This is trained on the opposite side of the face to the key light, and is less powerful and more **diffuse**. Why less powerful? Well, you are trying to create depth and contrast with the lighting. Using a fill light of even power to the key would give you a subject with an even amount of light on both sides. This would have the same flattening effect as one light pointing directly at the subject, resulting in an image that has little interest.

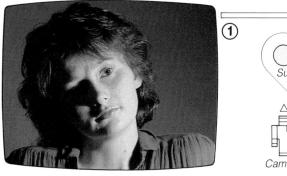
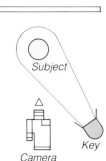

Step 1: Key light.

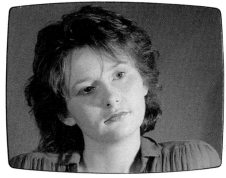
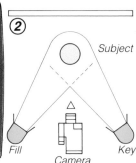

Step 2: Add fill.

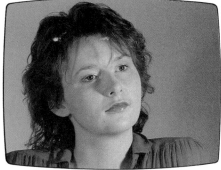
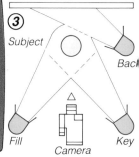

Step 3: Finish with backlight.

Finally, we get to the **backlight** (not to be confused with the background light, which is explained below). The backlight – as its name suggests – is used to illuminate the back of the subject to separate it from the background – adding more depth to the image. Lighting the back of the subject can add a halo effect to their hair and a focusing spotlight is best used for this. Otherwise you should use a very diffuse light that is less intense than the key.

Other elements can be added to this basic three-point system. An extra light could be used specifically to take out shadows, or you could use reflector boards to bounce light back at the subject. These are particularly useful for delicate filling in of shadows where an extra lamp would be too powerful. Background lighting goes a long way to improving your image quality. It can add depth to your pictures and is useful for filling in dark areas or picking out specific details. The best thing to do initially is experiment with different lighting set-ups while looking at the results on a color television.

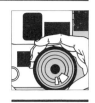

Lighting and atmosphere

You don't have to be a professional cameraman to realize that lighting is very important in creating atmosphere in a room. A single unshaded bulb, for example, gives a harsh unsubtle light. You can recreate the effect of this by pouring as much light as possible onto the subject from a high angle. This will create dark shadows under the eyes and chin. A warm inviting atmosphere, on the other hand, is created by soft, diffuse light. Placing several shaded lamps around your scene will fill the intervening spaces with an even, diffused light. The effect can be enhanced by using a slightly orange filter over the camera lens (see page 66), or by adjusting the camera's white balance (see page 44).

Creating a specific atmosphere is more a process of thought and consideration than anything else. According to Oscar-winning cinematographer Freddie Francis, there is no magic trick. He describes how he conceived the lighting for *Elephant Man*: "I tried to picture the scene. If I was in London in 1840 at that time of the year, where would the light be coming from? There probably wouldn't be much light. If there was light, it would be mixed up with a lot of smoke coming from fires. From these considerations and contemporary pictures, I could then decide where to put my lamps, how powerful they should be and what, if any, filters I should put in front of them."

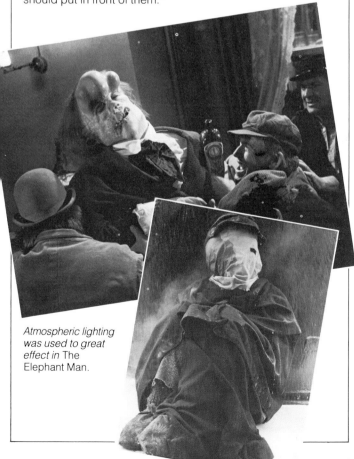

Atmospheric lighting was used to great effect in The Elephant Man.

Lighting words

Barn doors: Hinged flaps mounted on the front of a lamp which can be opened or closed independently to control the size and shape of the beam of light.

Blonde: Trade name that has become a general term for a particular type of 2kW QH movie lamp.

Color temperature: Describes what color the 'white' light produced by a source is going to be when viewed on the screen.

Diffuse light: Light that has been softened by filtering with a paper screen or a gauze filter. The shadows cast by diffuse light are 'softer' at the edges.

Filter: Transparent material fixed to the front of a lamp, or camera, which changes the nature of the light passing through it. Filters are usually colored, in which case the color of the light passing through them is changed. Filters can be used to modify the light in other ways, such as blocking ultraviolet rays.

Flag: Piece of wood or card which may be mounted on a stand. Used to stop stray light falling into the camera lens, or placed in front of a lamp to cut off part of its beam and so modify the pattern of light coming from it.

Fresnel lens: Lens mounted on the front of a movie or stage lamp, which focuses the light into a diffused but well-defined beam.

Gaffer: Name for the lighting electrician in a professional film or video crew.

Gobo: Piece of metal place which fixes on the front of a lamp and has a pattern of holes punched in it. Used to throw a varied pattern of light onto a scene or for a specific effect such as creating the shape of a moon or clouds.

Hard light: Quality of the light coming from a lamp which has hard, sharply defined edges to its beam and will create sharp shadows.

Kelvin: Unit in which color temperature is expressed.

Lux: Unit in which light intensity is expressed.

Photoflood: Used primarily in still photography. The photoflood bulb is similar to the domestic light bulb, but is 'driven' a lot harder to get maximum brightness – at the expense of shorter life.

QH: Short for quartz halogen, this is a particular type of high-power light source.

Redhead: Trade name that has acquired a general meaning. Used to describe a particular form of 850W QH movie light.

Snoot: A conical lamp fitting, which confines the light beam to a small area.

Daytime shots

Generally you need even illumination over the scene – the more diffuse the light the better. If the sun is bright and high in the sky, you will run into problems with deep shadows on your subjects' faces. You can get over this either by shooting in the shade, under a tree say, or by shooting next to a light-coloured building, which will reflect light back onto your subject's face, thereby filling in the dark shadows.

The best thing to do when shooting outdoors is to use some reflector boards positioned just outside the camera's field of vision. These can be made of large sheets of white card or styrofoam, or boards with cooking foil stuck to them. Flat foil gives a very direct reflection, while crumpled foil reflects a more diffuse light. Position these reflectors below and to one side of the subject, so that light is reflected onto the face – especially in the hollows under the eyes. There's no need to match the brightness on the sides of the face – a difference adds interest and depth to the image.

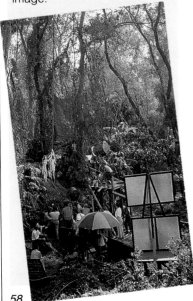

LIGHTING – OUTDOORS

Working outdoors, the obvious light source is the sun. It is without a doubt the best form of illumination for the home video user. The sun is bright – giving true colors and adequate depth of focus; it is an even light for the most part, although there are circumstances when this doesn't hold true; and it is always there!

But even with such a handy light source, you have to bear some things in mind if your shots are going to be entirely successful. The sun's brightness and position, for example, changes with the time of day and year. This is important if you're shooting something like a wedding where the church's entrance porch might only be in sunlight in the afternoon. Bright sunlight can cast harsh shadows which have to be taken care of, while light from a cloudy sky rarely gives such problems. And there are always going to be occasions when some extra light will be very useful for your shot.

Night-time shooting outdoors presents its own problems, but these are dealt with on page 63.

Home-light reflectors

The simplest reflector is a piece of white styrofoam. For more efficient reflection, you will need something a bit more shiny.

Cooking foil glued flat over a board is fine, and for a more diffuse reflected light use crumpled foil.

You can make reflectors to tint the reflected light by using coloured foil gift-wrapping, or by spraying ordinary foil with metallic paint. Gold foil will give a warm glow, blue foil a cool iciness. Green is eerie, while red can be used for sunset effects. By bouncing

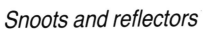

light from a lamp off a reflector onto the subject, you can get an even spread of light that is far more subtle than direct lighting. A flickering light bounced off a red reflector gives a very effective impression of being near a fire.

Snoots and reflectors

When buying photoflood lights, you can often choose the size and shape of the reflector dish behind the lamp. Generally speaking, the more shallow the dish, the more diffuse the light. Metal caps which go over the top of the bulb will accentuate this effect. A **parabolic** reflector will give a beam with almost parallel edges.

A **snoot** is a particular kind of 'add-on' accessory – a metal cone which fastens on the front of a lamp to give a very narrow beam of light. It can be used to accentuate

particular aspects of your subject – for example, a snoot directed onto the hair from behind will create a halo effect.

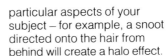
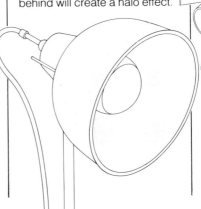
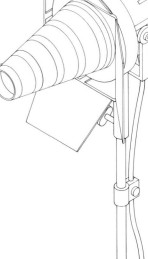

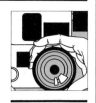

Time of day

Mid-morning/mid-afternoon:
Probably the best time to be shooting. The sun is angled at no more than about 30° in the sky even in mid-summer which means that shadows on faces are reduced. Watch out for dense shadows in doorways though, especially if the sun is very bright. Further into winter, and the further north you are, the lower the angle of the sun will be. This only starts to cause problems if you're shooting near tall buildings or the light starts to get particularly red.

Noon: Potentially the worst time for shooting if the sun is shining direct. This is the time when it's at its highest point and most likely to create deep shadows. This problem is reduced the further north you are, and the nearer to winter it is. With a heavy cloud cover, on the other hand, noon becomes the best time for shooting. This is because the sunlight is at its strongest but also its least directional, as the cloud cover diffuses the light.

Early morning/late afternoon:
A bad time for recording unless you're going for special shots. The light at this time is very directional and very orange in color. The sun is very low in the sky, so there will be long shadows with the light shining directly into your subject's face. The color temperature of the light is relatively low, which is why it is orange in color, but it is still much higher than artificial lights. You can have difficulty adjusting the camera's white balance to cope.

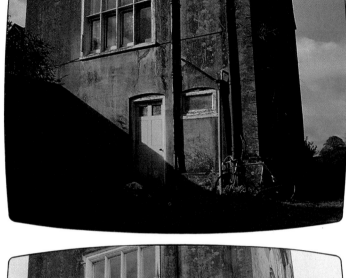

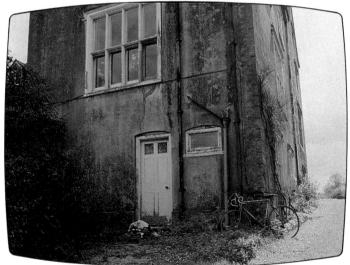

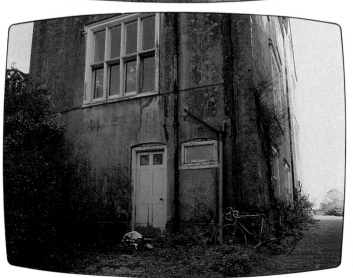

Fill-in light

There are occasions shooting outdoors when you need extra light to highlight a particular feature of your subject – usually the face – and a reflector just cannot do the job. The solution is to use a movie lamp or two, judiciously positioned so that the scene looks perfectly natural. Artificial light is used as a matter of course on most film locations – mainly because movie film isn't all that sensitive, but also to provide more complete control over lighting conditions.

There are two things to bear in mind here. The first is that your lamps must be giving out light at a daylight color temperature, so fit them with blue filters. Suitable material is available from most photo shops – an 82A filter is the one to ask for. Secondly, you use lamps in this situation in exactly the same way as you would indoors – to get rid of shadows but maintaining the same key light/fill light theory (see page 56).

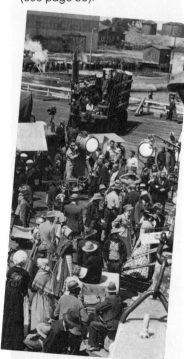

SECRETS OF INDOOR LIGHTING

The aim of artificial lighting is to make the people or scene you're shooting look the same on TV as it would if you were looking at it for real. We know that video cameras do not see a subject as we do, and we also know that, as TV is a two-dimensional medium, we must use light to create an illusion of depth.

A professional video crew will use any number of specialist lights to get the effect they want, but you can get perfectly acceptable results using bits and pieces found around the house. The important thing is to be aware of, and follow, the basic rules of lighting. The three-point system (page 56) is regarded as a standard for lighting particular objects and subjects, but lighting a room or larger subject calls for a little more ingenuity. In the end, there is no substitute for practice and experience. Video gives you the opportunity for endless experiment – just keep adjusting the lights until the picture on your monitor TV set looks right.

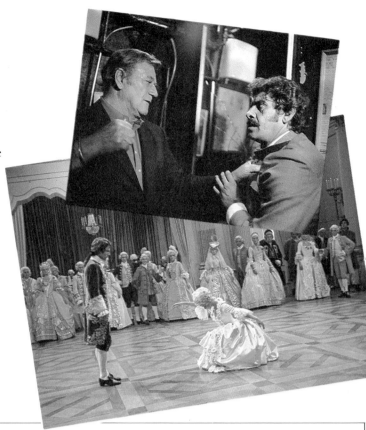

Real lamps do not light a room!

Shooting with ordinary room lighting will just give a picture with a few bright points in a background of darkness. A lamp appearing in the scene should be fitted with a high power bulb – substituting a photoflood bulb in place of the ordinary one is a useful dodge. This will illuminate a subject close by. To get a realistic looking fall-off in light, a second lamp should be placed out of shot above and behind this first lamp. It should give a wider pool of light that is, in effect, dimmer than the first and blends imperceptibly with it. A third light placed so that it illuminates the area next to the second is then used so we have yet another, but still

dimmer, pool of light. The overall effect is of a bright source, from the lamp we actually want in the shot, surrounded by dimmer (but still bright in video terms) light. Other lamps can also be used to highlight specific objects and parts of the room, but the overall effect on the TV screen looks as if the scene is actually lit by that one table lamp.

Obviously you don't have to light the whole room if you just want to shoot a subject in one small area of the room, but don't forget the background. A high-powered movie lamp pointed up at the ceiling will give an acceptable background wash of light.

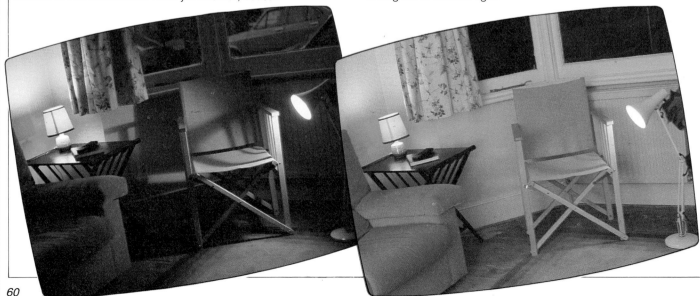

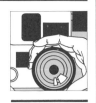

The bigger shot

A complete room: Point your lamps at the large reflective areas provided by the walls and ceiling, to get an even spread of light around the room. Providing your subject doesn't move about, these reflective lamps provide the fill and background light, while you use just one or more lamps for the key. Keeping the key light low will add a touch of intimacy to the scene.

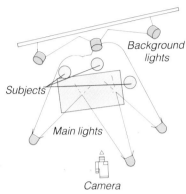

Lighting set-up for the scene below.

A group of people: Again flooding the room with reflected light will provide a good background. Careful positioning may well enable you to use one light as the key for several people. Setting it with as wide a beam as possible will mean that the light spill will act as a fill light for others. In a similar way, a second group's key lamp can act as the fill for the first group. Adding in a couple of other lamps should fill any gaps.

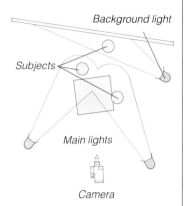

Lighting set-up for the scene below.

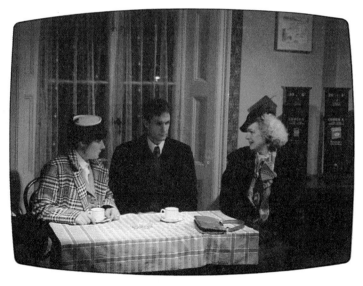

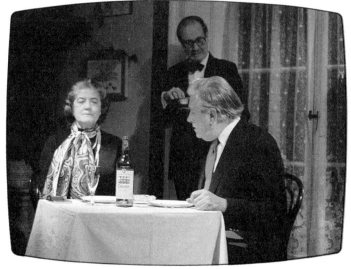

A few words of warning

Movie lamps are hot and they consume a lot of power. If you put a photoflood bulb in an ordinary light fitting, make sure that the shade fitted to the lamp is not inflammable and don't run the lamp for more than 10 minutes at a time.

Secondly, remember the power consumption formula from page 40. Current drawn (amps) = power rating (watts) ÷ voltage. Make sure that the power drawn from your sockets does not exceed their maximum supply rating. If in doubt use fewer lamps, or consult an electrician.

Moving subjects: Lighting moving subjects is one of the cameraman's nightmares. Obviously if you've set up key and fill lights in one position, as soon as the subject moves, he will be out of the light. There are two ways around this. Either you flood the area with as much diffuse light as possible and keep the key light in as general a position as possible, or you set up several positions and move the subject from one to another.

The latter course is often very effective – a subject moving between areas of light and shade has a lot of visual interest. Treat each area as a separate subject with its own key and fill areas.

Do not forget the background either. It must be properly lit for every shot. So if it looks OK for one shot, make sure that if you swing the camera around, the same lighting effect is maintained. Space behind your camera can become very cramped!

Color balancing and the window shot

Mixing natural and artificial light sources can be a problem for the video cameraman. The most common problem arises when you want to shoot a person sitting next to a window outside of which there is bright sunlight. So what happens when you train your video camera on this scene? The light sensor will pick up on the sunlight coming through the window and close down the aperture to cope. This will leave your subject almost in silhouette. If you open up the iris manually to recover the detail on your subject, then the window will be hopelessly overbright.

The best way around this problem is to light the subject strongly from the front with artificial light using the three-point principles detailed on page 56. So far so good, except that the lamps are at a lower color temperature than the sunlight. So you should set the white balance on the camera for daylight and raise the color temperature of the lamps by placing blue 82A type filters in front of them.

Generally speaking, if you have a situation with a mixture of light, you must first decide which color temperature you want to set the camera to, and adjust it accordingly. You can change the color temperature of the lamps, or you could alter the temperature of the daylight entering the room by putting orange-colored filter material over the windows.

Fluorescent lights pose a problem as they give out a greenish light. Although corrective filter material is available, they are best avoided.

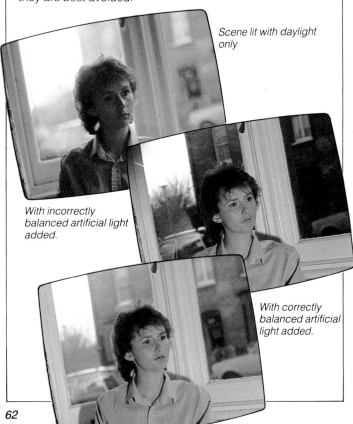

Scene lit with daylight only

With incorrectly balanced artificial light added.

With correctly balanced artificial light added.

Shooting in churches

A church presents a particularly difficult problem for video shooting, mainly because of its size and the fact that taking over the whole building in order to rig lights up is usually impossible.

The atmosphere inside a church is rendered with shadowy areas, the warm glow from candles, fairly dark walls and the windows showing up quite brightly. Following the room example from page 60, the area around a burning group of candles would be brightly lit – albeit with warm light – surrounded by diminishing pools of diffused light. This effect is repeated with the church's other lights and groups of candles. It is quite appropriate for your subject(s) to be seen to pass through very dark areas into pools of light.

If the church has white-painted interior walls then life is much easier. You can flood the interior with bright light by aiming your lamps at the walls or ceiling – preferably at the choir end of the church where the service actually takes place. A key light close to the couple would be an added advantage. Failing this, try and position the lamps as close to the couple as possible. Follow the three-point principle and be prepared for a shadowy result.

In all matters concerning churches – be they weddings or christenings – you must consult the minister first. If he is not happy having any lamps at all in the church then you will have to put up with low light levels or decide it would be better not to shoot at all, but record the service in sound only, and fake a few insert shots later to add in to the final edit.

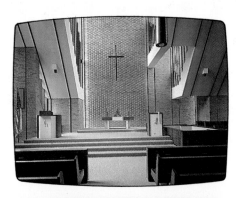

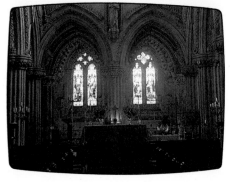

Top: Light, airy churches present few problems to the video maker. **Below:** Dark churches, however, need additional lighting for successful results.

Night shooting

Night shooting is really very much like indoor shooting – you have to build up the lighting from scratch with artificial lamps – except that the background is far more of a problem.

The simplest method is to use the news crews' 'flood-'em-with-light' principle. This means bringing along a handheld, battery-powered movie lamp and just pointing it at the subject. The lighting is very bright, but one-dimensional. The subject has no depth and the features more or less disappear – and the background is a stark black. This type of shot has a certain look and is very effective in some circumstances.

A more subtle method is to use available light patterns but exaggerate them. Take the example of a shot showing a man standing in the street under a lamp post, near to a shop window. This scene can be lit effectively by having a powerful lamp above and to one side of the man. A key light lower down, and perhaps at the same side, picks out the facial features. You may use another more powerful lamp, shuttered down so that there is only a slit of light, to illuminate the eyes. The light from the shop window could be reinforced with a photoflood, and another floodlight will increase the brightness of the pool of light spreading away from the lamp.

A variation on this is to strongly light a background object, perhaps a house or other building, and then have a key and filler light trained on the subject in the foreground. Although this creates a lot of dark areas, the building gives depth in an otherwise flat picture. Night lighting is very much like any other sort. You must ask yourself where the naturally available light is coming from and then reinforce it, at the same time picking out the important points.

Day-for-night shooting

This is a trick, well loved by Hollywood, used either to get around paying crews for unsocial working hours or to solve intractable problems such as lighting a man on a horse galloping across a 'moonlit' prairie.

So, you shoot the sequence in daylight. The sky appears much darkened and the sun becomes the moon. The biggest problem is the sky. Although the whole scene is shot underexposed (and this will mean fiddling with your camera's manual iris control until the picture looks right), the sky will still be very much brighter than the rest of the scene. A graduated (tinted at the top) brown or blue filter will often take care of this. Care must be taken not to tilt the camera upwards, however, otherwise the effect of the filter is lost.

Day-for-night shooting is usually most effective with film, as the image can be doctored in the processing stage. It is best avoided with video unless absolutely essential.

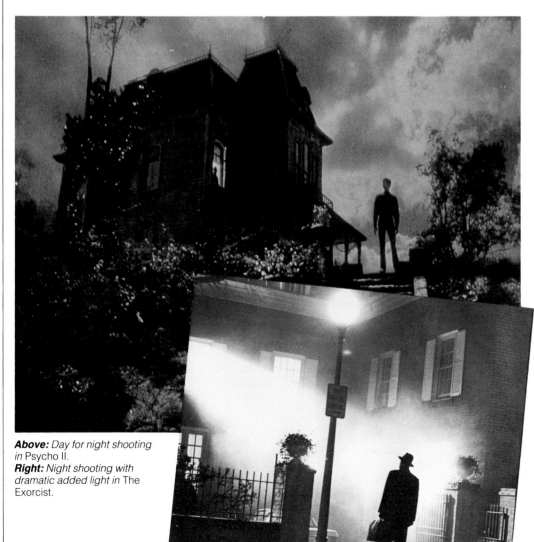

Above: Day for night shooting in Psycho II.
Right: Night shooting with dramatic added light in The Exorcist.

A look at make-up

Special pancake make-up for television went out with the introduction of color, but a little thought to what looks good on camera will work wonders. You will need to make sure that women's normal make-up is suitable for video, while checking that men are lightly powdered to reduce shine. If you're out for effects, for a dramatic production, then a stage make-up book would be a wise investment.

Basically make-up for video follows the same procedure as normal make-up, but with a few additional things to bear in mind. If you are shooting indoors under artificial light, then you must get the make-up done in that light, as cosmetics will appear to be of different colors in different types of light.

Bright reds and oranges are not a good idea for lipstick colors – these are the most difficult colors for a color TV system to deal with. As a final touch, try a dust all over with a translucent but matt face powder. Any shiny patches will reflect light, unmercifully creating over-bright patches on the image. This can only be cured by diffusing the lighting, which in turn makes the image flat and uninteresting.

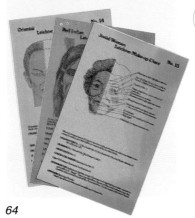

SPECIAL LIGHTING EFFECTS

So far we've looked at using lighting to make the image on the TV screen as lifelike and natural as possible. But lighting can also be used to create moods and atmospheres, which – although not realistic – are none the less interesting and absorbing to look at as part of a film or video.

Using the three-point method to light faces, your main concern is that the key light should come from one side, the fill light from the other and that the background be lit separately. By changing this basic set-up – lighting strongly from above or below or at an extreme side angle – you can introduce all sorts of sinister, dominating or unusual moods to the scene.

Using bits of board (called **flags**) to control the shape of light beams gives you other opportunities to manipulate the image. **Gauzes** are used to diffuse a light beam, and a **gobo** – a metal plate with a pattern punched out of it – can be used to cast a variegated pattern over the scene or project a shape onto the background. These are particularly useful for creating effects like clouds or fire.

Flags, gauzes and gobos

Flag: A piece of board or metal that is placed either in front of or close by the camera lens or a lamp to direct the light. In the case of the camera, it stops stray light getting into the lens and causing flares; in the case of a lamp it is used to control the beam. If you've ever seen any of those old black and white films where a room is in dim light with the only bright spot being the subject's eyes, this effect is usually accomplished by using a pair of flags to bring the light beam down in size to a narrow box. Care is needed so that the difference in brightness between the face and background is not so great that eyes are over-bright and the background is completely black.

Gauze: A piece of translucent material, spread over a frame, which can be used to control the light beam. This has the effect of creating a bright center to the beam with a dimmer surround. A round face can be made to appear narrower by being caught in a gauzed beam in which the center is a narrow V-shape. A face can be made the dominant feature of a subject if the light falling onto the rest of the body is diffused by a gauze.

Gobo: A metal plate which is punched with a pattern of holes. This fits in front of a lamp and when used with a colored filter can give a variegated pattern. These can be used to create all sorts of simple effects. For example the pattern of light through a window falling on a wall can be created by fitting a lamp with a gobo in which the pattern of a window has been punched.

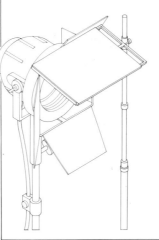

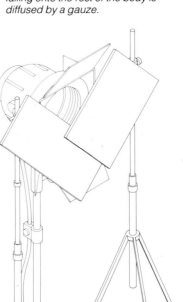

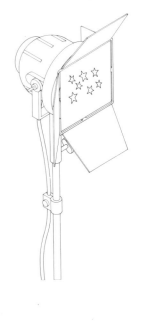

Lighting from below

This is a popular method of making a character look evil or dominating. It accentuates the facial features and gives the impression of height.

This particular set-up is very useful for low angle shots – the subject may be standing at a balcony – and when combined with a dark background or even no backlighting at all, can look very mysterious.

Adding an element of low lighting into an otherwise normal three-point lighting set-up can subtly suggest an evil intent without making it blatantly obvious.

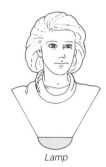

Lamp

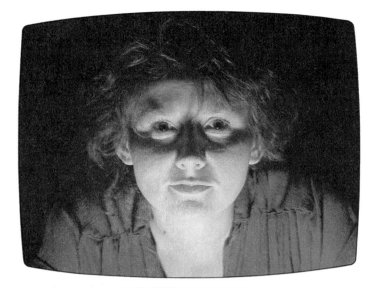

Lighting from above

A lot of top lighting has two effects. It diminishes the stature of the subject and makes him – and indeed the whole scene – look drab. In a situation trying to contrast two people, a combination of low and high lighting can actually be used to supplement their characters.

Another psychological effect of top lighting is that it is said to give the impression of being inside a pit, striving up for something. This may fit a dramatic point in your video. With a standard three-point set-up, a subtle hint of top light can bring out these qualities while accentuating features like wrinkles and other signs of age.

Lamp

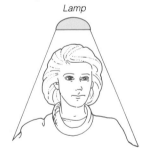

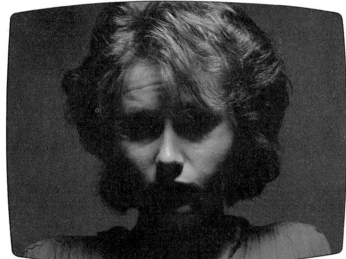

Side lighting

In effect this is little more than key light without a fill, but placed rather more to one side. It will bring out the contours on one side of the face, while leaving the other side dark.

If the subject is made up differently on each side of the face, intense side lighting can hide this difference. By gradually fading up a fill light, or cutting from this shot to another and back to a view of the same face but this time properly lit or lit from the opposite side, this difference – usually a scar or a birthmark – can be revealed with great dramatic effect.

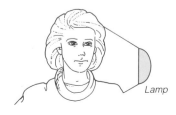

Lamp

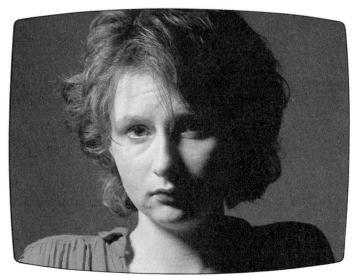

FILTERS & OPTICAL EFFECTS

WHAT IS A FILTER?

A filter is a piece of treated optical glass that screws onto the front of the camera lens. The treatment involved may be simply coloring the glass, or affecting it in some other way, either to screen out invisible rays or to modify the light's behavior in some way.

Your video camera will not need any modification to take a filter. Look inside the front of the lens barrel and you'll see a screw thread – its diameter will be listed in your camera instruction book. You can buy filters from any photo shop – just ask for one with the right thread diameter.

Most filters are sold mounted in screw-in holders, but there are several types that come in two parts – a holder which screws onto the camera and the unmounted filters which slot into it. These have two advantages – the filters themselves are cheaper, and you can combine several filters for multiple effects.

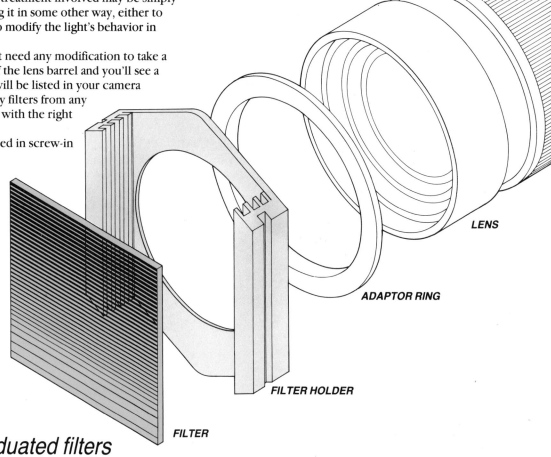

LENS

ADAPTOR RING

FILTER HOLDER

FILTER

Colored and graduated filters

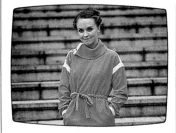

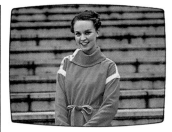

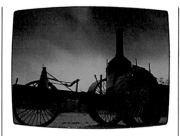

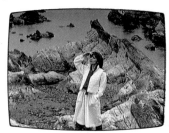

Warm tone or orange filters add warmth to light and a pleasant tan to skin tones. They can also be used to suppress blue casts on overcast days. The 81 filter is the standard orange filter used to convert the color temperature of outdoor light for use with a camera that has been white-balanced for indoor light.

Blue filters add a steely touch of cold to a scene. They can be used to create an evening mood in the middle of the day or the effects of pre-sunrise morning light. Combined with underexposure they will even help to create the effect of moonlight. The 80 filter color converts artificial light for an outdoor-balanced camera.

Sepia filters can be used to recapture the sepia tones that gave old-fashioned photographs their charm. They work particularly well with black and white pictures – try shooting close-ups of old family photos. Shooting live action in color can also look good. Try a sepia filter with a center spot diffuser.

Graduated blue filters are used mainly for shots with a wide expanse of sky. They deepen the color of the sky while leaving the color of the foreground unchanged. The graduation means that there isn't a sharp change in color. Graduated filters can be used for other effects – as shown here.

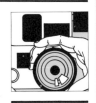

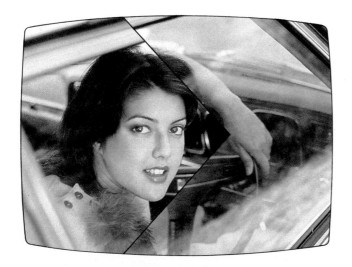

Non-colored filters

Polarizing filters can cut out irritating reflections from windows and shiny surfaces. They can darken blue skies and suppress surface reflections on water. They make it much easier to shoot someone through a car windscreen, for example, or subjects actually swimming below the surface of the water.

Neutral density filters are used to cut down the amount of light reaching the pick-up tube without affecting the overall lighting or color balance of the shot. This is particularly useful in video because it allows you a degree of control over the automatic exposure system by altering the amount of light going into the camera. Reducing the amount of light in this way is useful if you want to reduce the depth of field in a brightly lit outdoor scene, or to save colors from becoming washed out in very bright light.

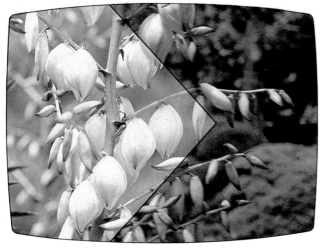

Diffusion, fog and dream

All essentially the same, as they give a slightly blurred, soft-focus look to the image. The diffuser is used to soften an image without suppressing detail. Fog or mist filters give an overall – or sometimes graduated – whitish misty cast and some detail is inevitably lost. A dream filter diffuses only the highlights of the image while leaving the rest perfectly clear.

Center spot versions of diffusion and fog filters are also available. In this case the filter has a hole cut in the center which means that the image will have the fog or diffused effect around the edges while the center part of the image will be perfectly clear.

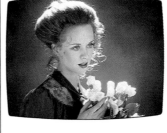 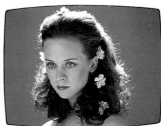

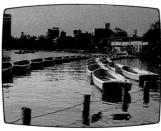 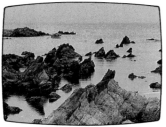

Graduated green filters are used mainly for special effects or landscape shots which have large bright areas of green which may need darkening in color. The dense area of the filter can be used either at the top or bottom of the image – or even to one side – depending on the composition of your image.

Graduated orange or sunset filter. With one of these you don't need to wait until evening – you can simulate the colors of the setting sun at any time. The dense part of the filter reddens the sky while the less dense area tints the rest of the image a more subtle shade of orange.

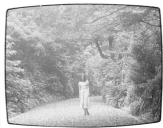 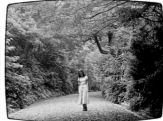

Star, diffracting and multi-image filters

These types of filter don't so much change the color of the image as its nature. The star filter has the effect of causing any bright point of light to give out 'rays' and the number of rays or points depends on the design of the filter. Star filters affect the light in this way because they have many very fine lines etched on their surface in the same pattern as the eventual stars. Bright spots of light are refracted by these lines into the star shape.

A diffracting filter is similar, in that it has millions of engraved prismatic grooves, but here they diffract bright points of light into the colors of the spectrum. Again different types are available. Some form a halo of diffracted light around the point of light, others create a star effect with the spectral colors. Like a 'proper' star filter, the direction of the points can be altered by rotating the filter in its holder. Used with a video camera, this rotational movement can actually be recorded on tape although the camera body must be held very still while the filter is turned.

A multi-image filter, as its name implies, produces a number of images of the subject when attached to the camera lens. This is more of an additional lens than a filter, in fact. If you are using a slot-in type, you can move the filter around so that the main image is anywhere in the frame.

The effects given by these filters can vary according to the camera's aperture. If possible try to view your pictures on a color monitor TV. You may have to use the manual aperture setting or neutral density filters for extra control.

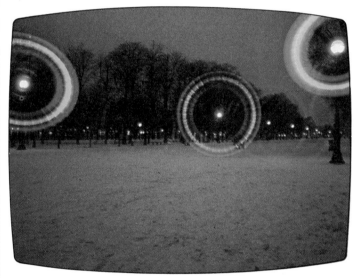

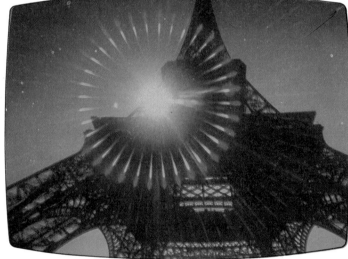

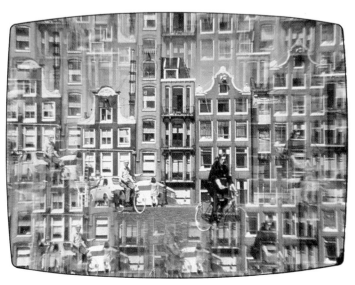

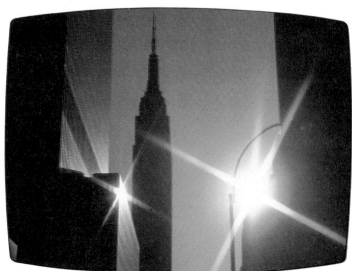

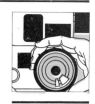

Do it yourself optical effects

Vignette and cut-out: If you have a filter system with a separate holder, you can create a number of effects with no more than stiff card and a sharp craft knife.

A vignette is a picture formed within an oval-shaped frame. Simply cut an oval shape out of a card, mount it in the camera's filter holder and see what happens. You could also have, for example, a keyhole shape or a double circle like a binocular's field of view. When using a cut out remember that the smaller the aperture (in other words, the brighter the light), and the further the cut-out is from the lens, then the sharper the cut-out shape will appear. Try and keep to the telephoto end of the zoom range (long focal length) for best results.

Fade in/out: Although some video cameras have an automatic circuit to fade to and from complete black, achieving this effect without such a circuit is possible simply by buying or otherwise acquiring a separate manual iris. These can be found in enlargers and as accessories to lighting equipment, as well as in old cameras. It may well be worth inquiring at your local photographic supplier, studio or processing lab to see if they are throwing out old darkroom or studio equipment.

When you get an iris, mount it on the front of the lens, with a filter holder, say. Fill any gaps which may let in stray light between iris and filter with card and tape. Opening and closing the iris aperture will fade in and out your video picture. As well as allowing you fades, the iris gives manual control over the light entering the camera and so gives more control over such things as depth of field.

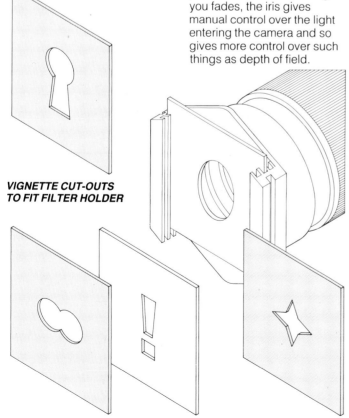

VIGNETTE CUT-OUTS TO FIT FILTER HOLDER

Add-on lenses

These are designed to modify the focal length of the lens already fitted to the camera. First, there are those which screw on to the front of the lens; second, there are those which are fitted between the lens supplied with the camera and the camera body; third, there are those which simply replace the standard lens.

You can buy the first type from a wide variety of sources. They will fit any brand of video camera, and are used just like a filter. Usually they allow you to get much closer to a subject and still keep it in focus.

The second type of lens is usually only available from the camera manufacturer and will be suitable only for cameras with removable lens systems. They generally have the same effect as the first type, but will give clearer, less distorted pictures because they are fitted in a better optical position to do the job.

The third type are for cameras with detachable lenses. They are really designed as different types of replacements for the lens already fitted. If your video camera has a detachable lens, then you will be able to buy an adaptor which will let you use 35mm still camera lenses in place of the standard lens. The standard fitting for video camera lenses is called a **C mount** (although some may vary) and the adaptor will slot onto the camera mount leaving all the pins and mounting points for one or other of the standard 35mm lens mounts on the other side.

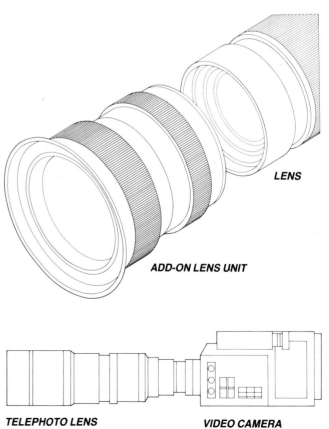

LENS

ADD-ON LENS UNIT

TELEPHOTO LENS　　　　**VIDEO CAMERA**

SOUND

THE IMPORTANCE OF SOUND

Sound recording check list

▶ Do not let anyone touch the mic while you are recording. You'll get loud bangs and scraping noises.

▶ Do insulate a table mic from the table by placing it on a foam pad. Otherwise any movement on the table will be picked up.

▶ Do keep microphones out of shot.

▶ Do make sure that cables are kept tidy, especially those attached to lavaliere mics, so that people don't fall over them.

▶ If you are recording an event that is not under your control, make sure that you position, and test, your microphones well before the event begins.

▶ When the camera is stopped, fade the sound down at the break point and fade it up again to the same level when the picture is resumed.

Sound is a secondary – and sometimes forgotten – element of a video program or film. However, just imagine even the most mundane of films or TV programs without sound and its importance soon becomes apparent.

Microphones fitted to most video cameras are omnidirectional types, which means that they will pick up sounds from all around (as you can see from the diagram below). This means that although you may well get the sound from the subject in front of you, it will also pick up sounds from behind and from each side, which may well not be what you want to record. If the camera is more than a few feet away from the subject, the easiest solution is to

either use a zoom mic attached to your camera – which changes from being very directional to omnidirectional according to the zoom lens setting. Otherwise, far better solutions come from deciding on the types of sound source you need to record, and then setting up the correct microphone for the job.

If you are recording material without lip-sync (dialogue with the speaker in shot), then recording the sound on a separate audio recorder is a very good idea. Otherwise the mic will have to be connected directly into the camera. Although the video recorder may well have a mic socket, this is usually automatically disconnected when the camera is plugged in.

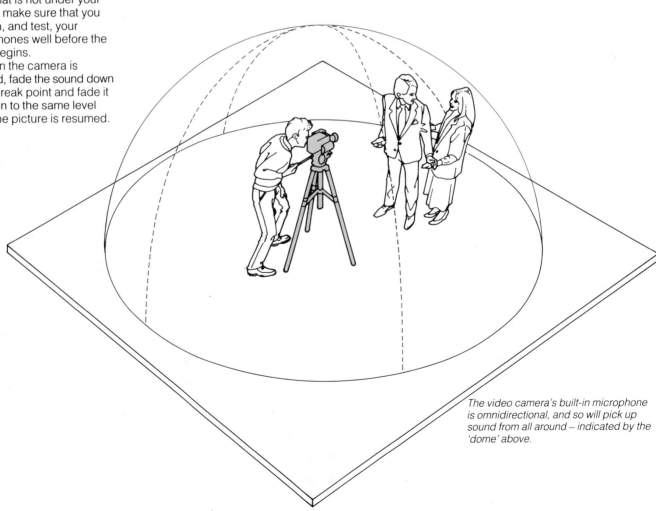

The video camera's built-in microphone is omnidirectional, and so will pick up sound from all around – indicated by the 'dome' above.

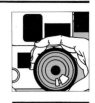

Using a separate microphone: If you want to record sound that's going to match the quality of the pictures then the best, perhaps the only, way to do it is to use a separate microphone, and to leave the sound to a separate person.

The types of mics available and their different properties have been listed on page 37. Their applications and uses are shown on this page and overleaf. The **sound recordist** should select the right mic for the job, wire it up, test it and manipulate the mic when recording, while monitoring the sound on a pair of headphones. In this way, you can get on with the job of getting the best pictures, secure in the knowledge that someone else will be taking equal care over the sound. The microphone usually plugs into the camera's extension mic socket. Some cameras have two sockets, for a stereo pair of mics. One of these should be used when only one microphone is employed. This is usually the left channel socket and will be marked L/Mono, but check your camera handbook anyway.

The socket will usually be a 3.5mm jack. However, most decent mics have a ¼-inch jack plug fitted as standard. This means that you will have to buy or make an adaptor.

Using the unidirectional mic with a group: Useful for picking up dinner table talk, the unidirectional mic can be hidden in a center piece on the table. Make sure it isn't standing directly on the table, though, or it will pick up bangs and thumps. A table cloth will deaden the sound of cutlery and plates. Try to position the mic closest to the main subjects you are trying to record and tell them not to clatter the objects on the table more than necessary.

Using the lavaliere or tie-clip mic: Most useful where your subject is moving about and you can't easily get any other mic close enough. The mic picks up sounds from the subject but not extraneous noise. The mic can be fixed on a lapel or tie if you don't mind it being in shot, or fixed under a shirt or blouse if it is to remain unseen. Make sure that the mic is fitted on the upper part of the clothing anyway, and kept away from dangling objects like necklaces, broad lapels or flouncy bows. The only problem is the cable, but this can run inside your subject's clothing. Make sure noboby trips over it and keep it out of shot.

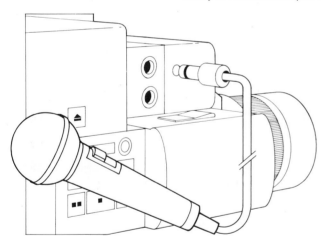

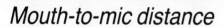

Mouth-to-mic distance

The distance between mouth and microphone is extremely important to the quality of your final recording. Too close, and the sound will be distorted with a lot of explosive 'pops' on the b, d, p and t sounds. Too far away and the voice will sound indistinct and barely intelligible above the background noise. An ideal distance is probably about 30cm although the sound recordist or cameraman should check this by monitoring the sound on headphones, and ask the subject to move or reposition the microphone if necessary.

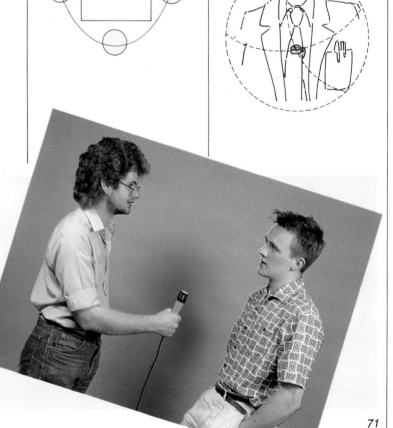

71

SOUND RECORDING STEP-BY-STEP

If you work methodically when recording sound and observe a few elementary rules, then you'll get good results every time. Having chosen the right microphone (see previous page), some advance planning is needed. The problems you will come up against will vary according to the location, but you should, like the Boy Scouts, always be prepared!

Shooting indoors gives you the most control over unwanted noises. It is quite usual to post someone at the door to make sure unexpected visitors don't suddenly burst in; the phone should be taken off the hook or unplugged; the doorbell should be disconnected and any noisy apparatuses, such as a fridge or heating boiler, temporarily switched off. It's amazing how irritating the relatively quiet background hum of a central heating pump can be on your finished video!

Next you should think about the acoustics of the room. If it's too 'dead', you will have to make it more 'live' and vice versa. This is described in detail on page 35, but be prepared to deal with either situation and bring along livening and deadening boards. Remember, it's what the subject sounds like through your monitor headphones that counts, so any adjustments to room acoustics should be made while listening on phones.

Shooting outdoors does away with worries about acoustics, but gives you the problems of extraneous noises you can't control. Traffic, passing aircraft and local industry are just a few examples. Moving the mic in close can minimize these problems.

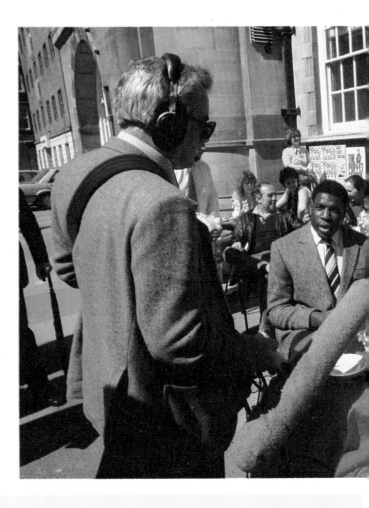

Recording indoors

Indoor sound recording is more controllable – you can modify the room acoustics and position your subjects. You should sort out the room acoustics first, then set up the microphone and group your speakers. For a two-person discussion at a table, use an omnidirectional mic on a stand between your subjects. This mic has a dome-like pick-up pattern. The two people should sit slightly at an angle to each other (to give you a good choice of camera positions) with their knees about 1 meter apart.

A larger group on 'location' is more difficult. If the people are sitting around a table, then an omnidirectional mic on a foam pad in the center is probably best. A randomly arranged group is probably best served with a more directional mic, turned towards each person speaking by the sound recordist.

'Studio' subjects are more controllable in the sense that they can be placed exactly where you want them. You can set up the acoustic beforehand and you will have some idea of what you are going to shoot. The person looking after the sound will know where the camera is going to be at any time, and so can make sure that the mic will be in the right place.

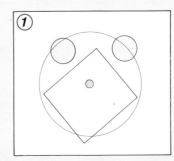

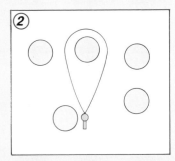

①An ordinary omnidirectional microphone can be used for a two person discussion.
②A larger group on location can be recorded with a directional microphone, turned towards each speaker.
③A studio set-up enables you to place microphones in advance.

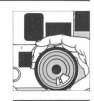

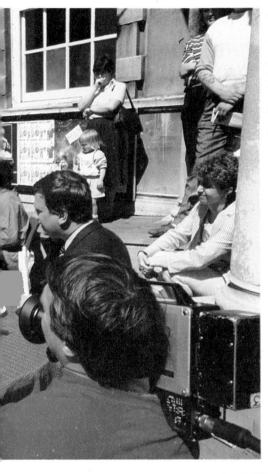

A professional news crew interviews boxer Frank Bruno. The sound recordist is using a super-directional microphone (in a windshield) which allows him to be very selective with the sound pick-up.

Sound words

Ambient sound: The bare sound of a particular environment – seashore, street, etc. – without speech and other additional sounds.
Audial design: The process of creating timed sound tracks for use with timed moving images.
Boom: Long-armed support for a microphone, usually held and manipulated by the sound recordist.
Crossfade: Fading out one sound as another is faded up.
Fade in/out: Bringing the sound up from silence to full strength, and vice versa.
Lip sync: Sound of speech synchronized to images of the person speaking.
Motivated sound: Name for sound that can be reasonably expected to occur with the pictures. The motivated sound to go with pictures of a steam train would be hissing and other steam train noises.
Post-sync sound: Sync sound added after the pictures have been recorded.
Synchronous sound (sync sound): Sound that fits the images exactly – synchronized with the pictures. Usually recorded at the same time as the pictures but can be dubbed on afterwards. Speech is a particularly important form of sync sound.
Wild track: A soundtrack that is not synchronized to the pictures. Can be sound recorded at the same time as the pictures, but on a separate recorder and not synchronized to the pictures, or may be other sound dubbed on in the editing stage.

Outdoor recording

The biggest problems here are unwanted noise and wind. Get the mic close to the subject and use an adequate wind shield. If you're shooting an 'on-the-spot' report, the speaker can hold the microphone. Make sure that he holds it tight, doesn't move his hands around on the mic body and holds it around 30cm from his mouth. You can experiment with this distance as the outdoors has a deadening effect on sound and it may be necessary to hold the mic closer. Holding a short loop of mic cable in the hand can cut down cable noise and also reduce the risk of dropping the mic.

If you don't want the mic in shot, then you should use a super-directional (shotgun) mic as close to the subject as possible but out of shot, or a more conventional unidirectional mic mounted on a boom held above the subject. Lavalier microphones can be fixed under peoples' clothes, but watch out for the trailing wires!

All sound recorded should be monitored on headphones. Like most mics, these are usually fitted with a ¼-inch jack plug, but video recorder earphone sockets usually have a 3.5mm jack socket. So you'll need an adaptor lead – with a ¼-inch stereo jack in-line socket at one end, and a 3.5mm jack plug at the other.

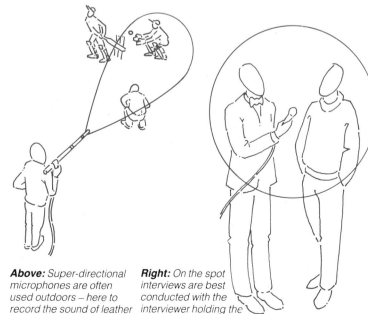

Above: *Super-directional microphones are often used outdoors – here to record the sound of leather on willow.*

Right: *On the spot interviews are best conducted with the interviewer holding the microphone.*

THE SEPARATE RECORDER

Using a separate audio recorder can have several advantages. You have much more control over the sound being recorded, the quality is usually far better, and the cables for both microphone and headphones are completely separate from the camera and so don't get in the cameraman's way. However, you will have problems if you attempt to use a separate recorder for sync sound. Putting the sound back onto the video tape so that it stays in perfect sync with the pictures is extremely difficult if you don't have access to a professional editing suite and so is best avoided.

Suitable applications for the separate recorder include those situations where the sound is important but you can't get good pictures to match – a wedding service where the camera cannot record acceptable pictures in the church, for example – and for sound that doesn't need to be accurately synchronized to the pictures – a steam engine rally or air display, say. You can also use it quite separately from the camera to record sound to be dubbed on (added) later, such as live sound effects or background noise like fairground atmosphere or the sea crashing on rocks.

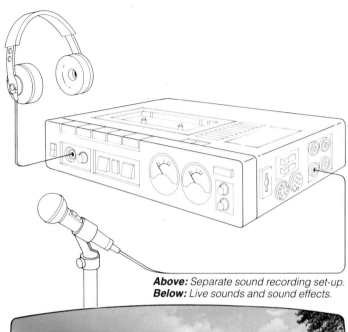

Above: Separate sound recording set-up.
Below: Live sounds and sound effects.

Using the audio recorder

There are two stages in making a live recording – preparation and the recording itself. First of all check over the recorder, microphone and headphones. Make sure that they are working properly by doing a short test recording. You should also check the batteries and replace or recharge them if they are low. Always carry a spare set of batteries, too. Check that you have sufficient blank tape and that it is suitable for your recorder.

When you come to make the recording, check that the recorder is set properly – that the noise reduction system is switched on and that the tape type selector is set to match the tape being used. Preparation of the subject and acoustics are the same as for recording into the video recorder – see page 72. Listen to a bit of the sound to make sure that everything is set up as you want it and then adjust the recording level. You usually have to put the recorder into record mode and hold it on pause to do this. The meter indicator should just be peaking into the red or +dB sectors of the scale on the loudest sounds.

When the level has been adjusted correctly, release the pause button and make the recording. It is useful to add a recorded announcement stating time, place and date before the start of the recording proper so that individual recordings can be easily identified. Keep on watching the level meters – if the sound pushes them more and more into the red, you may have to turn the input level down a bit.

Make sure that you also keep listening to the headphones, especially for odd background sounds. If these become particularly distracting, you may have to stop the machine, sort out whatever is causing these noises and make your recording again.

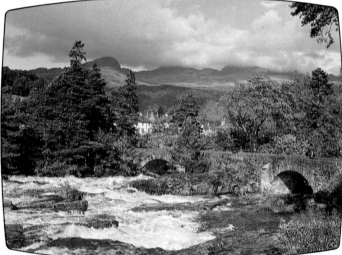

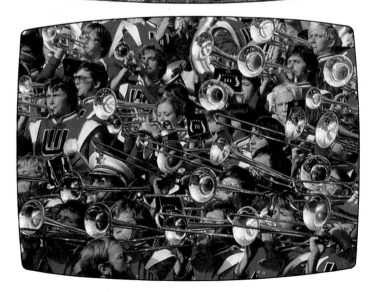

Sync sound

If you intend to record sync sound with a separate recorder there are several things you must look out for. Because the motor speeds of the video and audio recorders drift – that is, don't remain absolutely constant in relation to each other all the time – it is best to shoot only very short sequences. When you come to put the sound and picture back together again, they will stay synchronized throughout the sequence. Long sequences tend to gradually get out of step, even if they were perfectly matched at the beginning.

To help the process of matching up sound and vision,

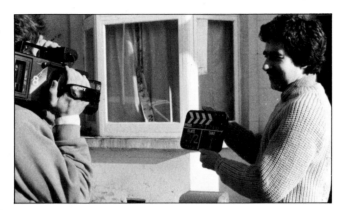

each shot should be marked with a clapper board. This makes a loud crack when the clapper is slammed shut, and this point can be seen on the image and heard on the

sound track. The point at which the two halves come together in the visuals should be adjusted so you hear the crack on the sound track at the same time.

Sound effects

You can buy some pre-recorded sound effects on records, but these may not always fit your video in terms of length or intensity. Recording some of the simpler effects yourself is fun, and not at all difficult.

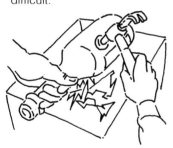

Breaking glass: You can break some glass in a cardboard box with a hammer, or 'cheat' like the professionals and drop some small pieces of metal onto a hard surface. The best sort of metal to use is heavy iron plate cut into pieces about 10cm square. Mix these up with some metal rods, nuts and bolts, old drain pipes and other things to alter the sound. A few more obviously metallic sounds can be added while recording if you're trying to get the sound of a car smash, for instance.

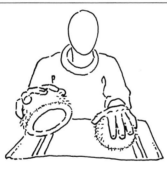

Horses: There's nothing simpler than a pair of coconut shells clip-clopped together, mixed with a few audible snuffles and snorts. For the sound of horses galloping on grass try drumming them on a table top covered with a wet tea cloth.

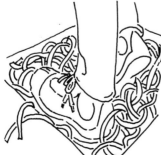

Walking in snow: There are various ways of doing this, but one method is to walk in place in a box packed with discarded recording tape. If you can't get

hold of any old tape (try asking your local radio or TV station) then experiment with shredded paper.

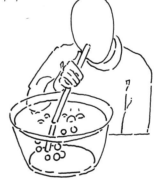

Horror: Let your imagination run wild. It's amazing how different everyday sounds can be, when recorded from very close up. Food bubbling on the stove can give the sound of a mad scientist's lab (although care must be taken when working near pans of boiling liquids), while every house must have a squeaky door or creaky floor board that can be made to perform for the recorder. Encourage your pets to make noises for that blood-chilling wild animal effect. Even the family cat's purring, when recorded close up, can sound remarkably menacing!

Separate recording checklist

Before you start:
▶ Do make sure that the equipment is working properly.
▶ Make sure that you have: blank tape, new or fully charged batteries plus spares, the correct microphones, headphones, AC adaptor lead (if you are going to power the recorder from the AC) spare cable for the mic and AC extension cable.
▶ Set up the room acoustics and position the mic in plenty of time before you're due to start, so that you can iron out any last-minute problems.
▶ Set up outdoors in plenty of time, especially if you don't know what there will be in terms of unwanted background noises.
▶ Before starting to record, check that the noise reduction switch is on; that the tape type switch is in the right position; and that you have set the recording level so that the needle is just peaking into the red zone.
▶ Label each recording with time, date and location by making a short statement into the mic.
▶ Leave a 10-second silence at the end of each recording. This makes editing much easier at a later stage.
▶ Keep a written record of each recording so that you can find and identify it easily on the tape.

PREPARATION

RESEARCH

Whatever sort of video you are making, whether it is a relation's wedding, or a serious documentary, careful research can make all the difference between the vitally interesting and the deadly boring in the end result. Take the trouble to delve into the subject matter you're going to be shooting.

Take the wedding example. You could just turn up and shoot things as you find them, but a little bit of research might reveal that your relation was going to marry a policeman, who intends to arrive at the church in a squad car. Wouldn't it look good if you were actually in the car with him and rushed out recording like they do in the TV cop shows?

The more complex the video, the more thorough the research should be. Above all think in terms of pictures – you are using a visual medium after all. If you're short of inspiration, just watch broadcast TV and films, and see how the experts tackle a similar sort of situation, and make notes of all the points you think are going to be relevant.

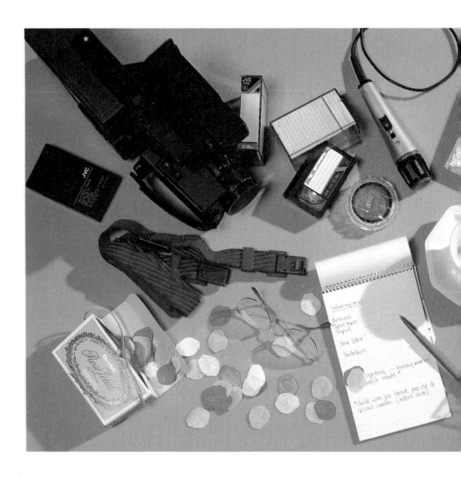

Scouting the location

This is something that is frequently considered unnecessary – until the day of shooting arrives and the site is nothing like you imagined. Often as not you spend half the time solving problems that could have been averted if you'd previously spent 15 minutes looking over the place. What do you look out for?

Looking around: Unless you're on the spot, you can't really imagine such things as the different camera positions you might want to use, or appreciate difficulties such as narrow paths, thick bushes and awkward railings – which could be very important if you're looking for good vantage points to shoot a wedding from, for instance.

Lighting: Outdoors this will be the sun. An obvious point is to check where the sun will be at the time of shooting. A church porch which may be in bright sunlight at 4 in the afternoon might be in deep shadow at 11 o'clock in the morning and so totally unsuitable for shooting. If you're looking over an indoor location, you will have to make sure that there are sufficient sockets to run your lamps from.

Power: A location check for likely sources of power is very important. This becomes all the more essential if you are using extra lights. You should check the position of all the mains sockets, how many there are and how much power they can deliver. This will tell you how many extension cables you will need to bring and how many multi-way adaptors you will need.

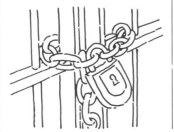

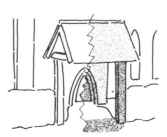

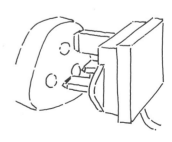

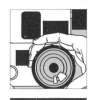

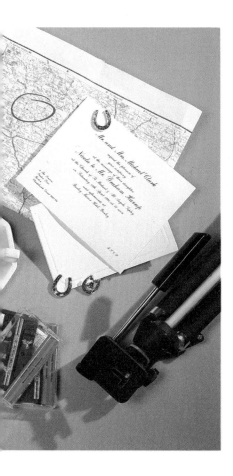

Notes

It's a very good idea to get into the habit of taking notes about anything and everything to do with your video making. The less that you commit purely to memory, the less you will forget. This is especially worth doing if you have a good idea or some particularly interesting point that has emerged from your research. It may not be immediately useful, but it could be just the answer to a particularly knotty problem that might turn up in six months' time.

If your research involves talking to people, you might like to use a portable audio tape recorder. This way you can be sure that nothing gets lost. If you use a high quality recorder, it may be possible to use some of the material in the finished tape. Even if you decide to come back and record a proper interview with the person, the recording of the original research chat may be better – people are rarely as fresh and original the second time round.

Permissions and problems

It's a fact of life that if you're not on your own property, you usually need permission from someone before you can begin to record even the most modest of material. Generally speaking, one person with a video camera and recorder on public property is usually OK, although it's as well to check exactly how public that property is – definitions will vary from country to country. You will also have to be careful where you actually point the camera. Shooting the outside of a police station will cause few raised eyebrows in the US, but doing the same thing in, say, Spain may bring an instant angry reaction from the local force. Military establishments all over the world are particularly sensitive, so don't risk an enforced holiday!

Once you turn up with even a small crew – and it doesn't matter whether you're amateurs or professionals – you immediately need permission to shoot from all sorts of bodies. Take a small street scene. The local highway authority needs to know – and give permission. The local police will need to know, especially if you may potentially cause an obstruction, and you will need the cooperation of local inhabitants if you want to move cars or keep people off the street while you actually shoot.

Moving off the street doesn't solve the problem. Parks – even public parks – and virtually all buildings open to the public are owned by somebody, who will need to give permission. Shooting a wedding needs the permission of the minister – especially if you're going to start trailing lighting cables all over the place.

If you are dealing with a public body get permission in writing – and stick to what you've asked for. Otherwise you may end up with a nasty bill if that extra shot meant that they had to pay staff overtime to clear up after you.

Asking permission is first of all a courtesy. Secondly, public officials are quite within their rights to stop you filming if you don't have the right permission.

Sound: When you get to the site, just listen. The human brain will unconsciously shut out unwanted sounds when you are concentrating on one particular thing – electronic equipment cannot do this. If the sounds coming from a position off camera cannot be stopped – a busy road, or a building site, for example – try to include the sources in an opening shot so that the viewers will recognize the sound and can then not worry about it. Quieter sounds such as fridges or air conditioning can be equally irritating – try and get them switched off. Finally, ask the locals about other hazards you may not be aware of – like the saw mill next to the church that does all its sawing on a Saturday morning when, of course, you'll want to record!

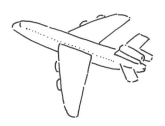

Continuity

Because it is quite common to record material in a more or less random order, the shots that go into a particular sequence may well be recorded at different times on different days. When they are put together, they must appear to be continuous, so props, costumes and other objects in the sequence must be the same throughout. For example, if there is a person featured in the sequence, and he is wearing a brown jacket at the start of the sequence, he must continue to wear that same brown jacket throughout – he can't suddenly appear in one shot wearing a grey jacket.

This job is called **continuity** and one person is usually assigned the job of making detailed notes of each shot so that they can be matched. This is extended to such things as lighting (if the scene is set in the morning with light streaming across the frame from one side then it must always come from that side) and sound (if there is a factory in the background then that sound must remain constant).

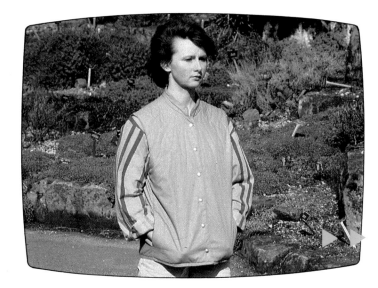

Programmed events

These are events that you may well want a video record of but cannot control. Although a wedding is a prime example of a programmed event, a school prize-giving might well be another. Preparation becomes even more important here than perhaps in any other situation – since you only have one go at shooting the event. If the event is being rehearsed, try and get into one of the rehearsals. This will allow you to see how the event is going to progress, where people are going to enter and leave the stage, and where you can reasonably expect to be able to position yourself. You should also be able to pick up a few clues about what 'unexpected' things may happen so that they don't completely throw you on the day.

You will also see how much available light there is, and find out if it is possible to use extra lighting in the event that it becomes necessary. You should also look at the possibilities for sound recording. Even if your visit only convinces you that the event is completely impossible to record, it has wasted far less time and effort than turning up on the day, complete with equipment, only to be disappointed.

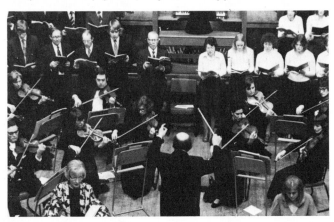

Putting things in order

Once you've done all your research and decided roughly how your production is going to go, the next stage is to put those thoughts in order. Even the most modest of videos can benefit from some planning. Take the example of the wedding video. You can't stop the proceedings and say, "Do that again. I missed it!" By planning which shots you want and the order you want to shoot them in, you will make sure that you get everything you want and won't miss something simply because you were in the wrong place at the wrong time. And if you're not going to edit later, then it's *vitally* important that you know exactly what you're after, and in what order.

The most elaborate form of planning is to create a **storyboard**. This consists of a series of thumbnail sketches, each one detailing a particular shot, with a full description underneath. These are then arranged in the same order as the final production. Often the shots are numbered and these numbers stay with the shot throughout the

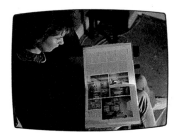

production. This helps the person in charge later in the editing stage as well as keeping all the notes for each shot together.

The shot list: Assuming that you're going to edit later, you could shoot material in any order (assuming you're not shooting a programmed event, like a wedding). A proper shot list is therefore a good idea. Put the most important shots first. That way, if the

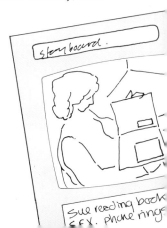

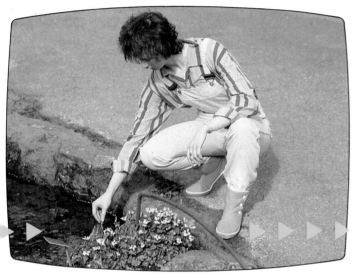

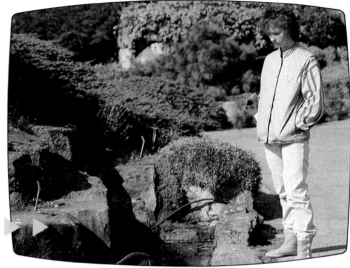

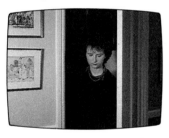
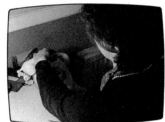

equipment fails or the weather gets nasty, you won't have wasted the entire day. This becomes very important if you're shooting outdoors and the weather needs to be of a particular sort, sunny for example, and the day itself is changeable. Make sure, too, that the list is as detailed as possible including any

movement or directions, so you know exactly what you want people to do and don't keep people hanging around unnecessarily. Complete all the shots you require from one camera position before moving on to the next wherever possible.

Options

▶ **Indoors or outdoors?**
A fundamental choice, or you can use a mixture of both.

▶ **Using a presenter or commentator?**
Outdoors – Is he seen in picture? Is he in costume or wearing normal clothes? Does he talk straight to the camera? Does he write his own commentary?
Indoors – Do you need more than one presenter, or separate interviewers and presenters? Do they wear normal dress or costume?

▶ **Graphics?**
Do you need maps, diagrams, drawings or animation?
Press cuttings – Could you use shots of these with or without camera movement, or with key sections picked out?
Captions – Are you using rub-down lettering, typed or handwritten captions, or those generated electronically on the camera's built-in character generator? Could you use special effect captions (made up from sand or rice, for example)?
Paintings – Do you want specially drawn artwork? How about historical prints?

Still prints – Can you use specially-taken archive photos, illustrations from books, catalogues and magazines, or archive illustrations? All can be recorded with or without camera movement.

▶ **Dramatization?**
Script – Are you working from an original play, or one that's been specially written? Are you using improvisation or re-enacting original historic works?
Studio or on location – Are you using the original locations of the story, historically accurate locations or abstract locations?
Actors – Do you need one actor for all parts? Several actors? Or an actor plus narrator/presenter?
Costume – Are you aiming to be historically accurate? Do you want to use abstract costumes or just everyday clothing?

▶ **Film?**
Archive or library film – Can you use sequences shot especially for video and dropped in without modification? Special effects using film?

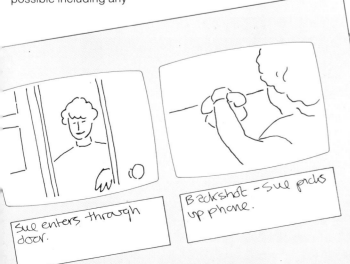

Sue enters through door.

Backshot – Sue picks up phone.

Before you commence
shooting, either indoors or
outdoors, make sure you have...
► Checked and worked out all
the possible camera angles.
► Investigated the power
supply situation.
► Listened for possible
sources of sound interference.
► Obtained all the necessary
permissions.
► Watched at least one
rehearsal if you're shooting a
programmed event.
► Looked at the access and
parking for the location,
particularly if you are working
with scenery and props.
► Arranged transport for
equipment.
► Told all the crew exactly
where the location is, when
they should turn up and how
long they'll be required.
► Determined exactly who is
doing what and when.
► Prepared a detailed shot
list.
► Checked over all the
equipment to make sure that
it is all working.
► Made sure that the batteries
are fully charged.
► Checked all leads to make
sure that there are no loose
connections.
► Assembled all the
equipment according to the
equipment checklist.

Power supplies

Indoors, everything can run
from AC. But check that the
supply is not overloaded.
When outdoors, power your
lamps from a multi-way
adaptor that is connected via
an earth leakage circuit
breaker, available from most
good electrical suppliers. The
recorder and camera can
then be driven either from
batteries or from another
socket via another ELCB.

WORKING OUTDOORS

One of the most important considerations when working
outdoors is how to power your equipment. There are three
options open to you – rechargeable batteries in the video
recorder (and in the monitor TV and audio recorder), the
possibility of AC power nearby, and power from a car battery
which may be available.

Rechargeable batteries: These are fitted as standard to all
portable video recorders and power the camera as well. Usable
time between charges depends on the power being consumed and
the air temperature. Although rechargeable batteries have a nominal
use time of between 30 and 40 minutes, this time drops when
you make a lot of use of features such as auto-focus and power
zoom, and when the weather is particularly cold. The continuous
use time between charges for the batteries supplied with a
monitor TV varies but is typically two or three hours, again
dropping off with temperature. A set of alkaline batteries for an
audio recorder will probably give five or six hours' service,
provided you don't use the monitor amplifier too loudly.

AC power: Obviously there's no time limit here, but you should
be extremely careful using AC power outdoors and don't use it
at all in damp conditions. An extension cable that runs from an
indoor power point to an outdoor location should be fitted with
an **earth leakage circuit breaker (ELCB)** for extra safety.
These are available quite cheaply from most electrical shops.

Car battery: A very useful compromise between the power
availability of AC and the safety of battery power. To use it, you'll
need a special adaptor which fits the car's cigarette lighter
socket. You might have to make a long extension power lead so
you don't get stuck having to work close by the car.

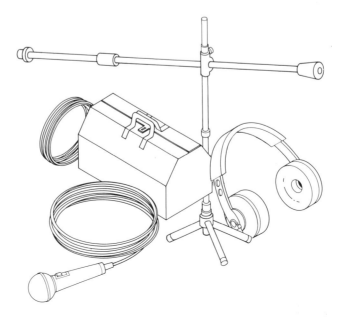

Making a video can require
little more than the recorder,
camera, blank tape and spare
batteries. For a more
complete shoot, this checklist
gives the equipment rundown.
► **Camera:** Obvious, but
make sure that it's working
and, if the lead's detachable,
make sure you bring it!
► **Recorder:** Again obvious,
but make sure that it's
working properly.
► **Batteries:** At least three,
all fully charged. They are
also useful for indoor shooting
if you want to get a shot that is
made inaccessible by trailing
cables.
► **Tripod:** Strong and light.
Don't forget accessories such
as dollies and any tracks.
► **Microphone:** Chosen
carefully for the situation. If
you're outdoors it's probably
a super-directional, shotgun
type. If it is an electret type,
make sure that you have a
battery for it plus a spare.
Check that the lead is long
enough and is fitted with the
correct plug or adaptor to fit
the camera's mic socket.
► **Fishpole or mic stand:**
Ideally you should have a
fishpole or boom, although a
mic stand will do.
► **Headphones:** Fitted with
enclosed ear pieces and the
right plug.
► **Monitor TV:** This isn't
essential, but a small battery-
powered color TV is very
useful for setting up shots and
checking color balance.
► **Cables and batteries:** For
monitor TV.
► **Video cassettes:** Perhaps
the most essential thing next
to the recorder and camera.
These should ideally be 30-
minute tapes. You should
bring at least three and
preferably four or five.

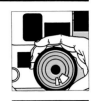

WORKING INDOORS

Separate audio recorder: Used for wild sound recording, or even sync sound if this is needed separately.

Batteries: For audio recorder. Either new alkaline or fully charged rechargeables, in addition to set already in recorder.

Audio cassettes: For audio recorder. At least three C60s and preferably four.

AC power units: Used to run video and audio recorders from AV and to recharge video batteries.

Lamps: Sufficient in number and type for the shots in mind.

Spare bulbs: At least one spare for each lamp.

Extension cables: One for each lamp, plus one each for the recorder, monitor TV, and audio recorder. A good supply of multi-way adaptors is also extremely useful. It is always better to have too many than too few.

Clapper boards: Used to identify all shots.

Props, scenery and costumes: To whatever plan you have devised.

Tool kit and sundry spares: Essential for on-the-job repairs. Sundry spares include fuses, insulation tape, etc.

In many ways the preparation for working indoors is the same as that for outdoors with the obvious exception that everything can be powered from AC. Basically, there are two sorts of indoor situation – location and studio. A location, as the name implies, is somewhere not primarily designed for video shooting – someone's living room, for example, or the interior of a church. A studio, on the other hand, is a room which has been set aside for shooting and is empty except for any set or other props you may have put there. It needn't be purpose-built – it could, for example, be your spare room cleared for the occasion.

Wherever your studio, in your scouting you should have checked on the position and number of power sockets, so don't forget to bring sufficient extension cables and adaptors. You should also have made a note of useful bits and pieces already at the location that you can make use of – drapes, furniture and so on. Also make sure you have plenty of spare bulbs for the lights, as well as fuses, spare batteries for any electret mics, spare connector cables, etc., and a simple tool kit.

Some paperwork is essential. Make sure that at least one member of the crew keeps notes of every shot – including any details that might be important later on. Comments such as "OK, but last 2 seconds spoilt by aircraft noise" are the sort of thing you'll be grateful for later on. At the end of the day you should be able to pinpoint any shot on any cassette. All this saves an enormous amount of time when you start editing.

The home studio

A video studio is essentially a room which is completely clear of all furniture, has a smooth floor, fairly dead acoustics and sufficient power availability to handle all the equipment without being overloaded. It should also have sufficiently good access to sets and props if you're going into video in a big way.

When it comes to converting a room at home, perhaps the most important point is to be able to clear it of all furniture. The walls should be a plain color, preferably a slight off-white color, or you can hang drapes. These can simply be lengths of rough cloth fastened to the wall with a staple gun. It's useful to have a set of black drapes, and a set of white ones. If you're not going to be overambitious with the lighting, you can probably get away with the standard domestic supply. Get an electrician to check over the system, however, before you start using it, just to be on the safe side. The floor is probably something you can do least about, and unless you intend to use a lot of dolly shots, the expense of laying a smooth floor is not justified. Similarly, unless you're going to be particularly ambitious with the sets, there shouldn't be any need to worry about access.

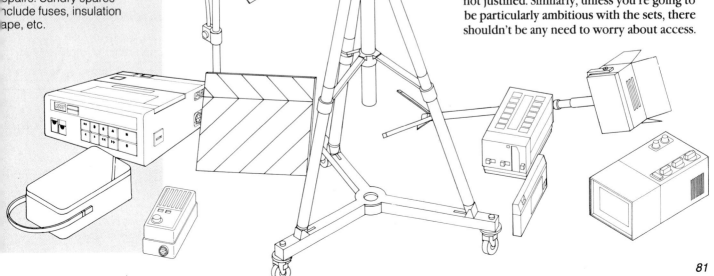

THE SHOOT

Having done all the preparation, you are at last ready to shoot. So what comes next? The obvious thing is setting up the equipment. Make sure that everything is working properly and make a quick test recording to check that you are getting a picture on the tape and that the sound is OK. The separate audio recorder should also be checked if you are using one.

Next set the camera's white balance. If you want to modify the colors slightly, this should be done while watching the results on a color TV. Before doing this, though, it is also useful to set the controls on the TV so that the picture is as lifelike as possible. This can be done by correctly setting the camera's white balance, then pointing the camera at some colorful object. Adjust the color, contrast and brightness controls on the TV until the image on the screen matches the real thing as closely as possible.

Next, set the lights – or adjust the position of the subject for the best effect if you're shooting outdoors – according to the first shot on your shot list. Brief everyone on exactly what they are meant to be doing and check the camera position and lighting on the monitor if you have one. At this stage you should have a rehearsal if the shot is particularly complicated. When you feel confident, then you can go for a **take**. (The word 'take' simply means each attempt at a shot.)

Each take should be marked with a clapper board. This has written on it the project title, and gives the shot number and take number. To

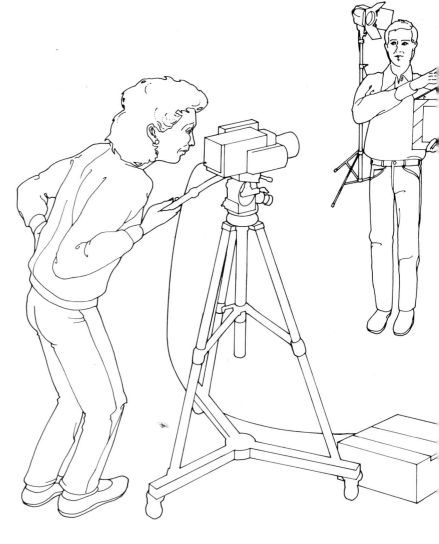

Shooting order – continuity and overlaps

Continuity is very important to the appearance of your finished video, but it is not strictly necessary to record each shot in the final running order, and there may be a good reason why that can't be done. A sensible compromise seems to be to shoot at least all the shots in each scene of the finished video in sequence. This means that the lighting and background sound will be constant and the subject can maintain the same mood throughout the set of shots. Careful notes must, however, be made of

everything before moving on. That includes the positions of all the lights, or the sun and cloud conditions if you are working outdoors, and the background sounds as well as props and costume. Taking Polaroid photos of the scene and your subjects is an easy way of noting all the small details. This will make it far easier to set everything back up in the same situation should that be necessary.

By varying the shooting order, you can also make best use of your resources, although this may mean moving the actual shot

order around. If you have one person available for just one day, then it makes sense to do the shots involving them all at once. Similarly if you have another subject who appears once at the start and a couple of times near the end, it makes sense to do all his or her bits together and avoid unnecessary waiting around.

Shooting overlaps is a technique which makes life easier for the person editing the video – you, in other words!

Suppose you are showing a man entering a building

through a door. The next shot shows him coming through the same door from the inside. When taking the first shot, you should make sure that the recorder is left running until the man has well and truly disappeared through the door. For the second shot, start the recorder running several seconds before the man comes through the door, and leave it running until the shot is completely finished.

The overlap allows a wide choice of cutting points when the video is edited.

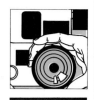

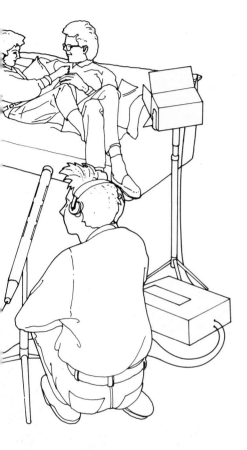

mark a shot, an assistant holds the clapper board in front of the camera so that the writing is legible, calls out the shot and take number, and brings the top half of the clapper down with a loud crack.

The procedure for each take

▶ Get everyone in their starting positions.
▶ Call for silence.
▶ Get video and audio recorders running.
▶ Mark the take using the clapper board.
▶ Wait for 5 seconds.
▶ Call "action" – the actual take can now begin.
▶ Hold the subject in his final position for 10 seconds after the end of the shot.
▶ Call "cut".
▶ Wait another 15 seconds and then stop the audio and video recorders. This is necessary because whenever you stop a video recorder, the tape rolls back and, if you don't leave a gap, the next shot can wipe the last few seconds off the previous recording. Never leave the recorder in pause mode unless you are going to go for an immediate retake.
▶ Make sure that you or your assistant makes a note of everything to do with the take.
▶ Reshoot the sequence again if you think it necessary. Otherwise set everything up for the next shot.

Make sure that every video and audio cassette is properly labeled and that its labeling corresponds to your production notes.

The clapper board

Used to mark each take as well as to provide a reference point to make it easier to match sound and picture when they are recorded separately.

You should write the project name and shot and take number on the board – these are either chalked on or you can use self-adhesive characters.

At the start of each take, someone should hold the board in front of the camera so it can be clearly read, call out the shot and take number, and bring the top of the board down with a sharp crack. The take then begins.

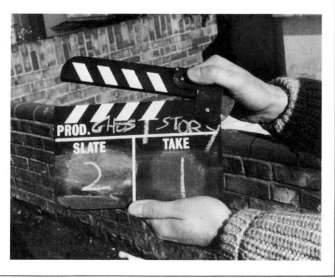

Directory of crew names

Boom operator: The person who holds and manipulates the microphone boom.
Cameraman: Looks after the camera, sets it up and operates it during each take.
Continuity person: Makes detailed notes after each take so that the scene can be reproduced exactly at some future date.
Director: The person with overall artistic control of the project.
Dubbing mixer: The person who puts the sound back onto the video tape when you are working with separately recorded sync sound.
Editor: Puts the shots together in the right order after they have been taken.
Focus puller: Keeps the camera in focus while it is being used for complicated moving shots.
Gaffer: The lighting electrician. He looks after all matters to do with providing power for the lights and maintaining them.
Grip: The person responsible for all the camera hardware such as tripods and dollies.
Producer: Oversees the whole project, finding locations, arranging for everything to be at the right place at the right time, and generally making sure that everything runs smoothly.
Production assistant: A general helper who carries out any and all production jobs that aren't specifically assigned to someone else.
Sound editor: The person responsible for assembling the sound track from both sync sound and separate sound sources, such as effects and music.

THE INSPIRATION

Having looked at the practicalities of using video equipment, the next step is to think about the creative opportunities. We shall start by seeing where the art of moving pictures came from – cinema has been around for the best part of 100 years, while television is hardly new. Then we will lead you – the home video director – through the sort of real situations you are likely to come across in your first few months with a camera.

Cinema

Although the first workable moving picture system actually appeared in Europe in the late 19th century, its development really took place early this century. The early film-makers were very much in the same situation as the home video maker today – they had a new toy and little idea of its scope and possibilities. However, they couldn't refer to a book and learn how other people put films together – they were completely on their own.

It was D.W. Griffith who had the foresight and inspiration to develop the ideas and techniques of film-making. The idea of telling a story by assembling shots, something we take completely for granted now, was very much a product of his work. In the earliest days of cinema it was common practice to simply point the camera at the action and leave it running. This gave very static shots, which didn't much change their point of view.

Griffith had other ideas. Gradually he introduced the idea of alternating long shots with close-ups, and the idea of parallel development – two plots running at the same time, the film cutting between the two to build up the tension. He also introduced 'tempo' and 'rhythm' to film-making, by varying the length of time each shot was held and the rapidity of intercutting. In other words Griffith introduced the concept of editing to the cinema. The climax of his career was probably his epic *Birth of a Nation* – made in 1915 and still regularly screened today.

As an example of the power of editing a young Russian, Lev Kuleshov, assembled a very simple experiment. He photographed five sequences – a man walking left to right, a woman walking right to left, their meeting and shaking hands, the man pointing to a large building, and the pair of them ascending a flight of stairs. Each sequence came from an entirely different location, yet when they were cut together it looked as if the events were all happening at the same time in the same place.

Even more startling was Kuleshov's next experiment. He filmed an actor with a completely expressionless face. Intercut with that footage were pictures of items such as a bowl of soup, a coffin containing a dead woman and a sequence of a girl playing with a toy bear. When the resulting edited film was shown the public raved about the acting. In fact the face was of course the same – totally expressionless – throughout!

These results led the Russians to conclude that editing was the most crucial aspect of film-making. The fact that these early rules

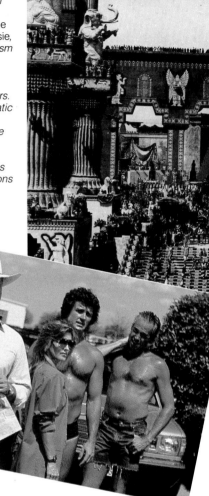

Right: *A scene from D.W. Griffith's lavish 1916 production* Intolerance.
Far right: *Still from Buñuel's* The Discreet Charm of the Bourgeoisie, *showing the influence of surrealism on 'arty' European film making.*
Below right: *Fred Astaire and Gene Kelly star in one of Hollywood's musical spectaculars.*
Below centre: *The great dramatic performance of actors such as Sir Richard Burton, characterize the 'human scale' approach of the British cinema.*
Below: *TV productions, such as* Dallas, *are now viewed by millions the world over.*

were formulated using film doesn't really make any difference in a video age as the basic techniques used are the same today.

In the years following the time of Griffith and Kuleshov the cinema developed in many different directions. In the USA the accent was very much on entertainment – making movies for commercial reasons. The wild flamboyance of the producers of Broadway musicals carried into the cinema, as did the powerful images of American history. If you want to make videos on a grand scale, then there are a million and one examples of the Hollywood tradition to inspire you!

The British theatrical tradition, along with rather more modest production budgets, has led to a tradition of cinema very much on the human scale in the UK. You only have to see performances by actors such as the late Richard Burton (*Look Back in Anger, Who's Afraid of Virginia Wolf, Equus, 1984*) to see how much can be put on the screen using very small resources – an ideal lesson for the amateur video maker.

Continental films can seem almost to be clichés in themselves – arty, inaccessible, the sort of thing you have to belong to a film club to see. But this *is* a grossly unfair exaggeration. Yes, a film in

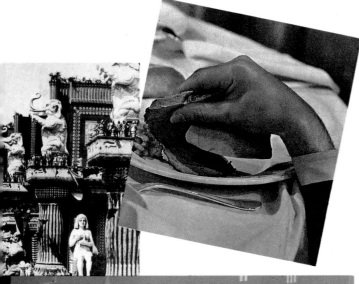

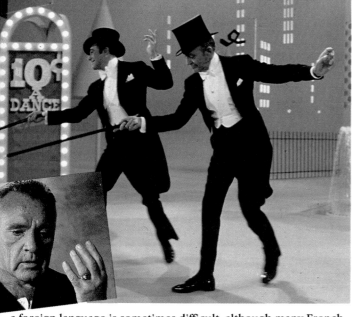

The term 'documentary' was coined by John Grierson in the 1920's. His interest in film-making was at first theoretical, but his examination of the media and their effects on society convinced him that film could be used as a force for 'social enlightenment'. In 1929 Grierson persuaded the British Empire Office to set up a film unit. The idea was to make films about the various areas of the British Empire to educate and inform the British public. This he did with such originality that his Empire Office film unit, and later the GPO film unit, became world-famous. His ideas were very influential and many of Grierson's colleagues set up film units in private companies. During the war Grierson carried his work on in Canada, setting up the Canadian Film Board and making wartime propaganda films.

Documentary has developed in leaps and bounds since those early days. We have come to consider such mammoth TV series as *Life on Earth* or *Cosmos* as standard TV documentaries. Brilliant as these are, they are the product of huge teams of people with many years of expertise behind them.

When Grierson and his team were making films, there weren't any rules to follow – they were as untutored in documentary film-making as the newcomer to video making. Their subjects were also much more down to earth – and it is in the solution of similar basic problems of program production that the home video director can readily learn.

Television

TV, unlike the cinema, has had a much shorter history – less than 50 years. But in that time it has managed to take over as the medium of mass communication and entertainment, while cinema now exists as a 'luxury' entertainment.

However, throughout the history of television, much of its output has come either directly from the cinema – in the form of feature films and shorts – or in cinema-inspired formats such as the TV newsreel. Until very recently all outside news material was recorded on film, while many prestigious TV dramas and serials are still made on film – simply because film gives a superior image in terms of color quality and range of brightness.

But TV has of course developed forms and ideas of its own. Because of the unique position of the 'box' in the home, TV can report the news literally as it happens, often with dramatic results. In the London Iranian Embassy Siege in 1981, the reality was more riveting than TV action drama, not least because it was being broadcast as it happened.

In many ways the forms and ideas of TV are closer to the amateur video maker than are those of the cinema – although there is no reason why you should restrict yourself when it comes to ideas or inspiration.

The technical parameters of TV obviously have a large bearing on the home video director. Huge panoramic views are almost always avoided – they may look good on the cinema screen but are lost on TV. On the other hand, drama which concentrates on people and their relationships (so called kitchen-sink drama) works rather better on TV than in the cinema, because of the small size and intimacy of the screen itself.

a foreign language is sometimes difficult, although many French, Italian, German and Spanish directors have made English-language films. The difference is rooted in the continental approach to the arts themselves. Directors such as Antonioni and Buñuel come from backgrounds in art, and conceive stories very much more in visual terms. They are very concerned with the way the film looks, as much as with the story it is trying to tell. Although film and video are different media, a look at films of this sort is a rich source of new ideas for the amateur video maker. They can help you to visualize everyday events in different ways which can make your own programs that much more special.

The documentary

Most video makers are likely to want to make documentaries when they first start using their equipment. A video about a family wedding is a documentary, as are shots of the children playing with their presents at Christmas. Documentaries form a very high proportion of most TV output, so there is ample opportunity to study and gain inspiration from the professionals.

THE WEDDING

WITH THIS RING...

Learning all about your video equipment and how it should be used is one thing; applying the technology to recording a real live situation is another. Over the next eight pages you'll find a step-by-step account of how to record a wedding – covering the whole process, from initial preparation to final post-production. And of course there is much more to home video making than weddings, so we'll go on to look at many other ideas and situations.

Although you'll find descriptions of specific steps to take, the best thing you can do is observe as much as possible before you start – use your eyes and ears – and watch as much professional work as possible. The things that seem perfectly natural and easy when seen in a TV production probably took a great deal of time and thought. If you can, record a few wedding sequences – and the material leading up to the wedding – from TV shows and watch them several times. See how each shot is constructed. Make a note of its length, camera angle, who's in it, what they say. Make a note of how the service is broken up, how many shots stay on the bride and groom's faces, how many on the minister, how many on the congregation. See how many shots are of the building, how many are insert shots away from the church, and their nature and length. You can observe the contrasts between, say, a fictional wedding in a soap opera and a documentary or newsreel film of an actual event.

There are many feature films in which a wedding occurs at

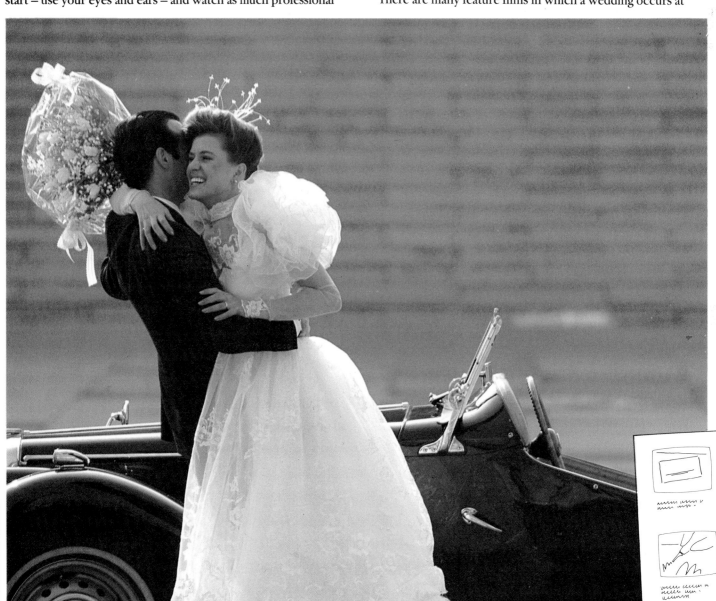

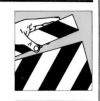

one point or another. *Love Story* with Ali McGraw and Ryan O'Neal is a particularly romantic film. *The Graduate* ends with a society wedding which is abruptly aborted by the intervention of Dustin Hoffman. Weddings occur on a lavish scale in *The Godfather* and *Camelot*, and on a rather more modest scale in *A Kind of Loving* and *The Family Way*. You may even pick up some ideas from the slightly macabre weddings in such films as *The Bride Wore Black* and *Chamber of Horrors!* Finally, and very importantly, watch the 'real-life' wedding videos that any of your friends may have. They are often a good source of ideas and should give you an idea of what others have done, and may show you which things **not** to do!

With your ideas in mind, you can then proceed to the initial stages of planning and shooting your own wedding production.

Remember that it is a family occasion. You are preserving something personal that will be treasured for many years, so you must go for personal shots; reactions of friends and relatives; the sheer joy on the faces of the bride and groom; and all those other little events that make such a day unique.

Don't be tempted to sacrifice these important elements to some 'grand aesthetic design'. The bride and groom will want to see themselves as the center of attention, not as bit-players in a grand spectacular. By all means re-edit at a later date to suit whatever 'artistic' ideas you might have had, but don't make this the first and only interpretation of your material.

Preparation

This involves two stages – the creative and the practical – and they go hand in hand. The creative stage involves finding out as much as you can about the two families involved. If they're friends of yours you will probably know a great deal about them anyway, but try and delve a bit more into their past. Ask them about their childhood, where they were brought up, what sort of jobs they wanted to do. Talk to their parents. Doting moms – and dads – will often reveal anecdotes about the bride and groom's past, which you could work into the production. Have a chat with the best man and chief bridesmaid – they may have a prank planned, which you could be prepared for.

Decide when you want the 'live' coverage to start. You could, for example, stay with the bride while she gets up, has her hair done, dresses and finally leaves for the church. Use this sort of material to show the buildup of tension, nerves and excitement as the moment approaches. You can do the same thing with the groom, but it is often said that the bride provides the center of attention at a wedding. If you are fortunate to have a friend who is also equipped with camera and recorder, one of you could cover the bride, the other the groom and intercut the footage in the final edit. You may like to shoot some of the groom's stag night or the bride's hen night. You can of course fake some of these

scenes if you can't cover two places at once.

Whatever you decide to shoot, you next come to the practical stage of preparation. It is essential that you have an advance look at the church and also the place where the reception is going to be held. At the church you should talk to the minister and find out first of all how much of the service he will allow you to record and under what conditions: will he allow extra lighting; will he allow you to get close in to the couple; will he allow any recording at all? The answers to these questions will dictate how you are going to record the service itself. If no shooting at all is allowed, you will have to discreetly record sound only and find insert shots such as church exteriors, photos, invitation cards and so on to show over the soundtrack.

Assuming that shooting is allowed, you should next check the availability of power points and work out how much extension cable you will need. Look into lighting positions and above all check camera angles, both inside and out. Find out where the sun will be at the time of the wedding and check for obtrusive exterior noises.

Repeat the process for the place where the reception is being held and make sure that the management gives you full permission to shoot. They are often very helpful and may give you practical help in the form of loans of lights and extension cables, or perhaps by letting you into restricted areas to get better camera angles.

Don't forget to work out the logistics of getting from one place to another either. You want to be sure that you can get from the church to the reception in advance of the bride and groom, set your equipment up and be waiting for them as they arrive. You may like to post your friend with the second camera ahead of you at the reception. Alternatively you might consider leaving as soon as the couple have emerged from the church. There is often quite a wait while the 'official' photographer takes his pictures – which you can of course use as inserts later.

Finally, you should draw up a rough shot list/storyboard. This will ensure that you won't forget all those bright ideas you had in the planning stage, and you won't be continually worrying about which shot to take next.

Remember, you can't stop a wedding and say, "Sorry, I missed that, could you do it again?" You only get one shot at it!

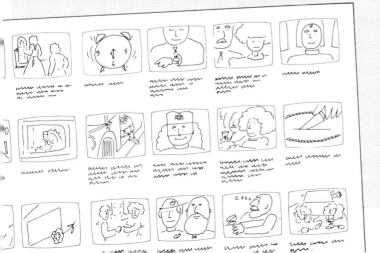

THE SERVICE

From your preparation, you should have a very good idea of what's going to happen and when it's going to happen. If you've never been to a wedding before, get hold of a copy of the service and read it through a few times just to be sure. Better still, sneak into someone else's and take notes. You will, of course, have talked to the minister beforehand, so ask him if you have any doubts (creative or spiritual).

Assuming that you've sorted out any pre-service shots, your first task on arriving at the church is to set up according to the plan you devised in your preparation. This may have to be pretty speedy, as there will probably have been another wedding in the church immediately before the one you are covering.

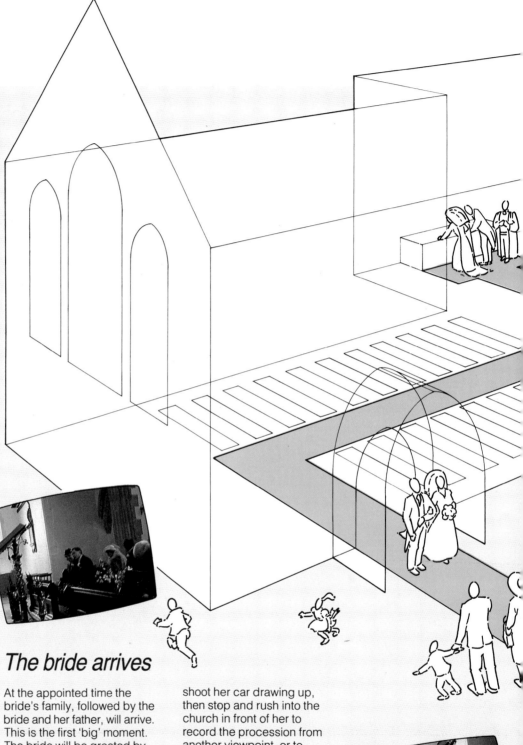

Get there first!

Aim to arrive before any of the guests. Once your equipment is set up you can record a few general shots to use as inserts later on. From around 30 minutes before the service is due to begin, the guests start to arrive and are shown to their seats by the ushers.

The groom will arrive with no particular ceremony. He will probably greet some of the guests and pace around looking worried and nervous before taking his seat indoors.

The bride arrives

At the appointed time the bride's family, followed by the bride and her father, will arrive. This is the first 'big' moment. The bride will be greeted by the minister in the church porch and they immediately begin the procession into the church and up the aisle. This is where the service begins. A second camera in the church to pick up the bride as she comes up the aisle would be very useful here. Otherwise you have to decide whether to

shoot her car drawing up, then stop and rush into the church in front of her to record the procession from another viewpoint, or to simply follow and record the procession from the back.

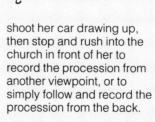

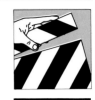

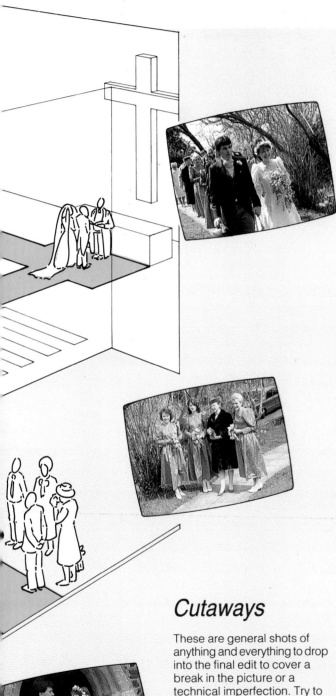

The marriage itself

Most marriage services usually begin with a hymn. You can use this opportunity to reposition the camera so you're in the right place for the actual marriage service. If you are recording a separate soundtrack, you can still include the hymn on the final version. Keep on the bride and groom for the first two lines, stop, reposition, and come back to them for the last verse. The intervening music can be filled with cutaway and general shots you can record at any time (and not necessarily during the service).

Next comes the service proper. This runs through to the point where the minister states "I now pronounce you man and wife". Throughout this you will have to decide on where to cut to close-up and wide shot. Again, with a separate sound recording you can afford not to worry about the sense of the words but just get the best pictures. Without a separate sound track remember that you will chop the words every time you start and stop the camera.

At this point the register is signed. You have to decide whether to follow the bride and groom into the vestry to witness the signing or stay with the congregation. There may be another hymn beforehand and perhaps a short sermon from the minister.

Following the signing of the register, the bride and groom proceed back down the aisle and out of the church. Again you have to decide where you want to be to get the best shots. If you want to pick them up as they emerge from the church, you'll have to get out of the church before them. It may be best to position yourself towards the back of the church where you can shoot them as they come down the aisle and then walk in front of them as they emerge from the church.

The departure

Next, the official photos in the church grounds are taken, followed by the departure for the reception. You must decide whether to get over to the reception in advance of the party or shoot the departure and arrive at the reception behind them. With two cameramen this problem is easily solved – you have one in each location.

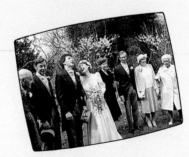

Cutaways

These are general shots of anything and everything to drop into the final edit to cover a break in the picture or a technical imperfection. Try to get a shot of every member of the family and the guests – this is even more amusing if you catch them doing something 'unconventional' (especially the children). It also makes everyone feel more a part of the day's events. Other cutaways can be the organist playing or prominent features of the church.

If you find you're short of cutaways when you get to the editing stage, it is quite easy to go back to the church and shoot some extra footage. If you want shots of the organist for instance, you could get these in ten or fifteen minutes after a Sunday service.

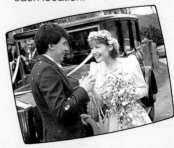

THE RECEPTION

This is where you need to have your wits about you most. There is never a set formula for wedding receptions. They can be held in many different places, following any sort of order. From your research you should have discovered exactly where the reception will be held and what will go on.

There are however a number of common elements. The reception will start with the bride and groom welcoming all the guests. There will often be quite a wait until this part of the procedure is over – time to set up inside and check the equipment. You may even do a few on-the-spot 'interviews' (vox pops). These little off-the-cuff comments are very useful as inserts and serve to involve all the guests in the final result.

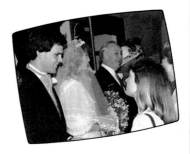

Welcoming the guests

On arrival the bride and groom will welcome all the guests. Try and cover this so that the receiving line is clearly visible as a diagonal across the screen, intercut with facial close-ups.

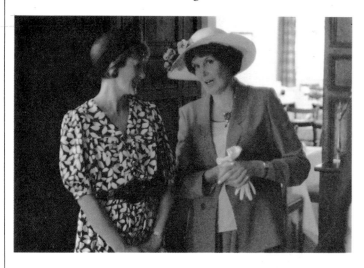

Welcome drinks!

Following the initial greeting, things can follow a number of courses. Drinks usually follow until the bride and groom have welcomed all the guests and then they enter the main room and the guests are invited to eat. This may be a formal meal or a standing buffet. The room may be indoors, it may be a marquee or it may even be outdoors. The best sort of shots to take of the meal are short clips of people eating and the more unusual antics of both children and grown-ups alike.

After the main course the cake will be cut, and the best man will call for order and speeches will be made. Following this the gathering will become more informal and will end with the departure of the bride and groom.

They may be leaving for their honeymoon at this point. You should be ready to shoot their departure and the car driving away, together with any pranks or tricks that may be played on them.

More often than not, there is also an evening event. It is here that people get silly, and you can be equally silly and outrageous with your coverage. Try and get as many vox pops as you can. If you have a friend who's a good actor, get him to play the professional interviewer, walking round gathering comments from the assembled crowd. Again, your closing shots could be the bride and groom driving away.

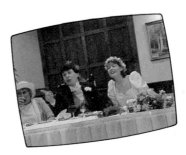

The speeches

Although these tend to look very much like a political gathering, try and pick up the nervous fidgeting that goes on. Reaction shots of the guests are also very useful here – especially of the bride, when the best man reads out some of the greetings messages.

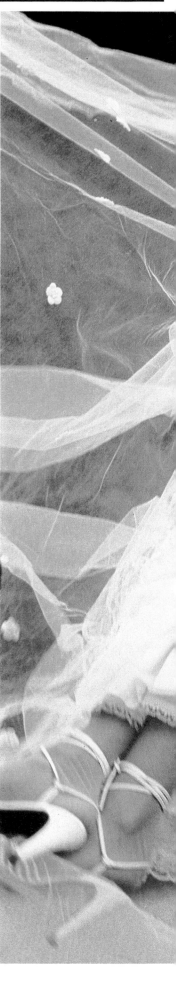

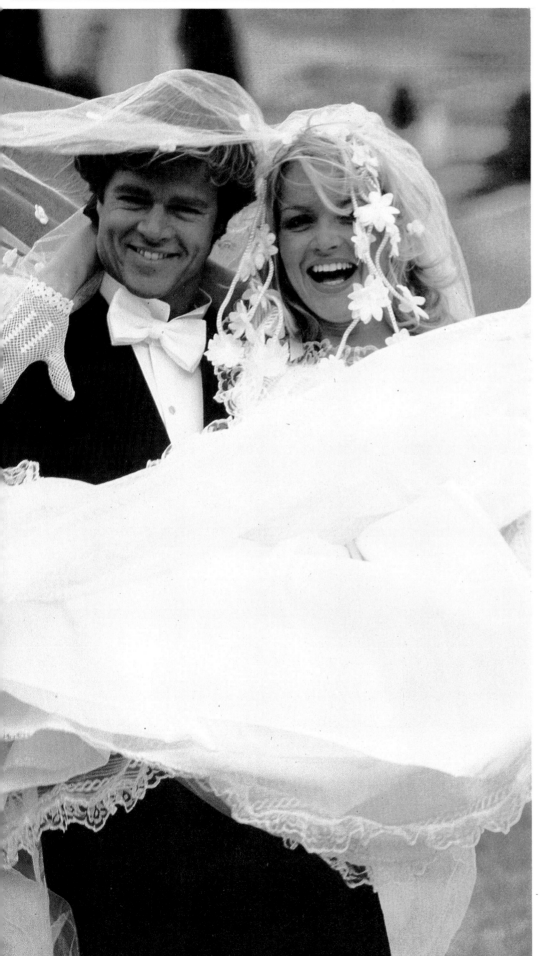

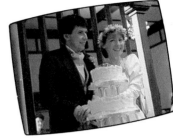

The cake

Highly symbolic. Although you can get the usual angle – and the photographer will probably pose the couple for his own use – try to get an unusual angle. Either shoot very low or very high or even from the bride and groom's point of view.

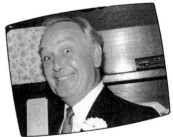

The evening event

A time to be silly, as things descend into chaos. Try and reflect this feeling with unusual camera angles, shots of people being very silly and the odd cutaway of the guest who might have had too much to drink, or the new romance blossoming in the corner. Vox pops with the guests are particularly good here, as the drink and general atmosphere will have relaxed everyone and removed much of the camera shyness that might have existed earlier.

SHOT AND EDIT ORDER

The basic elements of the final video are the shots taken on the day. But there are other things you can include – the most obvious being artwork materials such as invitation cards, orders of service, pages of the hymn and prayer books, the hotel brochure (if the reception is being held in a hotel), record sleeves (if there is an evening disco), pages of the bridal-wear catalogue, the actual still photos of the bride and groom, and so on.

As this is a strictly domestic and private enterprise you could include material from TV, films, books etc. Old family photographs and memorabilia of the bride and groom as children are very interesting here, as well as material illustrating their jobs.

If you have a continuous sound recording of the ceremony it may be possible to include the entire service in the video. Those bits of the service that don't have matching pictures can be illustrated with the cutaways you will have shot. You may want to shorten or edit the service – most weddings last around 30 minutes, which is an awfully long time in TV terms. Recordings of the reception and evening event will be a random selection of shots with no connecting thread unless you re-edit them into some sort of narrative form.

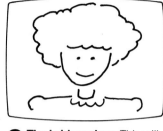

1 Opening credits: A shot of the invitation card usually looks very good, or perhaps a spread of wedding magazines with the invitation sitting in the middle. Pan around the magazines and finally settle on the card, zooming in until it fills the screen.

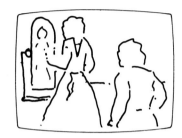

2 The bride wakes: This will probably be faked, but shoot the bride-to-be in bed asleep, cut to alarm clock, cut to bride waking up. This sequence can be developed – bride leaving house and arriving at hairdressers. Cut to bride arriving home with new hair-do.

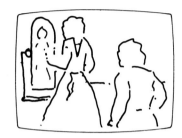

3 The bride prepares: The tension mounts. Shots of bride dressing in wedding gown. Intercut with rest of family getting ready and fussing around.

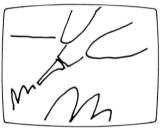

8 Signing the register: The bride and grocm usually disappear into the vestry during the final hymn to sign the register. Follow them to the vestry door, fade to black. Rush round to the vestry and get close-up shots of their hands on the register and of the faces of relatives as it is signed.

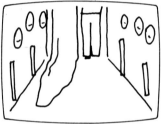

9 Final procession: This can be shot either from your vantage point or from the back of the church. In the latter case you can stay on the couple until they've completely left the church. As soon as they have disappeared out of shot fade to black.

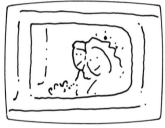

10 Bride and groom's departure: Pick up bride and groom as they walk down path to car, pan and follow them to car door. Pick them up through car window getting into car. Get a final shot of them getting into car, waving goodbye and car driving off.

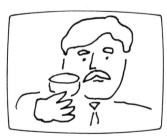

15 The speeches: More general shots bridge between the cake and speeches. Start with medium close-up shot, intercut with fingers playing nervously with notes or table furniture. Try and get guests' reactions to some of the jokes and funny anecdotes.

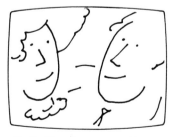

16 The departure: More general shots, including guests collecting coats and saying their goodbyes. Follow bride and groom. Close-ups of their expressions to each other – hold for two seconds then intercut to them walking outside. Cut to outside as they get in car and drive away.

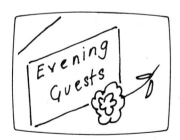

17 Credits or link card: If there is no evening event, this will be where the final credits go, otherwise you can link to the evening event by showing a shot of the invitation card for this part of the proceedings.

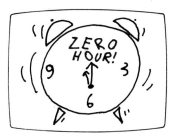

4 The departure: Start with close-up of a clock with the hands pointing to 'zero hour'. General panic, knocking on door as first of cars arrive. Noise and bustle will diminish as more and more people leave. Final shot of bride and father alone, then leaving through front door.

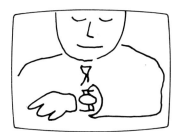

5 Groom and church: As the last sequence is running, intercut with shots of groom arriving at church, pacing around, the guests arriving, and him looking anxiously at his watch.

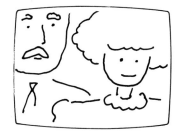

6 Bride's journey and arrival: Pick up as the car arrives at the church. Bride and father get out, are greeted by the minister. A brief pause for the photographer, then they enter church. Follow behind and keep them in shot as they walk up the aisle. Fade to black.

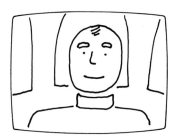

7 Take up position in organ loft: Fade up. Pan to minister and zoom to medium close-up of his face as he starts the ceremony. Throughout keep fairly close in to whoever's speaking. Fortunately nobody will move very far and a pan from person to person is acceptable.

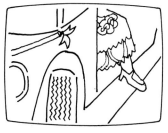

11 Arrival at reception: Pick up car as it draws to halt at curb. Shoot bride and groom getting out of car, and follow them back 'news-footage style' into reception building. The more bustled this looks the better.

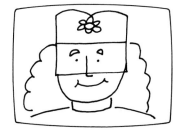

12 The greeting: A line of people – bride, groom and their respective parents. All guests file past to be formally greeted, try an unusual angle and bride's point of view, intercut with close-ups of guests' faces.

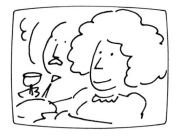

13 General shots of people eating and drinking: Long shots intercut with close-ups of particularly interesting moments. Intercuts with vox pops if this is possible.

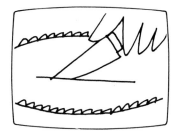

14 Cutting the cake: There is usually a speech. A long shot can be intercut with close-ups of bride and groom's faces, close-ups of cake, shot looking down knife and shot from bride's point of view.

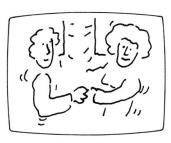

18 General shot: General noise and bustle at the evening event, loud music and people enjoying themselves. A good opportunity to try out some special effects filters.

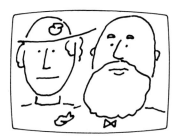

19 Vox pops: Try interviewing as many people as you can on camera – ask them what they think of the event, the bride and groom. Ask them if they have any funny stories about the bride and groom.

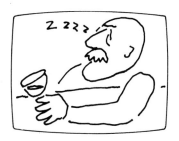

20 'Sub-plots': Intercut into the evening, shots of the guest who's fallen asleep on the floor, or the couple getting to know each other very well – the start of a new romance? Tact is obviously important here, but this shouldn't put you off gathering the pictures in the first place.

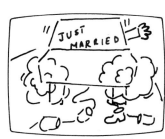

21 Final departure: As with the previous 'departure', shots of people collecting their coats, intercut to bride and groom leaving and driving away. Fade to final credits.

VIDEO ON VACATION

So you want to go one-up on your friends' snap-shots and capture your holiday on video?

On the practical side, you must first decide whether the inconvenience of carrying about expensive and heavy video equipment is outweighed by the thrill of recording your own moving pictures. Apart from the recorder you will have to take 3 or 4 spare batteries and an AC power unit to recharge them. Also give a thought to taking a lightweight tripod or monopod.

Customs regulations are also something to be aware of and the equipment must be adequately insured. Other hazards on holiday include theft and damage, especially if you are on the beach. Sand and video cameras do not mix!

On the creative side, some preparation will be necessary if you are going to get good shots or be in the right places at the right times to capture local events. The sort of things to be thinking about are local conditions, local customs and events. We are not suggesting you plan things like a military operation – a holiday is there to be enjoyed after all – but if you go to the trouble of taking the equipment with you then it's worth spending some time getting those shots which ordinary holiday makers might miss. Finding out a bit more about your holiday destination will also help you to have a better time generally – so the research is never a waste of time.

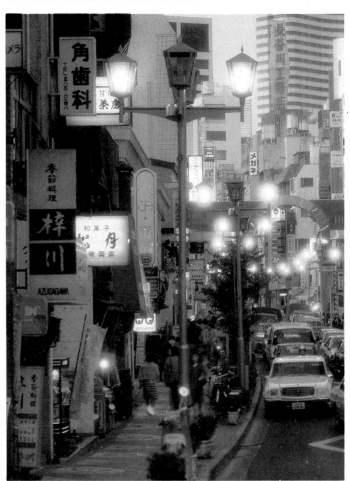

The paperwork

Customs regulations: If you're taking the equipment out of the country you must check with your local customs office exactly what paperwork you need to complete, so that you can take the equipment into your destination country, get it back out at the end of the holiday and re-import it into your own country. You may need no more than the purchase receipts, or you may have to fill in a special declaration form too. Don't forget that just because you have permission to take the equipment out of one country, it doesn't automatically mean you have permission to take it into another. For example, you may have satisfied British customs that the equipment is your property for your own use, as you step on board the cross-channel ferry. That doesn't mean that French customs on the other side automatically assume the same thing. They may demand another quite separate set of paperwork to allow you to take the equipment into France. And vice versa when you come back.

Insurance: Not quite as daunting as customs and, in fact, not strictly necessary – except that unless you can stand the financial loss of your equipment, plus the possibilities of third party claims should you cause an accident while using it, it is well worth the modest outlay. Video equipment is a popular target for thieves all over the world, and the chances of recovering your equipment abroad are pretty negligible. See page 148 for more details.

The preparation

In essence this means finding out as much as possible about your intended destination so that you don't miss either a particular event or some not so obvious feature of the area. It also means that you won't waste your holiday time deciding what you should shoot, when this can be done before you set off. The points to consider are:

Buildings: Of course you have the usual tourist haunts such as big cathedrals in large cities, but don't ignore the less imposing buildings, especially in far-flung countries. A Provençal farm house can be just as interesting visually as say London's Westminster Abbey. For the more well known

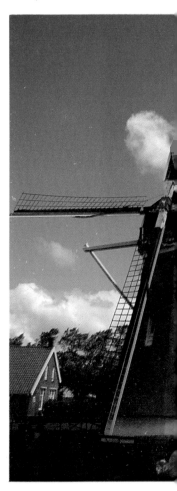

buildings you can find out something about their history – a big church might have a crooked tower, or an abrupt change in architectural style brought about because it couldn't find any money to continue building for a hundred years. Studying photos from guidebooks or postcards can give you some ideas for unusual camera angles, or show you views that tell as much about the people using the building as the building itself.

Countryside: This is as varied as the architecture of a country, especially in color and form. Photos in the guidebooks will show you something of what to expect. Shooting in a country like Tunisia, for example, you immediately think of cacti and long dusty roads. The geometric shape of a yellow, cactus-lined highway that runs dead straight for mile after mile is particularly strong and this can be contrasted with the lush vegetation of the towns and oases. On the other hand, Scotland immediately makes you think of lush green glens and the highlands. There are vast sweeps as one hill descends into a bank of mist to meet another high peak.

People: Perhaps the most interesting, colorful and varied element of all in a holiday video. As with most things, if you go a little off the beaten track and find the 'real' people of the country (rather than those who are the 'professional' tourist groupies), they are very often only too glad to perform for your camera. Most people are proud of their country and will do anything to carry that image abroad. Look at people doing even the most apparently ordinary things – when they are part of another culture they have a charm of their own. There's something particularly Gallic about a group of Frenchmen sitting outside a pavement café on an early spring evening. There's something uniquely Latin about an Italian mother calling in her children for their evening meal. These are far more genuine and authentic than the 'local color' laid on to entertain the tourists by the tour companies.

Local customs: In a sense an extension of the activities of the people of a country, but local customs tend to be the 'organized' events and rituals that are peculiar to one location. Reading up about your destination will tell you about the more obvious events, like major religious festivals etc. But if you read a bit deeper, you may well find out about customs that happen because the local people want them to happen, rather than being arranged specifically to entertain tourists. A remote Austrian town might have a custom of ringing a special bell at 6:45 every Thursday evening because that was the time and day they were liberated from Napoleon's army two hundred years ago.

Wildlife: Although you might not consider this quite so important unless you are a nature lover, the local wildlife contributes just as much to the atmosphere of a location and deserves consideration. The alligators of Florida are as much a part of local atmosphere as the weather or the landscape or the people.

The practicalities

What to take with you:

Camera – Make sure that it's been properly serviced and if you're going anywhere with extremes of temperature, that it will work in those conditions.

Recorder – As with the camera, it should be serviced and checked for suitability.

AC power unit/battery charger – This is essential to charge the batteries and run the recorder for checking recordings. Check that it will run off the power available in the country you are visiting.

Batteries – Take at least three, preferably more. Check that they aren't damaged and will retain their full charge. You might consider a battery belt instead which will give continuous power for far longer periods.

Support – A lightweight tripod is handy, but if this proves too bulky try a monopod.

Blank tape – Take at least four 30-minute blanks with you. It may be difficult to buy more if you are in some out-of-the-way location.

Other options might be a battery-operated lamp or two, and a small portable monitor TV. These are available with screen sizes down to as little as 3½ inches and are perfectly adequate for this application. Also take a sound recorder, microphone, batteries and blank tape. These are very useful for capturing long tracks of background sound, that would be a waste recording onto video tape. You can also record in sound only any particularly shy locals who won't perform for the camera, and then dub them onto the video soundtrack over views of the area which don't have their own sound.

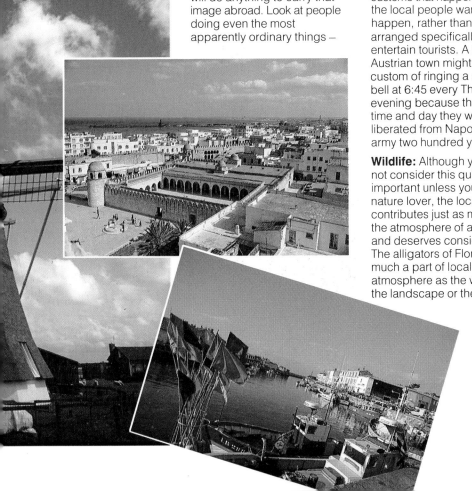

FINDING A THEME

Having read up about your holiday destination and arrived to see how the reality compares with the books, you will need to think about some shape and form for your video. Let's take a day at the seaside. The most obvious common factor of the beach, the town, its people, and its sights, is the sea. Use the sea, therefore, to link everything together.

You could probably open with a shot of the sun rising over the sea – this can be faked to some extent with a graduated orange filter. Cross cut to a picture of waves crashing on rocks and pull back to take in the beach scene as a whole. You can use this to work in shots of the children playing on the sand, pictures of gulls circling in the air, the cliffs, the Punch and Judy man and ice cream sellers. This sequence of pictures can then be shot in reverse order – perhaps far quicker – so once again you end up with waves crashing on rocks. Now, though, you've chosen your angle so that when you pan left you pick up the fishing boats in the harbor. This can lead into a series of shots of boats and most importantly the people who sail them. Perhaps they're sitting on the quayside mending nets or just having a drink in the local bar.

Keep at it throughout the day. Each sequence of pictures can be joined by a view or aspect of the sea, which may just be dimly visible in the background; or the sound of it may be played on the soundtrack and not seen at all, but it will still be there.

The beach – problems & possibilities

The practical problems of shooting on the beach and at the coast stem largely from the fact that sand and water have a sneaky way of getting into mechanical and electronic equipment, unless you are very careful. Don't leave the camera or recorder anywhere where there's loose sand. By all means record on the beach, but always leave the camera in the car or hotel when you're not actually handling it. You can even power the recorder from the car battery if you are working sufficiently close by, or use the car battery to recharge the recorder's batteries. It is worth experimenting with taping your equipment into plastic bags for protection – leaving the camera lens and viewfinder poking out through holes, with the plastic taped around them. Better safe than sorry after all!

Having said this, water is wonderful for sparkly effects. Try using a star filter on reflected sunlight. Beaches are also very lively places with lots of things happening. It is quite an entertainment just watching the people and if you can record them discreetly you will get a marvellous video – a continental beach is even more fun, as quite apart from people's general oddities, different holidaying nationalities each have their own distinct ways of behaving. A crowded beach also tends to attract vendors and traders of all descriptions. These are usually wonderful characters and well worth observing and recording.

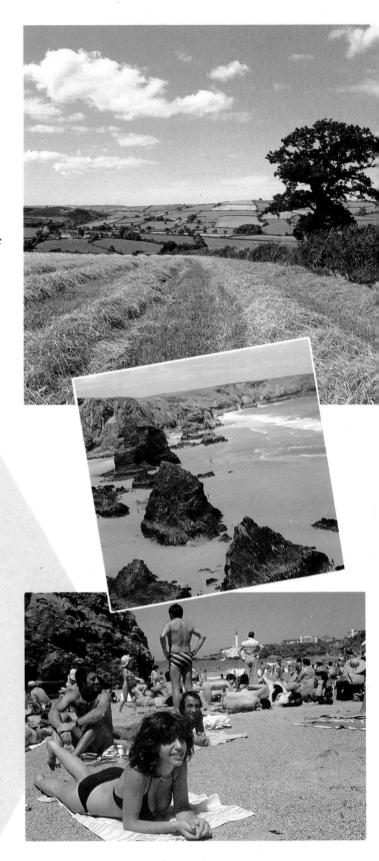

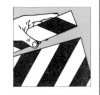

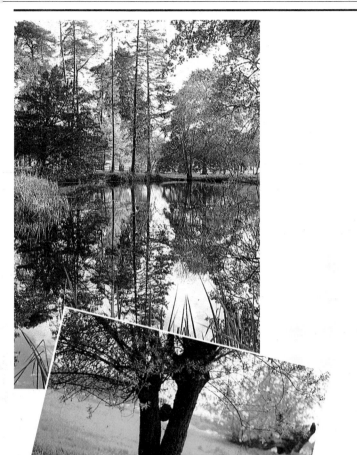

In the country

The country is altogether different from a crowded place like a beach. There are huge open spaces, and everything is on a grand scale. You might say that this is the province of the still photographer rather than the video cameraman, but remember that vast open spaces still have a life of their own. The vastness of a landscape can be accentuated by passing clouds, especially if the wind is high and is pushing them along. Reflections in water are another example of movement. Look for geometrical shapes that are changing with light or wind. A tree-lined avenue may appear to be completely static when viewed from a standing position, but shot from a moving car will take on an almost hypnotic quality.

Video can be used to show contrasts. A shot of a waterfall can be cut next to the vast mountain that created it. A close-up shot of a rabbit darting across a field can be contrasted with a wide-angle shot of the flat countryside.

Don't forget that certain aspects of a view can be modified and changed using filters. Graduated blues darken and enrich the sky; graduated orange turns midday to dusk; and graduated green can intensify the color of a landscape. Star filters look good on water; a polarizing filter helps you to see under the surface of water, and fog and diffusion filters can add a touch of mystery to the scene.

In the city

A holiday based in a romantic city such as Venice, or an exciting place like New York, can provide a rich source of images for the video maker. Your first problem is usually deciding what and what not to see and record.

From the point of view of your video, it helps if you think in terms of a theme – the sights of London are an obvious one, but that doesn't really help the process of selection. In many cities you will find that just by looking down little alleyways, lanes and doorways off what might be a well-known but unremarkable street, could provide more than enough material for a video tape. It will tell you much more about the city and its people than the well-known tourist sites could ever do. How about 'The Hidden Treasures of Fleet Street' as a title? Everyone knows that the street is (at the time of writing at least) the heart of national newspaper production in the UK, but do they know about Bert's hairdressing shop that hasn't changed in 50 years, or the medieval well, or the river Fleet that runs under the street and gives it its name?

Having said all this, the predominant interest in a city will be its buildings – and these demand certain considerations not found with other situations.

The first one is perspective. With a video camera you are fortunate in that you can pan along a vast facade to take in the whole of its detail, but this in itself demands that you

(Continued overleaf)

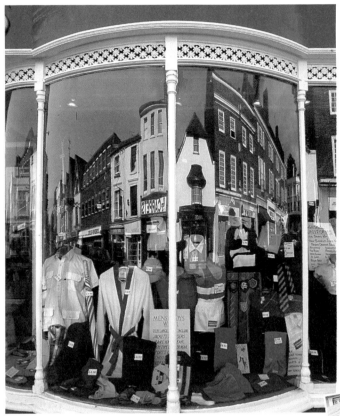

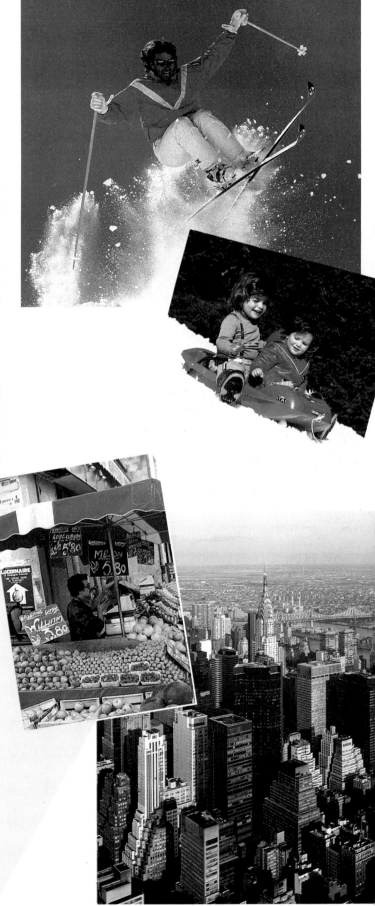

(Continued from previous page)
choose your viewpoint carefully. The first thing to remember is that the wider the angle of your lens, the more distorted the perspective of the picture will be. This can be used for effect, but doesn't necessarily give a true picture of the building being photographed. Try moving further back if you want a wider, panoramic view.

The converging horizontals of a long building can look effective, especially if you are shooting about halfway up it. The hard edges of the building can be softened by including some foliage around the edges of the frame.

Don't forget that buildings have details – a door knob or carving can be intercut with shots of the building as a whole. Light in itself can be a feature of architecture, and the movement of changing patterns of light as the sun comes and goes is something that can only be captured on video.

Don't forget that buildings are designed for people – or should be – and shots of people using a building can be equally revealing. A shot of people entering and leaving an elevator and dispersing to other parts of the building can be very revealing. Including people in shot also gives the viewer an idea of the scale of the building. By using passing figures to establish the camera's point of view, you can then tilt upwards to show the sheer scale of a church interior, for example. It at once assumes a vast and gigantic character – especially if the further reaches are first glimpsed in an out-of-focus blur.

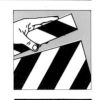

In the snow

The most likely situation in which you are likely to find snow is on a skiing holiday. There are two problems specifically associated with snow – cold and light.

Let's take them one at a time. From a practical point of view snow is cold and wet, although paradoxically the actual air temperatures in some resorts can be quite high simply because of the snow's reflective qualities. The main effect of cold is to reduce the battery capacity. A battery is principally a chemical device – a chemical reaction takes place which drives current out of the battery and into the recorder. The colder it gets, the less efficient any chemical reaction is – that in the battery included. This means you will have a shorter time for recording between battery changes, so you will need more spare batteries.

The question of wetness is really one of common sense. Don't put the recorder down on snow. The battery does get quite warm when you are using recorder and camera, and it is quite likely to melt the snow immediately below it. Nobody wants their recorder sitting in a puddle of water!

By far the most important problem will be light. Because snow is white and reflective, you may find that the camera is constantly setting the auto-exposure to light coming off the snow and so underexposing the rest of the picture. You may well find faces are very dark and colors equally shaded. One way to compensate for this is to have the backlight switch in the 'on' position, or perhaps even set the exposure manually if your camera has a manual adjust facility.

From a creative point of view, a skiing holiday probably best resembles a cross between a beach holiday and one set in the country. You have all the people and the social scene of a beach, as well as the countryside and views of a holiday in the wilds. There are some splendid opportunities for action shots – passing skiers, tobogganists and so on. Try to keep the camera angles very low – as if the skier is looming over the camera.

Although we wouldn't recommend that you take a video camera on skis, you may be all right on a toboggan – especially with a small camcorder. If the camera does get dropped, dust off any snow immediately before it has a chance to melt and get inside. Waterproof housings for cameras do exist, and some manufacturers are launching sport versions of camcorders which are water resistant and would be ideal for this sort of application. Failing that, experiment with taping the camcorder or camera and recorder into a plastic bag.

The waterproof housing

Underwater photography is a commonplace part of many a wildlife program and there is no reason why the amateur can't get similar results with the right preparation and equipment.

A word of caution first of all. Video equipment runs off electricity, which doesn't mix with water! So don't under any circumstances run your equipment from AC anywhere near water. Battery-powered recorders are OK when used with proper housings.

Waterproof housings have been available for still and film cameras for a number of years. With the invention of the video camcorder there is now no reason why the same housings cannot be used for these. Housings for a camera alone with waterproof connectors for the camera to recorder cable also exist but are less widespread.

In essence the housing is simply a waterproof bag with a clear glass plate at the front to which the camera lens is fastened. The camera controls can be manipulated through the bag and the camera used in the normal way. These housings are usually water-tight down to a specific depth, which varies according to the design and specification of the housing. The biggest drawback is their price. For something that may be only rarely used by the amateur they are very pricey – several hundred dollars – so renting one from a film equipment shop might be an attractive proposition.

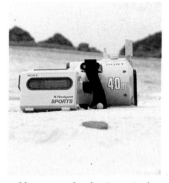

You may also be tempted by water-resistant housings such as the one for the Sony Handicam. These are fine for messing about on the beach – they keep out the water and sand – and will protect the camera if you accidentally immerse it in the sea. They are not actually water-tight and are not designed for prolonged underwater use.

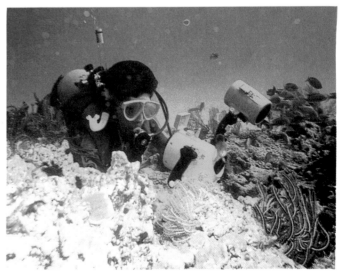

FROM STAGE TO SCREEN

THE STAGE PLAY

Every video cameraman is bound to be asked sooner or later to tackle a recording of the school play or the amateur dramatic club's latest production. Although you could just stand the camera at the back of the room and let the recorder run from start to finish, this is a great waste of a valuable opportunity to create a lasting document that will not only be a memento of the production, but also something interesting and entertaining in its own right.

It has to be said, however, that if you are using video as a training medium, then a clear and unambiguous recording will probably be needed – especially when applied to performing arts such as dance. This aside, there are so many possibilities offered by video that it seems a great pity to waste them.

There are two options to consider when recording a stage play. Either you leave the play much as it is and create an interesting document of a stage production, or rethink the play in film terms. This latter course offers more possibilities and, naturally, involves more work.

Whichever option you choose, some preparation is needed. This is discussed in detail below.

From the information gained from your preparation, you can plan exactly how you are going to tackle your recording. A live document is detailed on these pages – on the next spread we look at ways of expanding the play into a video program.

The on-stage document

If you simply want to create a permanent document of the play and don't want to expand it by reshooting and adding in more material, this is how to proceed.

First and foremost you must get to know the play thoroughly. You need to know who is speaking at any given moment; to whom they are speaking; when they enter and from where; and when and where they exit. You also need to know if a character is reacting to dialogue addressed to someone else.

Obviously you need to have read the play, but also try to attend as many rehearsals as possible, so you can actually see the size of the stage and where the exits and entrances are. You will also have to look at the lighting. Fortunately a properly lit play should photograph

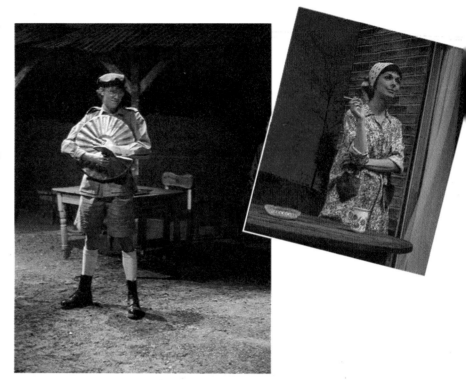

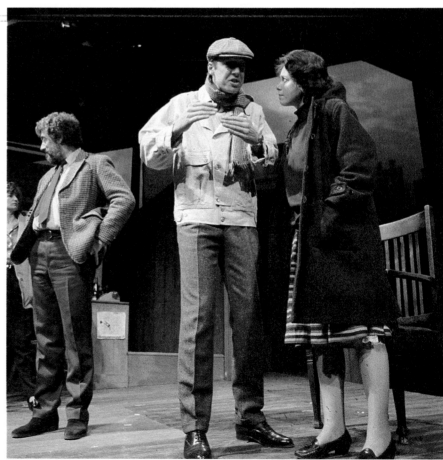

well on video (if you set the white balance of course) although some particular lighting effects such as dark browns and deep reds may not record particularly well. At the very least the faces and not the floor should be well lit.

At this point you will know whether you are going to be able to edit later or whether you have to record straight through in one go. If you are taking just one continual shot then you will have to plan a shooting strategy to make sure you keep the speakers in shot as much as possible, without swinging from one character to another and back again. It is OK, incidentally, in some shots to keep the camera on one character even when he or she isn't speaking. Their reaction to another person's dialogue can be as interesting visually as seeing the speaker, and it stops you having to continually move the camera from person to person.

To pick up people as they enter you can stop the recorder, move the camera, and restart the recorder. With some practice – and prompting perhaps from an assistant – this can look remarkably smooth in the end.

With added editing...

If you have the opportunity to edit so much the better. The procedure is to record the play four times as follows.

The first time through you elect to keep the camera on the main person speaking throughout each scene. If there is a group and each member speaks in turn with little break you may have to keep two or three people in shot. You record the characters' dialogue and their reactions as they are spoken to.

The second time around you keep the camera trained in each scene on the other person who wasn't there before.

During the third time around you should record wide-angle general views of each scene.

The fourth taping is used to pick up reaction shots and other bits of business that come from people not immediately involved in the action previously recorded. You could even include some audience shots here.

When you come to edit you have the choice of three different angles for each line plus some optional cutaways – the equivalent of recording with four different cameras in a television studio. You can then vary the shots to always keep the most important view on the screen while never losing a line or important reaction or gesture.

Lighting and sound

Every stage play is lit and many have sound effects. Although the lighting is designed for the stage, there are several important aspects that are common to both stage and video lighting. The first is to make sure that all the areas of the stage from which characters deliver their major speeches are adequately and properly lit – unless their faces need to be hidden for dramatic reasons. As many video shots are fairly close in – often showing no more than shoulders up – this becomes even more important. If everyone seems to be in perpetual shadow, try as diplomatically as possible to get the lighting designer to adjust some of the lamps to cast more light on the faces.

Sound, to the video maker, is less of a problem in these circumstances, as most sound effects can be added in quite successfully after the material has been shot. Perhaps the greatest problem here will be sound effects that are OK when played in the theatre but awful when re-recorded back onto tape. If there's no dialogue at the sound effect points, then there's little problem. If they run under dialogue, then you may well have to just live with them.

Placing the microphone(s) in a theatre can be a problem. The ideal place is dangling

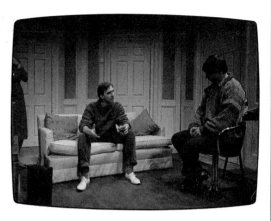

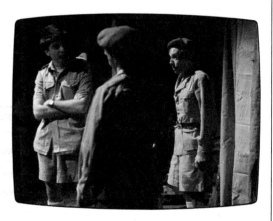

from the lighting rig above the stage, but if this has to plug into the camera then you will need a very long cable. The best compromise is probably to use an extremely sensitive rifle mic fastened to the camera. This will at least pick up what the camera is actually being pointed at.

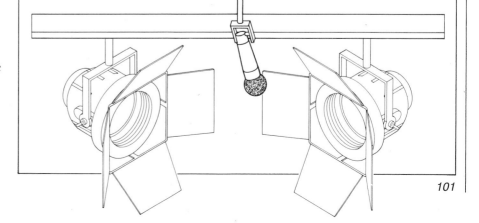

CREATING A SCREENPLAY

Although recording a play faithfully from a stage production will take a fair amount of work, it is, in a way, a terrible waste of an opportunity to create something new. Take the typical amateur dramatic production. A lot of people will have worked very hard to put their play on stage – they will have learned lines, found their characters, and put a lot of effort into giving their best performances for the audience. All this work can be utilized to produce something that is original and new for very little extra effort.

It may be obvious, but the stage and the screen are not the same. Each has its own styles, conventions and possibilities – the chief ones being that on the stage you have a small number of fixed locations that may or may not be 'realistic', and the drama is played in one stretch to a live audience. On screen you are not limited to a few locations, you can roam freely in time and the actors do not perform to a live audience. This freedom of location unfortunately means that film and TV audiences automatically expect any film to have a realistic setting.

The other chief difference is that on stage the audience member is free to look anywhere he likes on stage. He is free to

look at the person who is talking or the person who is being talked to – or neither. In film and TV the director chooses the viewpoint, which may include close-ups that are impossible to actually see in the theatre without opera glasses. It follows that the images chosen by the film/video director must be the ones important to the story. So, a simple close-up of a hand on a door handle or a discarded gun has an importance in a video that would be lost if the same objects or actions were seen on a theatrical set.

When it comes to adapting a stage production for video, you have two options. Either you shoot the play live, having chosen the shots you want to go into the final production, and then shoot extra new material to edit in with these shots, or you reshoot everything from scratch, but using the same actors and dialogue.

Which of these two options you choose depends on two things – the play itself and the availability of your cast and the locations to shoot them in. Your course of action may well also depend on your imagination in making a small stage set look good on video.

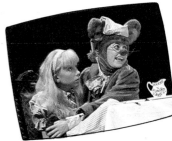

Being able to zoom in for close-ups of action on stage adds a new dimension to any production.

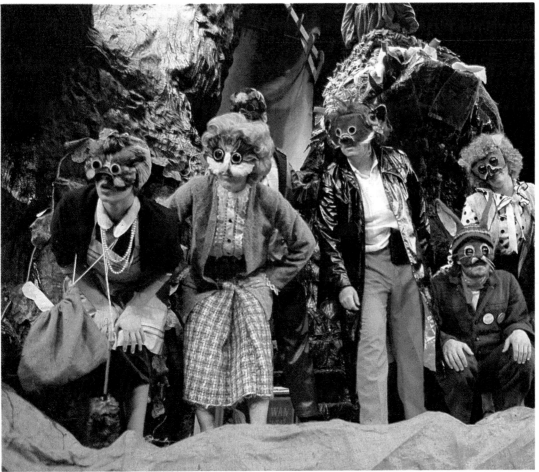

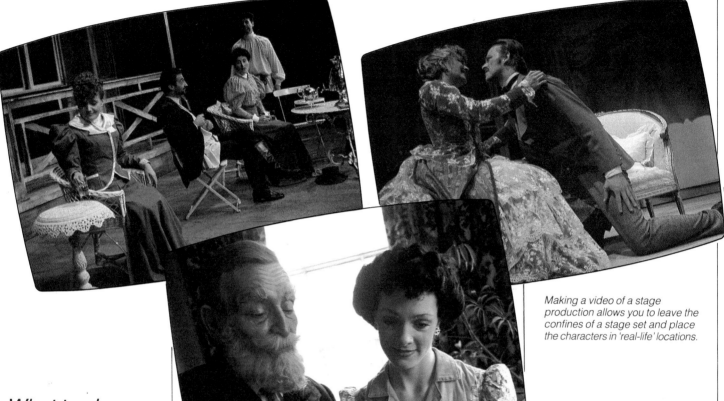

Making a video of a stage production allows you to leave the confines of a stage set and place the characters in 'real-life' locations.

What to change, and what to leave

Let us assume at the start that you are completely familiar with the play, the characters, what happens to them and where it happens.

Things that stay the same:
▶ The obvious thing to leave the same is the story – although you can tinker with one or two details, changing the storyline radically means you are really starting to create something completely new.

▶ The major characters obviously stay the same – if you take out the hero or heroine, it's patently not the same story, although you can drop one or two minor characters whose function may be just filling in time on stage, while main characters change costumes and so on.

▶ The basic time, period and location of the action stays the same although some details can be changed.

Things that can be changed or added:
The biggest advantage of video is that you can add things to a stage play that move the action on far more effectively than several lines of dialogue or a world outside the set that can only be suggested.

▶ The order of some scenes and the placing of certain lines of dialogue. This, to some extent, happens in the theatre, but is much more usual in adapting stage plays for the screen.

▶ The location of some scenes. If you are taking the play out of a single stage set and into the 'real world' then you can place some key lines, say, out in the street or in another room. This doesn't

affect the rule of keeping the play in the same time and general location.

▶ If a play is set in a single room, you can add shots of what's happening in the outside world. Be careful when you do this to listen to the dialogue. If one character describes the scene outside then your shot should match that description. Alternatively, putting in the shot dispenses with this dialogue altogether and the speech can be cut.

▶ **Extra characters:** Although a play may only have, say, five characters, others may be referred to. On video it is possible to actually bring these characters into play. There may be a scene where one of the characters describes a

situation involving her son and husband. This speech could be cut and a dramatized version actually showing them inserted instead.

▶ **Close-ups:** The close-up is very much a part of video and film which has no equivalent in the theatre, but is a powerful way of moving the action on. A close-up of a doorknob turning can be as useful as half a page of dialogue in which a character describes how a house frightens her.

▶ **Music and sound effects:** Incidental music is a common cinematic convention which is used for building a mood. This is rarely ever done in the theatre. Sound effects are another device used far more in film and TV than in the theatre. Again, a carefully chosen and placed sound effect can say as much as a pageful of dialogue.

STAGE TO SCREEN –
THE PRACTICALITIES

Having looked at the possibliities that video can offer a stage play, how can you put them into practice? To illustrate the process of turning a stage play into a screen version, let's use the David Lean film *Brief Encounter* as an example. This particular movie has been shown countless times on television all around the world and is also available on video cassette in most countries.

The film began life as a short 40-minute play, *Still Life*, part of a series called *Tonight at 8.30* written by Noel Coward. This is still a favorite of amateur dramatic societies. It is set in a railway refreshment room, and in five scenes, it follows the meetings and the love affair that develops between a suburban housewife and an equally suburban doctor.

In *Still Life* the action is confined to the same refreshment room throughout and anything that goes on outside that setting is inferred. The dramatic climax (and we never actually see this moment on stage) comes when the couple are interrupted at a friend's flat as they are about to make love. Running through their developing affair are the much lighter relationships between station ticket collector and refreshment room manageress, and a waitress and the porter.

The screenplay

Your first decision is based on how you want the final structure of the video version to look. In *Brief Encounter*, the film narrative actually starts at the point where the play ends, and extends the final scene (where the heroine, Laura, has just parted from her lover, Alec, for the last time) to the point where Laura arrives home. The narrative of the play is then told as one long flashback, eventually arriving at the point where the film originally started. Throughout the film we hear Laura's voice telling the story, moving on the narrative.

Your next decision is how much of the original dialogue to leave in and how much can be replaced by images. It is here, more than anywhere else, that *Still Life* and *Brief Encounter* seem to diverge. In the stage play we simply see Alec and Laura's brief meetings in the station buffet. Although their main topic of conversation is about themselves and, as they play progresses, their overwhelming love, we catch snippets about what they have done during the rest of the day. The film version actually fills in those bits·of action. Because the original stage play was only around 40 minutes long, Noel Coward felt quite free to extend and adapt it, writing in new dialogue to fill these moments and extend their thoughts. Having said that, a fair amount of the original play has still been cut.

Your third decision is how much additional material you are going to shoot and what form it should take. You can obviously set the location and time of the play much more accurately with film. *Brief Encounter* opens with shots of trains hurtling through the station and then a shot of the station ticket collector crossing the tracks and entering the buffet.

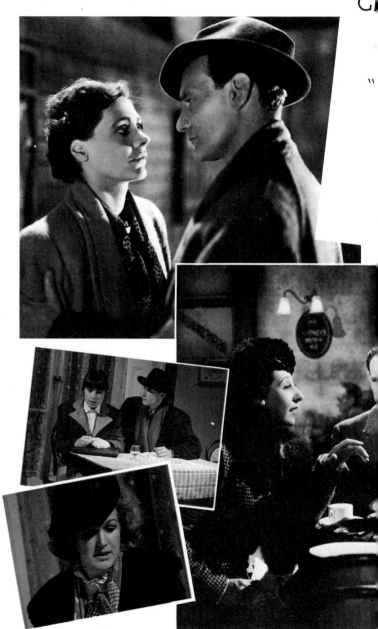

Having established the time and place, you must then decide how many of the times and places referred to in the dialogue you are going to actually shoot. These can either replace dialogue or be shown over the existing lines. In *Still Life*, for instance, Laura tells Alec how she spends her day in the town. In *Brief Encounter*, we actually see Laura going into shops, eating in the café, going to the pictures.

Next you need to decide on the order of dialogue. Although you can't switch dialogue around completely at random, there's no reason to keep it in exactly the same order. At the start of the film, for example, we are at the end of the play. As the film opens we are taken into the refreshment room. Alec and Laura are sitting at a table looking unhappily at each other. From this we cut to dialogue between the ticket collector and buffet manageress.

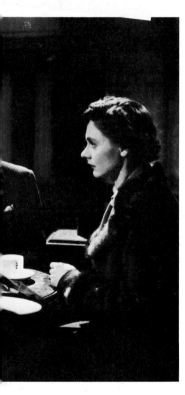

JOHN C. WILSON

presents

JDE LAWRENCE

EL COWARD

GHT AT 8.30"

LAYS by NOËL COWARD

ED by THE AUTHOR

by G E CALTHROP

Transferring a play from stage to screen opens up a number of creative possibilities for the director. Here we see two approaches to Noël Coward's Brief Encounter – *the original film version and an amateur stage production.*

This dialogue, in fact, occurs at the start of the play. Throughout the film version bits of the original stage dialogue occur, although not all of them are spoken in the refreshment room. The climactic scene in the friend's flat actually happens there and the whole film is punctuated by shots of trains rushing through the station.

Shooting

With a definite idea of the screenplay firmly in mind, you may well have prepared some sort of rough storyboard. The next stage is to plan exactly how you are going to shoot the material.

If you don't have the resources to shoot dialogue actually on location, the best plan is to keep much of the action within the confines of the stage set. The closer you go in on faces and other objects, the less the viewers will notice the background set – so any deficiencies will be less obvious. Try to make costumes and hand props as authentic as possible. Record the whole play under these conditions several times, concentrating on a different actor each time. This will give you all the shots you need while not interrupting the flow of the performance.

The next thing is to shoot the exteriors. Obviously shots that don't involve the actors cause a minimum amount of fuss. If one or more characters are involved it gets complicated. Don't forget that all exterior shots must match the time and period of the play and the characters must be wearing the same costumes if interior and exterior shots are meant to interconnect. Be very careful of writing extra dialogue. Unless you keep it down to a mere 'yes', 'no', and '12 o'clock madam', or are a very talented writer, it may sound silly and could possibly not fit at all.

The point where it all comes together is in the editing. With your new screenplay firmly in front of you, it is time to assemble shots from the play, material shot outside as atmosphere without any of the play's characters, and material shot with characters either mute or with dialogue.

At this point, the amateur making a video strictly for his own pleasure can also add in 'stock shots' recorded from TV or other films.

Don't be afraid to slightly rethink your idea if something isn't editing together quite successfully. You can often get over the problem of an awkward transition from one scene to another by means of a cutaway or close-up. Laura's hand on the waiting room door as she leaves could cross cut to her being seen opening the friend's flat from within the flat.

This is also the point where you can add incidental music. *Brief Encounter* uses Rachmaninov's 2nd Piano Concerto, and this is first introduced as part of the scene as Laura turns on the radio. From then on it fades in and out, punctuating and highlighting the growing romance, as her voice-overs come and go over the live action.

You could, indeed, add a voice-over or even extra dialogue at this point. A couple arguing can be recorded on sound alone and then dubbed onto a tape that shows feet pacing up and down a carpet. Don't forget that sound is very useful for establishing places, especially when you don't have ready images on tape.

Video vs stage

Stage:

► Restricted to a few different settings.

► Need not have realistic sets to look good.

► Has a live audience.

► Members of audience can select which part of the stage they observe at any one time.

Video:

► Can move freely in location and time.

► The director selects what the viewer will see within the setting of the scene, not the audience.

► Is recorded.

► Is expected to have realistic settings.

Adaptation checklist

► Decide on the structure of the video – is it going to be the same as the play or different?

► Decide which elements of the dialogue you are going to leave out – which are superfluous and which can be replaced by exterior shots.

► Decide what external material you are going to shoot. Work out how much needs new dialogue, and how much is going to incorporate dialogue from the original play, which might have been spoken in another place.

► Decide on the order of the remaining dialogue, and how much needs changing or rewriting.

► Decide on any special visual effects and also choose suitable music and sound effects.

THE VIDEO ALBUM

A FAMILY HISTORY

Although we have talked about using video as a moving visual medium, it also has tremendous scope for bringing together a number of different still images – photographs, maps, books, newspaper clippings, family heirlooms, etc – to tell a story. This set of visuals can be further combined with a well-chosen soundtrack and commentary to make a video program that is every bit as interesting and informative as something involving live action and people talking to camera.

If we take a family history as an example of the possibilities that the video album offers, we would start by assembling as much visual material as possible, covering the period from, say, when Granny was born to the present day. Old family photographs are an obvious place to start, but to put them in their context of time and place, try to find some contemporary illustrations of her home town, some of the magazines and newspapers that were available at the time, old maps of the town and so on. They need not be originals – reproductions or even books with old photos in them will do just as well.

As the story progresses, don't forget to keep the viewer well in touch with the time and period. Particular events in world history – such as the start of the war – can punctuate the story, provide natural breaks and point the way. All the time remember to mark these points with pictures that illustrate the event. A newspaper headline saying "War Declared" would be just right in this case.

Video is, of course, a moving medium so old movie film could be incorporated into the mix of the program. This can be particularly effective for those great moments such as weddings, and if you have video recordings of world events use those to mark the points in time.

Sound, in a project like this, is equally important. If you have old tape recordings of various relatives, these can be dubbed onto the sound track at the points where you are showing still pictures of those members of the family. If you were more ambitious you could record Granny reminiscing about her childhood and dub that over scenes of that era. In addition to this, there will be some sort of commentary, but these dialogue tracks can also be mixed with music, and specific pieces of music can be chosen both to fit the period (they may have been popular songs of the day) or to fit the mood (they may have been a particular person's favorite).

On the right, we have outlined an imaginary video family history. What you put in yours of course depends on the material at your disposal.

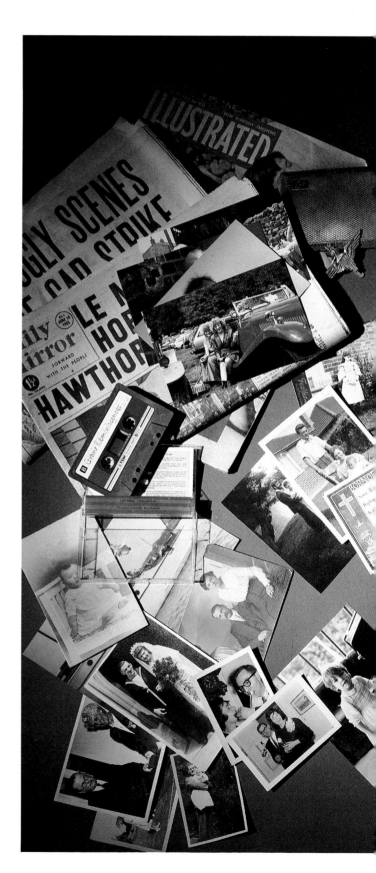

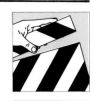

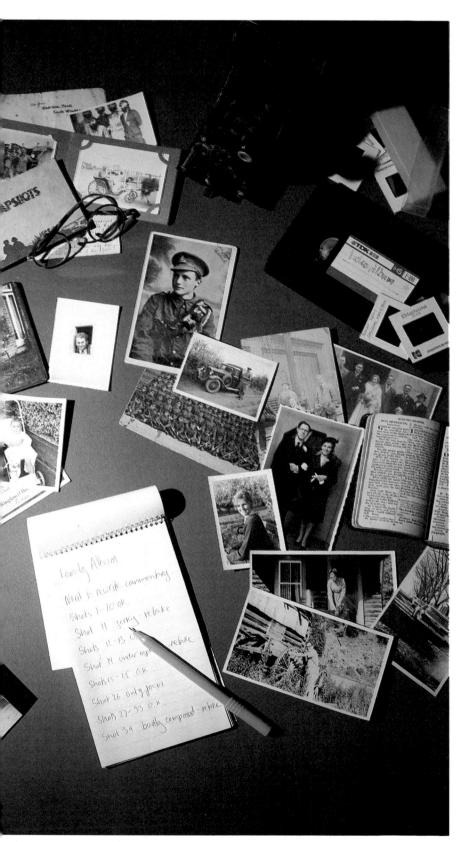

Shot sequence outline

1 Opening credit. (Rub-down lettering or title generator.) Run over photo of Gran's home town as it was in 1900.

2 Photo of Gran's christening. Voice-over with details. Cut to other photos of christening.

3 Old photos and maps of home town, with modern material. Music of the time on soundtrack.

4 Outbreak of World War I. Illustrated by newspaper headlines, recruiting posters and other available printed material. Wartime sound effects. Photo of Gran at school

5 Photo of Gran at her first job. Other available material showing similar industry from this period. Sound effects to match.

6 End of war. Illustrate as before. Then photo of Gran's husband-to-be. Photo of his work-mates and family. Voice-over with details.

7 Gran's wedding. Photos and other memorabilia. Wedding bells on soundtrack and voice-over: Newspaper headlines to fix point in time.

8 Three years later first child – Victoria – is born. Then second child – Eric. Sequence of growing-up pictures. Voice-over with details.

9 Outbreak of World War II. Newspaper headlines. Perhaps archive newsreel material 'borrowed' from TV programs. Winston Churchill etc. on soundtrack.

10 Britain at war. Pictures of the family. Eric leaves to serve his country. Photos of him with his unit. In 1943 Victoria falls in love with an American airman – Chester. Photos of him in uniform. Voice-over reminiscences etc.

11 Big headline – V.E. day. War is over. Newsreel footage. Photos of celebrations. Eric returns home. Chester has to return to the United States. Victoria is to marry him and go too. Photos. Voice-over with explanations.

12 Eric courts and marries Mary Brown. Photos to match.

13 – **to end of 'album'** As the family expands there is more ground to be covered. Being more recent, most of the family should be familiar with events, so more details can be conveyed in voice-overs. Intercut details of Victoria and Eric's families growing up on different sides of the Atlantic, contrasting changes and differences in lifestyles. 'Archive' material will be more readily available from TV coverage, so references to world events will be easier to handle.

RECORDING ANIMALS

LIVING THINGS

In terms of video making we can say that animals come in two sorts – pets and wild. Wild animals can be in the wild or in a zoo. Recording animals, therefore, will depend on type and location. One thing is certain – a lot of patience is necessary if you are going to get the best results, especially if you are after good pictures of animals in the wild.

The first rule is to observe your subject very carefully. For example, pets and captive animals become very restless before feeding time and are placid afterwards. By discovering your subject's daily routine, you can often anticipate when they are going to perform the particular sequence you are trying to shoot.

You should also be prepared to shoot an awful lot of material just to get that perfect sequence. Fortunately with video this costs nothing more than a lot of time.

Getting any animal to perform as you want it to, is very difficult, and you must usually do something to attract the animal's attention – even if the 'pose' will only be held for a few moments.

You can increase your chances of getting a good shot by being fully aware of the animal's physical appearance and habits. A bulldog for example will always look its most imposing when shot face on. Remember that dark fur absorbs a large amount of light and so dark-coated animals will need to be shot with the camera's backlight switch in the 'on' position. Camouflaged

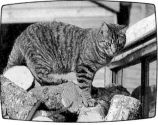

animals present another problem and should be taken against a contrasting background.

Recording animals in the wild presents its own problems. Some animals are positively dangerous to approach. Others are too timid to allow people very close. Be prepared to use your lens at its telephoto setting and to move fast.

For tiny animals facilities such as macro and low light capability really come into their own. Having said that, it is as much the ingenuity of the photographer that gets the picture as any expensive equipment.

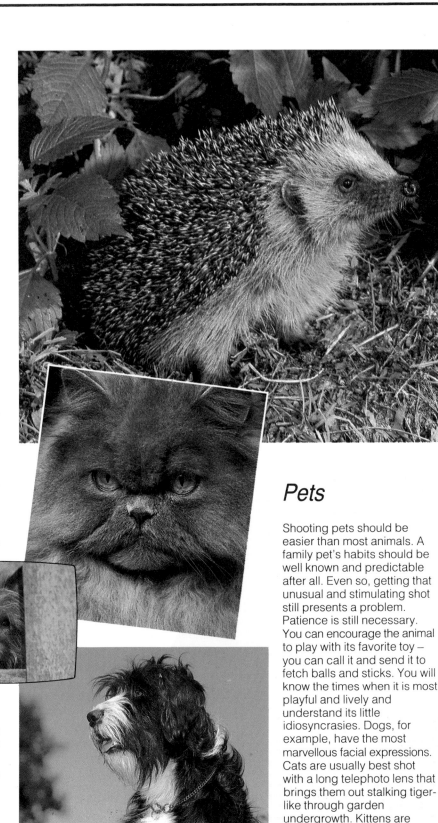

Pets

Shooting pets should be easier than most animals. A family pet's habits should be well known and predictable after all. Even so, getting that unusual and stimulating shot still presents a problem. Patience is still necessary. You can encourage the animal to play with its favorite toy – you can call it and send it to fetch balls and sticks. You will know the times when it is most playful and lively and understand its little idiosyncrasies. Dogs, for example, have the most marvellous facial expressions. Cats are usually best shot with a long telephoto lens that brings them out stalking tiger-like through garden undergrowth. Kittens are sweet when seen together playing in a basket.

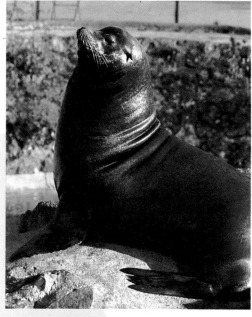

Animals in zoos

Zoos give you the advantage of finding exotic animals reasonably close to hand without the dangers of pursuing them in the wild. First priority is getting to know the animals' routine. Have a chat with the keeper – he'll know when the animal is most lively and co-operative, when it is being fed and any other quirks it might have. He will also tell you what is and isn't permitted. Never use bright movie lights (or flash still photography) unless you have express permission. They could seriously upset the animals, not to mention the zoo's management!

Slow-moving animals, such as elephants, don't make particularly good subjects unless you are able to show up the texture of their hide – they simply appear as grey motionless hulks. Wait for moments of activity, such as trunk waving and trumpeting.

Inevitably some animals are kept behind bars or netting. This can be minimized by getting a long way away from the animal and shooting it at the telephoto end of the zoom lens. The netting will go out of focus and become less visible.

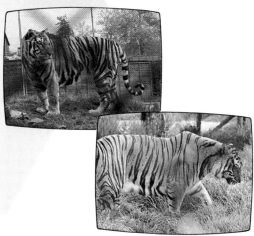

Birds

The variety of different birds is enormous – there are colorful ones, drab ones, night hunters, day hunters, and so on. Fortunately they are creatures of habit, returning to the same places to roost or nest or feed their young. Birds are particularly easy to shoot when busy at their nests. Even so it is essential to keep quiet and still, especially when the young are still being reared. It is very easy to scare birds away and they will rarely return once they have noticed you.

To observe birds in the wild, it is more usual to use a blind – an inconspicuous 'hut' set some distance away from the bird's nesting site. Video recording is possible through slits and windows in the blind, but you may need a really long telephoto lens fitted to the camera. This means using a camera that will take SLR camera lenses – a 250mm or greater telephoto is recommended.

Photographing birds in the back garden can be equally rewarding as perching on a high cliff top in a makeshift blind. The same principles still apply – quiet, stillness, and the long-distance approach.

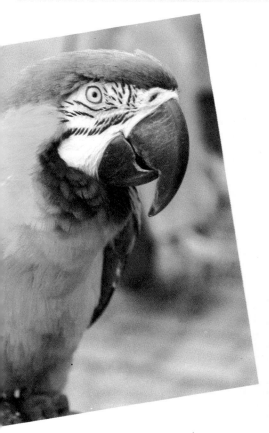

Special tricks and close-ups

Although some animal pictures seem natural, they are in fact faked. Shooting a picture of a fish or frog in a tank can present enormous problems. The answer is to trap them in a small area of the tank while

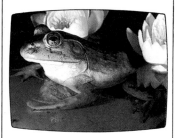

you shoot, using a sheet of glass which doesn't actually show up in the final picture.

Sometimes a magical picture of something in nature is obscured by a distracting background. A tree branch swathed in ice will not look very special when set against other tree branches, but shot against a black backdrop it immediately comes to life. Subjects like an early morning picture of a spider's web picked out with dew can also look good if backlit.

Experiment with the macro facility on the camera. Everyday items like flowers can look completely different when photographed close up, while photography of tiny creatures is much easier. You must, however, take care over lighting these situations.

Some of the most exciting nature photography is obtained by constructing artificial environments for animals that look real. Many children have made worm or ant farms as projects and this principle can be extended to, for example, constructing whole runs for foxes or a complete environment for mice.

THE FAMILY OCCASION

CHRISTMAS DAY

One of the first uses that most people apply their a video camera to is recording a particular family event. This could be a birthday or anniversary, a wedding or christening, or a time when the family are all together, such as Christmas Day.

Although you would never want to plan such an event down to the last detail – making each member of the family play a pre-determined role – you should nevertheless give the day some thought. You must first ask yourself exactly what you are trying to achieve. The answer to this is really a record of the family celebrating Christmas. The second question is, what topics will it cover? (Waking up, opening presents, Christmas dinner, playing games, and so on.) The theme is of course quite obvious, although different angles can be added due to any 'pecularities' of your family.

Your next step should be some brief jottings to guide you

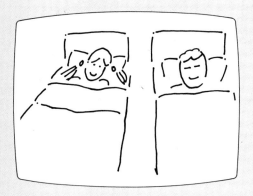

Establishing shot of children in bed. They wake up, rush excitedly out of the room. Catch them in long shot as they creep down the stairs and into the living room.

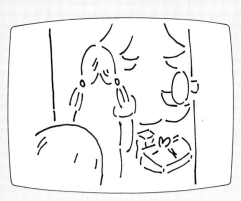

Pick children up as they enter through the living room door and pan around as they make their way to the tree. They open their presents and you can show each child in turn opening something in mid shot, each child in close-up, close-ups of the presents, some long shots of the tree as a whole and some cutaways.

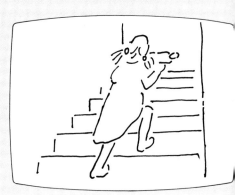

The children each grab one of the toys and rush out of the room. Pick them up in a long shot disappearing up the stairs and then another shot as they burst into Mom and Dad's room. Perhaps they leap on the bed to wake them up. Reaction shot from Mom and Dad (or just Mom if Dad's doing the shooting or vice-versa). Fade out.

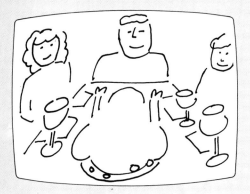

Fade in to long shot of family sitting at table ready to eat. Turkey is ceremoniously brought in to loud applause. The meal commences. Close-ups of people enjoying themselves can be intercut with shots of the contents of the table being devoured. Try some low 'turkey's-eye view' shots and big close-ups of items on table. Cut to...

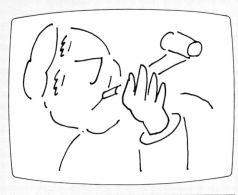

...after-dinner jollities – Christmas crackers being pulled, jokes and games, brandy and cigars. Fade out.

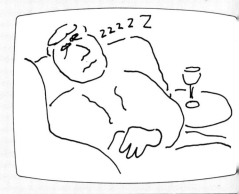

Fade in to picture of Dad snoozing in armchair. Intercut with pics of roaring fire, and guests slumped in front of the TV set. Cross cut to...

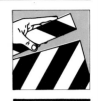

around the various shots you might think you need. With careful planning you may find that no editing is needed at all, although it would be much better if you could drop in a few reaction shots and cutaways to cover awkward or unwanted moments.

If you're feeling very ambitious your next step would be to draw up a storyboard. This can only be approximate as this type of situation is bound to throw up all sorts of unexpected opportunities. You should not stick rigidly to the storyboard if the unexpected does happen!

Whatever happens, don't forget to record a few still shots away from the main action. These can be views of the Christmas tree, or the snowy scene outside, or the cat asleep in front of the fire, etc. You could even try a few 'arty' shots, such as a candle viewed through a wine glass or big close-ups of the turkey or Christmas pudding. Using special effects filters, such as starburst or dream are 'naturals' for shots of the tree.

With a plan in mind, you only have to shoot away.

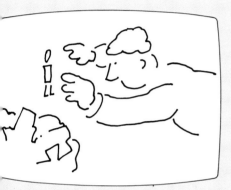

Fade into the living room – a different area or the mess of wrapping paper now tidied up to show passage of time. Children are now playing with their toys. Intercut this with...

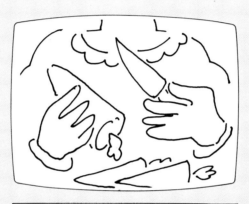

...the kitchen. Christmas dinner being prepared. Mid shot of person at the sink or stove can be intercut with close-ups of pans bubbling on the cooker, vegetables being peeled in the sink and other cooking activity. Children can run into kitchen to be given knives and forks to lay on table.

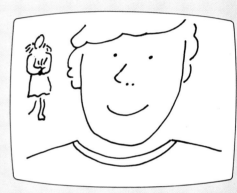

Pick up children as they emerge from kitchen door and go to table to set out cutlery. Again use a long shot, intercut with faces of children as they go about their task. Take low angle shots that represent the children's point of view. Fade out.

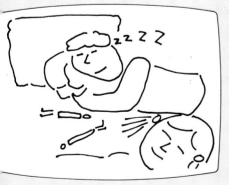

...children playing once more with toys, but this time very sleepily.

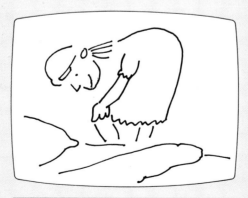

Children undressing for bed, being put to bed, perhaps being read a bedtime story.

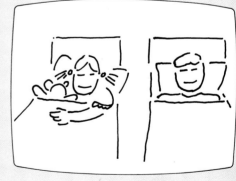

As a closing shot you can start where you finished – the children in bed asleep. Close the video by snapping the light off.

MORE VIDEO USES...

Although video is primarily a creative tool, it can also be of great benefit as an aid to other interests. Its role as a training aid is probably the most widespread, but video has other uses as a recording medium – as a sort of visual notebook.

The use of video for sports coaching is becoming particularly widespread. You can, for example, record your golf swing and then play it back frame by frame. A good coach will immediately be able to spot where you are going wrong and tell you how to correct it.

This facility for individual coaching can be extended to give an overview of a whole team's performance. A recording of a game can be played back, stopped, started and run in fast or slow motion and any of the players' weaknesses will be shown up and hopefully then corrected.

Actual coaching tapes are also available, which allow you to compare your own performance with that of the professionals. This makes side by side comparisons possible, as well as giving you the luxury of being taught your sport or game by experts.

This idea of coaching can be extended into the performing arts. A dancer or dance troupe, for example, can record their performance and then analyze it frame by frame. A musician may want to study playing technique – he can record his own performance and then replay it frame by frame. Fortunately TV coverage both of sports and the arts is so good that you can record the professionals at work from TV, and then compare your own performance with theirs. Beware of copyright restrictions though. Taking these sorts of recordings outside the home could land you in trouble – and that includes using them in schools.

Apart from looking at various performances, video can also be used as a visual notebook. Although you can record aspects of architecture by still photography, actually recording moving shots of buildings can capture a whole lot more. In this way you can see the way that the light can change (even within a short space of time) on the building, and you can assess the way people interact with buildings (a very important, and much neglected, aspect of architecture). By panning, and to some extent, zooming, a video tape of shots can give an overall idea of the size and scale of a building. These principles can also apply to sculpture and other large items such as boats, trains, aircraft, and so on...

The video scrapbook is a very simple idea. You collect TV programs or bits of programs that relate to your particular hobby (cookery or sport, say). Of course, most people do this 'naturally' when they begin using a video recorder, but applying a little thought to the editing together of your 'collection' can make an interesting program from snippets.

Video can also be used to construct a catalogue. On page 136 we show you how to record any flat artwork onto video. You can use these techniques to keep a running catalogue of any pictures or slides, and valuable reference material you have that might be damaged by frequent handling.

Sports – the individual

Perhaps you are a keen golfer, and want to record your swing to see where you're going wrong. You should set up the camera head-on so that everything you need to see is included in the frame. Lighting should be no problem as you are outdoors, although you shouldn't have the light behind the subject. A tripod is a must – don't be fooled by those photos of people taking handheld shots in the product brochures – any movement of the camera will blur the image and you won't be able to tell whether it's the golfer's technique that's at fault or the cameraman's. Because the recording may well be played and replayed many times, it is worth recording on a very high grade tape.

If you want to compare your own action with that of a professional (which may be recorded live off-air or watched on a coaching tape), try and match your shots to the ones of the professional as best as possible. In this way almost frame by frame comparisons can be made.

With all the shots recorded, it's up to you and your coach to go through them. You can go over them again and again, backwards and forwards, frame by frame. If you are comparing your own action with that of a professional, try and get hold of two recorders and televisions, and set them up side by side. By playing the recording of yourself next to the one of the professional, you will be able to see the differences very clearly.

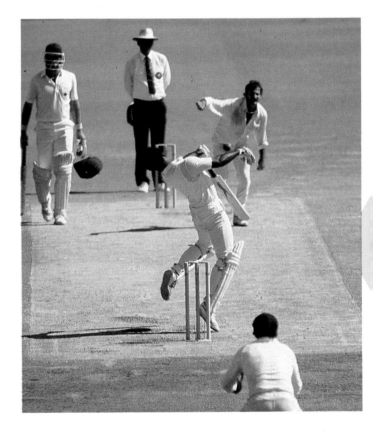

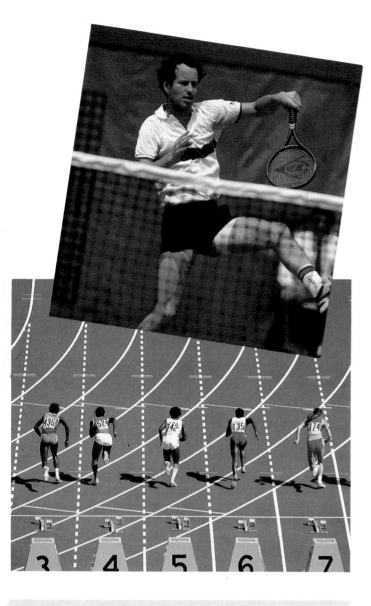

Coaching tapes

One of the earliest forms of programming for the pre-recorded video industry was made up of tapes of various sporting events. This was so simply because there were few copyright problems and sport is (of course) a relatively popular topic. More recently actual coaching tapes have been produced, which not only show highly talented professional sports people in action, but also attempt to pass on some of their skill and knowledge. The range available is huge. Whatever sport you play, there is bound to be something for you.

You can use these tapes in a number of ways. Obviously just watching them is of interest, but unless you are able to enact the lessons they teach as they are being taught, then the immediate impact is somewhat lessened. This means, in the first instance, standing, golf club in hand, in front of the TV set! Some sports are easy enough to follow this way – setting up the TV in a gym, or perhaps even your garage, means that you will have enough room to practice things like a golf or tennis swing without bringing down the light fittings.

For team games such as soccer or basketball, the drill should really be to watch a section of the tape perhaps in the corner of the gym, and then go out and actually work on the lesson with the coach. Which brings us to our second application...

Passively watching video is one thing, but it is much more useful to record your own performance onto tape and then play it back side by side with the professional version. Yes, you do need two video recorders and two TVs, but in a team there is bound to be at least one other video recorder owner and virtually all the members will have a TV set.

Again beware of copyright. Copying tapes is definitely illegal – and the video companies are not afraid to prosecute.

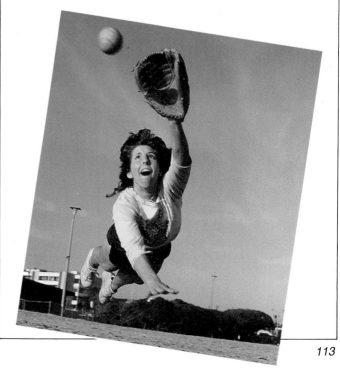

Sport – the team game

Individuals within a team can be recorded and their technique analyzed and improved in the same way as a single sportsman. But video has other uses.

When you're in the middle of a game you obviously don't have a view of how the team is playing as a unit. By recording a whole game, or a large section of the game, from a vantage point that takes in the whole field of play, you can see how every member of the team is performing in relation to the whole team. By speeding up the action you can see more easily how the team reacts to certain situations and where the deficiencies lie. In a soccer game, for example, it might be the case that when the opposing team takes a corner from the left hand side, they often score. By watching an overview of that situation, you may well see that there is always a gap in the defense that no one on the field was aware of. Having found this, you can then suggest a way of plugging that gap.

You can also record the set pieces of a team sport – the corner in soccer, the foul in basketball, the field goal in football – and analyze them both in slow and fast motion to see how the team performs. These could then be compared to similar situations in professional games and improvements suggested.

The video scrapbook

It is quite often the case that people interested in a particular topic will keep cuttings, photographs and other memorabilia or practical material, perhaps mounted in a scrapbook. Someone interested in cookery will keep recipes cut from various magazines or the backs of various food packets, the gardening enthusiast will keep hints and tips cut from magazines, planting charts and other material cut from the back of, say, seed packets and free give-away leaflets.

You can take this concept one step further by saving a particular blank tape and recording bits of TV programs and features on your special topic. This can be augmented by shooting still pictures and charts of various materials to go with your hobby.

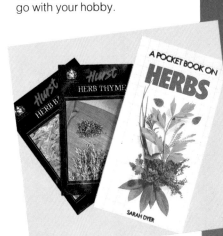

Architecture and sculpture

Although it is wrong to regard a video camera as something to record 'still' views, the sheer size and scope of a building is something that lends itself to being recorded onto video tape. There are three elements to consider when recording a building.

The first is the shape and scale of the building. It is a waste of video's unique abilities to simply end up with a tape of ten seconds of this feature, then ten seconds of that one, and so on. However, if you start with a shot of a particular feature – a gargoyle on a church for example – then zoom back to show that it is in fact only a small feature on a huge tower, you achieve the double effect of recording the feature, and showing its size in relation to the rest of the building. Although the video camera can take in huge expanses of building by panning and zooming, never lose sight of the fact that you have the ability to relate different parts of the building to others.

The second element of architecture is the way light falls on the building. You can, for example, capture in real time the effect of, say, the sun suddenly coming out from behind a cloud and the resulting changes in color and shadow. If it is a day when the light is constantly changing, then these effects can be continually recorded – something that is impossible with a still camera.

The third element is people, and the way they react to various aspects of a building. It is useful to set up a camera at a point where people have to react to features in a building – a set of doorways for example. By playing this back at high speed you get a good idea of how well designed these features are and the interest they create.

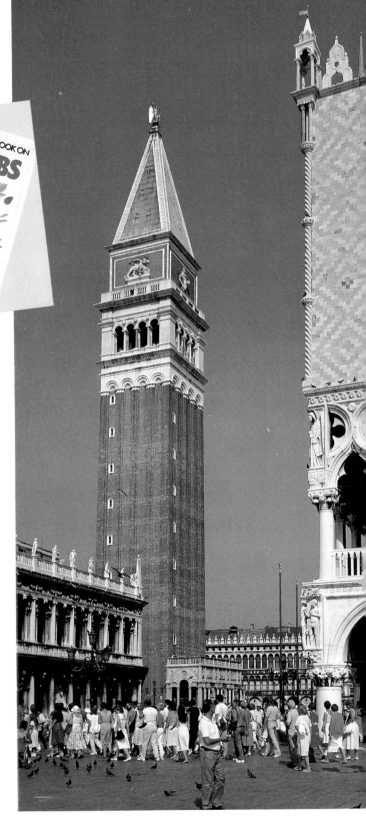

The visual arts

Just as you can use video to analyze sport, it can (as we have said) also be used for performers of all sorts. For example, as a training aid for dancers – to analyze their movement for aesthetic and artistic reasons. If you are studying choreography, a recording of a particular ballet can be played over and over again, both in real time and in slow motion, and the movements noted. Different choreographies for the same ballet can be compared, different leading dancers' techniques can be observed and analyzed.

An instrumental performer's technique can also be recorded and analyzed in much the same way as your golf swing. The different angle of the video camera is often very revealing. What the performer couldn't see with his own eyes, is often blatantly obvious from the camera's point of view. There is also the opportunity to compare your own technique, frame by frame, with a recording of a professional performer.

The actor – professional or amateur – will also benefit greatly from seeing his performance on video tape. Again the different point of view shows up faults that are glaringly obvious to everyone but yourself – the nervous scratching of the head or continual tugging of an ear for example.

The video album

Video also has uses as a cataloguing medium. Suppose you are a still photographer with a huge number of valuable transparencies. Rather than having to look through them either by holding them up to the light or putting them onto a light box, you can record each one onto video tape, together with a reference number. When you need to find a particular one you can run through the tape on picture search. A written index will tell you which tape you should look on and roughly where on the tape the particular slide is. Use short tapes (30-minute) otherwise you could be scanning through a lot of tape. Other valuable items such as stamps, old documents, prints, etc, can also be catalogued in this way.

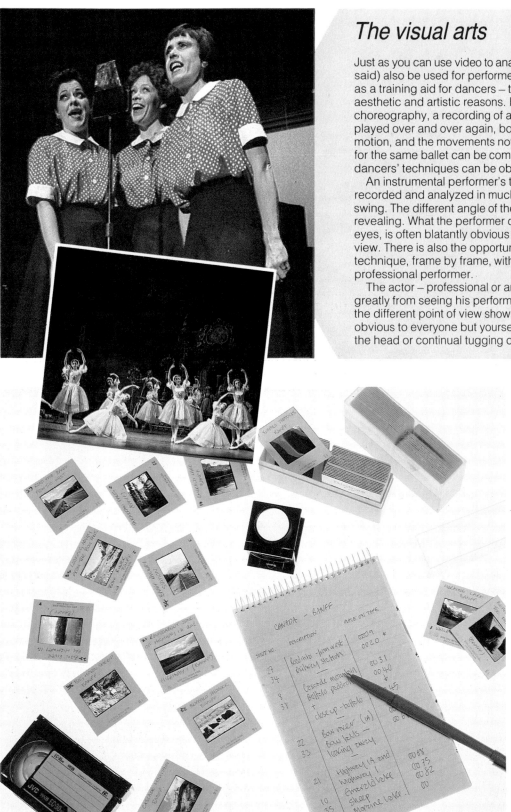

PEOPLE ON VIDEO

THE NON-ACTORS

In the first instance the likely subjects for your video camera are almost certainly going to be friends, family and people around you. Even as you gain more proficiency and confidence with the camera these people will still form the focus of your attention.

This makes it doubly important that your subjects look their best on the screen – that they give a good 'performance'. But what is a good performance? Well, simply one that makes them appear to be as they really are, rather than acting for the camera or looking shy or ill at ease.

As with most groups of people, there is usually one member of the family who is a born performer. Most, however, will range from slightly put off, to downright frightened of the camera, and it is these who need most encouragement.

There are two ways of getting good pictures of non-actors. Either you record them while they are not aware that the camera is running, or you put them completely at ease before you start shooting. Whichever you choose will depend on the situation and the people involved.

Children seem to worry less about being photographed than adults so you needn't worry quite so much about camera shyness. On the contrary, you will have to curb their natural inquisitiveness as they take more interest in the person holding the video camera than in the activity you are trying to record. Pets also come into this category, although of course they are even more unmanageable.

Adults – the best performance

Assuming that you can't shoot people unawares, your main task as director is to coax the best performance out of your subjects on camera. Although some people are born performers, most will be nervous, shy and apprehensive, especially if you have a complicated lighting set-up as well as a full production crew!

From the start, you should aim to put your subjects at their ease. If possible leave all the setting up to someone else. As director you can talk to the subject and discuss what they are going to say, how they are going to say it, and so on. Encourage them, make them feel important, make them feel welcome and part of the team. Nothing makes somebody more nervous and anxious than standing about all alone and ignored, while others are busy setting up equipment, rigging lights and so on.

When it comes to the actual recording, the process of encouragement should not end but, if anything, intensify. Nothing builds up someone's confidence better than being told that they are doing a good job.

If the subject is speaking to camera, then stand just to one side of the camera and encourage them to speak to you – and look as if you're listening and responding. If you're working to a written script and things appear not to be going well, try asking the subject to use their own words to express what's in the script.

Another way of encouraging a subject to speak with confidence is to interview them. Assuming that you are going to edit afterwards, you can structure your questions so that they can be edited out leaving only the replies – which should make perfect sense on their own. The interviewer should be seated near the subject but just behind the camera so that the replies will appear to be addressed to the camera itself.

Finally, leave the recorder running when you've arrived at the end of the shooting script. You'll be surprised just how chatty and voluble people will be when they think that they've finished. If you plan things carefully you could save all your awkward or difficult questions until this time – or at the very least ask them again in a modified way. If the subject thinks that they are not being recorded they may well reply in a more relaxed and coherent manner.

Children – the best performance

In a sense, children are the complete opposite from adults. If you point a video camera at them they become inquisitive about the camera and forget about what they were doing – which was what you wanted to record! Older children do develop a sense of shyness and some encouragement is often necessary to overcome this.

Candid photography

One alternative for taking shots of people who may otherwise not want to be photographed, is to use a variety of devices that make the camera less conspicuous or even completely unnoticed. Here we have three different ways of fooling your subject. We are assuming, incidentally, that you're not doing anything illegal or antisocial and that your subjects genuinely do not object to being photographed even if, in the normal course of events, they would not record well.

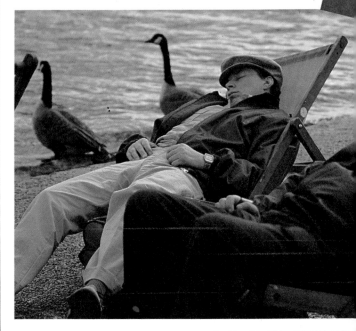

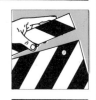

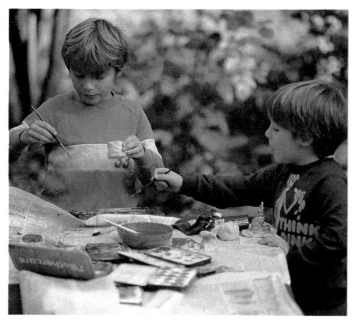

Starting with young children, your first task is to get them thoroughly acquainted with the video equipment. Show them how it works and what they look like on TV. A few doses of this and the novelty will soon wear off – you can encourage them to think that it's a game if this seems to make them act as you want them to. The most important thing, however, is to make sure that they have some absorbing activity to carry on with while you are shooting. A birthday party is an obvious example. With cakes and jelly in abundance they aren't going to be too interested in the video camera. Opening Christmas presents will be another. Try and stay well back and use the telephoto end of the zoom lens.

Older children pose a slightly different problem, and tend to be more like adults. Those children who are natural show-offs and performers will probably need no encouragement at all – the others should be dealt with as shy adults, except that you should be extremely patient and lavish with the praise. If, for example, you are asking a child to recite a poem, have his favorite aunt or uncle sitting just off camera. Ask the child to say it for them and to them. The aunt or uncle should, of course, be listening, responding and encouraging. The same would apply if you asked a child to perform with a musical instrument.

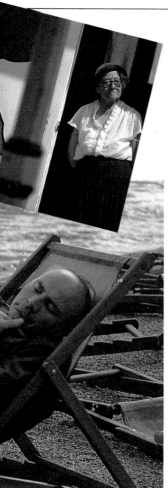

The long lens: Really only an alternative for those with cameras that feature a removable lens assembly. With the appropriate adaptor ring you can attach standard 35mm camera lenses onto the video camera. For candid photography this means using something like a 200mm (or greater) lens, otherwise you could do just as well from a long distance with the standard zoom fitted. Don't forget that the longer the zoom lens, the more secure the camera support has to be. You really need to be in a position where you can use a tripod to get pictures that look steady.

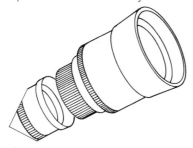

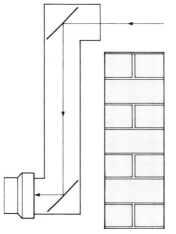

The periscope: In its simplest form this is a vertical tube with mirrors at both ends. It allows you to see over the top of objects without showing any of your body. Periscopes available for use with video cameras range from simple cardboard 'stick-together' models, to fully professional metal units. You could even construct a simple model for yourself. The periscope is of most use when you have dense bushes or a wall to hide behind.

The anglescope: If you can't find somewhere to hide with the video camera, you can fool people into thinking that you are pointing it elsewhere, when in fact you are pointing it at them. The anglescope is like the top end of the periscope. It looks like a simple lens attachment and screws onto the front of the camera. There is, however, a hole cut into the side of the anglescope behind which is mounted a mirror. This bends the light through 90 degrees, so the camera actually sees objects to the side, rather than straight in front of it.

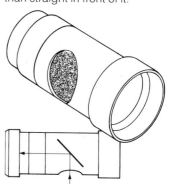

THE ACTORS

Eventually every video director is going to want to turn his hand to putting some sort of drama on the screen, whether it is an original screenplay, or an adaptation of some stage play. This means he will be working with actors.

It's sometimes forgotten in the highly complex and technical world of video making, that acting is just as complex and time-consuming a task in its preparation and execution as anything else to do with the production. An actor doesn't simply 'turn up and do it' on the day, but undergoes extensive preparation, as wide ranging as the video director's, if a bit more cerebral.

What does this preparation involve? In essence it means taking all the steps necessary to make the character up there on screen seem believable, and it is the director's job to coax that performance out of his cast – whether they are experienced professionals or talented amateurs. By believable we mean that the person watching the video should think that those characters actually exist in the situations portrayed, rather than thinking that they are watching actors impersonating other people. Take the TV soap opera for example. To many viewers the worlds of *Dallas* or *Dynasty* are as real as their own lives. They believe that J.R. Ewing or Alexis Carrington are real people. This is amply demonstrated by the amount of mail the actual characters receive from the viewers telling them how to cope with a particular crisis, or even asking for advice!

Although there's no substitute for talent, there is nevertheless a working method which you can follow that will allow you to get much nearer to the truth of a part than you could unaided. This is based on the so-called 'method' which was devised by the Russian actor-manager Konstantin Stanislavski. Method acting is taught in one guise or another in virtually every drama school in the world.

Stanislavski's method was a reaction to the highly artificial and stuffy acting styles prevalent at the turn of the century. It involves drawing on particular experiences of life and recreating those relevant to the character. Although this may sound extremely daunting in theory, in practice it means little more than putting yourself into the position of the character and acting how you think you would act if you were in the same situation.

Don't forget that in the end acting is just that

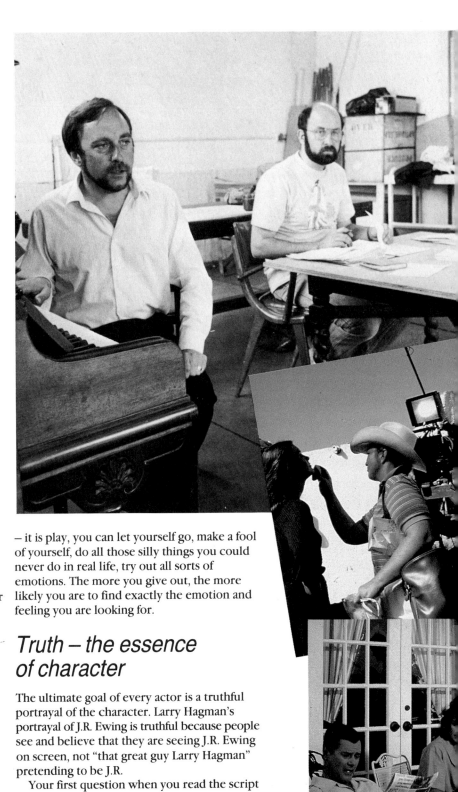

– it is play, you can let yourself go, make a fool of yourself, do all those silly things you could never do in real life, try out all sorts of emotions. The more you give out, the more likely you are to find exactly the emotion and feeling you are looking for.

Truth – the essence of character

The ultimate goal of every actor is a truthful portrayal of the character. Larry Hagman's portrayal of J.R. Ewing is truthful because people see and believe that they are seeing J.R. Ewing on screen, not "that great guy Larry Hagman" pretending to be J.R.

Your first question when you read the script for the first time must be, "so who is this person?" Obviously you can find out a lot about him from the character description and comments made by the other characters. You

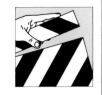

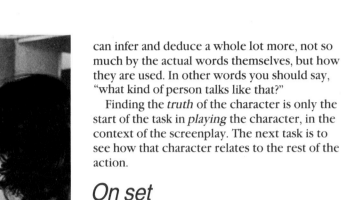

can infer and deduce a whole lot more, not so much by the actual words themselves, but how they are used. In other words you should say, "what kind of person talks like that?"

Finding the *truth* of the character is only the start of the task in *playing* the character, in the context of the screenplay. The next task is to see how that character relates to the rest of the action.

On set

Having found the character and worked out the objectives for each scene, the final stage is the practical one of getting in front of the camera and playing it.

The first – and obvious – point is to learn the lines. You can't play a part in character if the only thought in your head is "my God, what's the next line?"

Beyond this, you are now applying the character you have developed to the objectives of the scene. If you're having difficulty finding a feeling that goes with the specific situation, try to rethink the situation so that it relates to something you've experienced. Suppose you're asked to play a pregnant girl, turned out of her home because of her condition. This may be a situation you've never experienced, but you are far more likely to have experienced rejection in some other form – you may have just broken up with your boyfriend, for example. Try to recall and use this very personal feeling of rejection when you play the girl. Try to remember how it felt to be rejected, and hold that remembered feeling at the front of your mind.

If you feel that a particular scene is not working well – if it feels stiff or artificial – try approaching it in a totally different way from the one you've considered to be 'right'. Take a funeral scene. An obviously sober occasion, but try playing it cheerful and happy, or perhaps drunk. If you've wormed your way sufficiently into the character, this new approach may well reveal things, when played with the other characters in the scene, that were completely hidden when played straight. It is not unknown for an apparently wrong interpretation to be in the end much more dramatic and appropriate.

Finally, a word for directors. It is important for actors to be like children, to be inquisitive, not to have the inhibitions of adults, and not to go over the top. It is equally important for the director to be in complete control of them, to be the parent, and to instill the discipline.

Objectives and resistance

It is true to say that for every dramatic situation each character will have a goal or objective. There will also probably be something stopping him achieving that goal – the resistance. It is this conflict that makes drama interesting and exciting. Take the early scene in Shakespeare's *Macbeth* where Macbeth is being encouraged by his wife to kill the king while he is sleeping. His objective is to kill the king and inherit the crown of Scotland, his resistance is his fear of the consequences. There is a similar objective and resistance for every character in every scene. By finding each one and working for it, you know exactly where you're going in each scene and what you are supposed to be doing.

Although we have mentioned only scenes, don't forget that the whole film has an objective which shapes the whole structure and you must work within that. For example the objective for James Bond in virtually all Bond films is to stop the villain carrying out whatever dastardly deed he has in store and thus to save the world. The resistance is made up of the efforts of the villain to stop Bond interfering in his plan for world domination.

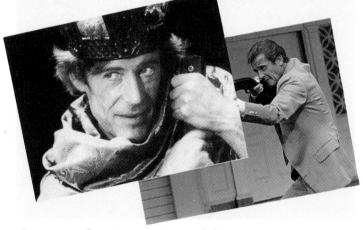

Simon Callow plays Mozart

How did British actor Simon Callow find the character of Mozart in the British National Theatre's original stage version of Peter Shaffer's play *Amadeus*? "I knew that his tempo and emotional volatility were greatly in excess of mine. As the weeks went by I began to work my own inner speed up to fever pitch. I ate my food twice as fast as I'd ever done. I spoke at twice the speed and darted from place to place. If I went for a drink I drank twice as much as I

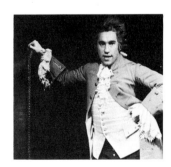

would normally have done. It was necessary to accustom my body to a completely new metabolic rate."

POST-PRODUCTION

FINISHING OFF

What is post-production? This term covers all the operations that turn a mixed jumble of shots and recorded sounds into the finished video. It is during post-production that you convert those random and unordered shots you took at your cousin's wedding, into a family document that will be treasured for years to come. It is during post-production that you put together your baby's first recorded words, the still photographs of his christening and shots of his first steps, to make something that will again be a unique document – more than a photo album, more than a set of moving pictures, more than a random set of sound recordings.

What exactly can you do in post-production? Essentially you are ordering the visuals, ordering the sound and putting the two together.

Let's take the visuals first. Whether you are working on domestic or fully professional format, video editing is a process of copying the selected shots from your original tapes onto a master tape in the right order. Unlike audio tape or cine film, you can't cut and splice video tape. You would lose the control signals that tell the electronics in the TV where to start scanning each picture – and most likely ruin your recorder's heads straight away!

Because editing is a copying process, the final master's quality is never quite as good as that of the original shots. This is one of the reasons why it is very important that the original material is bright and clear with as little low-level lighting as possible.

At the editing stage you can process your shots – turn them into black and white, run them in slow motion, and so on. And you can also add in still pictures as well as titles and graphics, including computer-generated ones.

Sound too!

Turning to the sound, when you're at the post-production stage you can create the soundtrack. You can add in music and special sound effects, insert those special snippets of sound you recorded on location, and modify the sound track already recorded. If you've recorded your sync sound separately, this is the point at which it is added back onto the video tape.

Although a professional editing suite costs many thousands of dollars, you can get very good results by simply using two domestic video recorders for picture editing. The first will be with an audio cassette deck and a simple audio mixer for the sound. There are some technical limitations, but the possibilities of even a simple set-up such as this are limited only by your imagination and ingenuity. The way to find out if something will work is to try it. The only thing you might waste is your time.

You will need two video recorders for editing. The first will be the portable you've used to shoot your original pictures. The second might be the AC machine you already own, or you could borrow one from a friend. The format of the machines doesn't have to be the same, but it's better if they are. And at least one machine must have the **insert edit** facility.

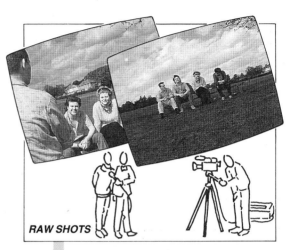
RAW SHOTS

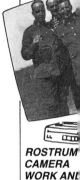
ROSTRUM CAMERA WORK AND TITLES

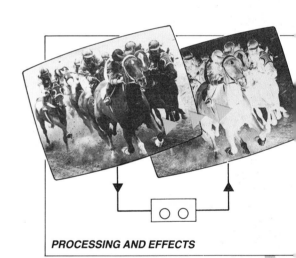
PROCESSING AND EFFECTS

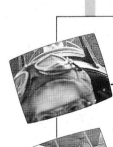

EDITING

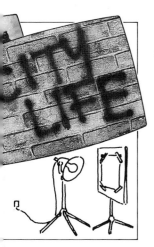

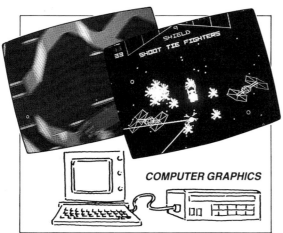

COMPUTER GRAPHICS

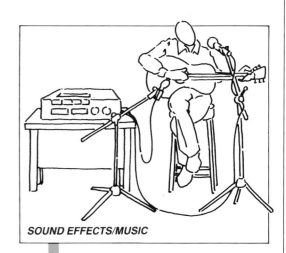

SOUND EFFECTS/MUSIC

The editing process: By combining every element of your previously recorded video and audio material with other processing and graphics, your tape will be complete!

FINISHED TAPE

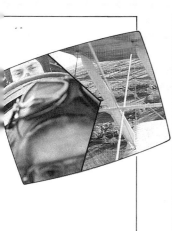

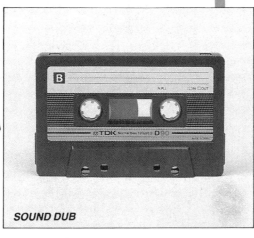

SOUND DUB

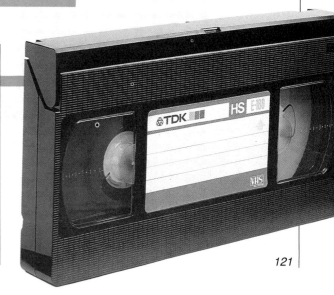

EDITING

PREPARATION

Careful note-taking while shooting will now start to pay off. Before you even start thinking about editing, you should have written down a detailed description of each shot as you intended it to be taken, and a list of everything on each tape. Next you should decide on which takes you are going to use and in which order. At this stage you should also be thinking about special effects, titles and any other special material you may want to add in – such as computer graphics.

It might be a good idea to recap on what we mean by the words **shot** and **take**. A shot is a particular visual sequence that is recorded in one go without stopping the recorder. Each actual attempt to record that shot is called a take.

Although you should have some idea of what order everything will go in before you start shooting, you must now start to think in detail about your specific shots and takes. The first step is to watch everything you have shot. Make a note of the takes you want to use (see why each one was labeled with the clapper board?) and the order in which you are going to use them.

Although the sound is prepared separately from the visuals, you should be thinking about the soundtrack at this stage, especially if you have a piece of dialogue (or music) that you want to fit exactly to a set of images – for example the words of the wedding service that you recorded separately because you couldn't shoot in the church. In a case like this, the visuals you do use should fit the sound. Ideally, you should prepare your sound edit order before starting work (see page 131). This will mean that all the elements of the video have been considered and you won't have to re-edit some of the pictures because the visuals were seconds too long or short for a piece of dialogue.

Careful preparation has one other advantage – it means that you won't suddenly want to insert another segment in the middle of the sequence you've just completed, simply because you forgot about it. If you do want to insert a new segment, it's going to mean re-editing everything that comes after it – definitely something to be avoided!

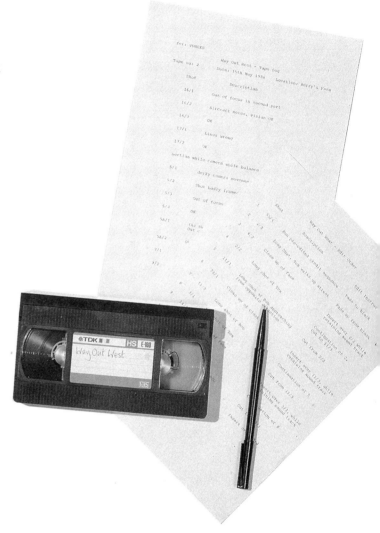

Taking care of your tapes

Editing is a copying process, and the quality of your original material therefore becomes very important. This means taking great care of your tapes and the images stored on them.

Tape care starts while you're shooting. Don't have the recorder in pause mode any more than is absolutely necessary.

It is even more important that you look after tapes once you've finished recording. It may sound obvious, but you shouldn't drop cassettes or otherwise mishandle them. This could damage the tape guides inside the cassette which may cause it to jam. The shock can also slightly demagnetise the particles on the tape, degrading the image.

You should keep your tapes away from stray electro-magnetic fields – this means loudspeakers, TV sets, microwave ovens and anything that contains an electric motor. Cables carrying large amounts of electrical current should also be avoided. These things tend to alter the tape's magnetic patterns, ruining both picture and sound.

Once you get the cassettes home, it is a good idea to make copies, and use them to view the material and choose your edit order. Playing a tape over and over again, stopping and starting, running sections in slow motion, and so on, will eventually degrade picture quality quite noticeably. If you can't make copies, try to play the originals as few times as possible, with as few stops and starts and as little use of picture search as you can manage. In this case it is even more essential that you should keep an accurate record of what's going on each tape when you're shooting.

Home editing – what you can do

You can get some very good results using the simple set-up of two domestic video recorders and a TV. One machine – the **slave** – plays back material which is recorded in edited order by the other – **master** – recorder. These are some of the facilities offered by such a home editing set-up (further details on how to carry out each one can be found later on in the book). It is by no means an exhaustive list – you're bound to have your own ideas to add to it.

▶ **Cuts from shot to shot** – accurate to around one second or perhaps half a second with practice.

▶ **Image conversion** – from color to black and white.

▶ **Still frame, slow motion and fast motion** – quality will depend on the slave (playback) recorder being used. If this has noise-free still frame and slow motion facilities, then you will get interference-free still frame and slow motion in the final edit.

▶ **Solarization** – a special effect that is achieved by massive overexposure. You can do this by running the sequence you want to turn into a solarized image on your TV screen and re-recording it with your video camera onto the other recorder.

▶ **Image reversal and fade in/out** – can be achieved in a similar manner as solarization by re-recording a TV image.

▶ **Addition of titles, still images and photographic and filmed images** – recorded using the camera and either transferred 'live' into the final edit or recorded on tape and then edited in.

▶ **Combining titles and images** – either by using a camera that will mix the image with the built-in character

generator or by using a home video production console.

▶ **Adding in computer generated titles and images** – achieved by setting up a graphics sequence on a home computer and adding in to the final mix either 'live' or pre-recorded.

▶ **Adding in a new sound track** – This can include sound effects, new dialogue, commentary, and music. Depending on the type of video and audio recorders used this can be in ordinary, hi-fi or digital sound.

There are, however, some things you *can't* do with this system. These can be summarized as follows:

▶ **Frame very accurate cuts** – which would allow you to almost drop in separate words or cut very quickly from shot to shot.

▶ **Fades and dissolves between shots** – cannot be achieved with this basic set-up. But by preplanning fades, you should be able to do them 'in the camera' when shooting.

▶ **Accurate insertion of sound** – including sync sound that has been recorded separately.

The list isn't very long, but basically you can also bear in mind that home editing operations are easier and more convenient to carry out in a professional editing suite, where quality loss is also likely to be less. Although using a professional editing suite might sound extravagant, the cost may very well be justified for special projects, which may be cherished for a lifetime.

Insert and assemble edits

When video material is edited, by transferring it from the slave to the master recorder, the insert edit facility is used – for a very good reason. When you make a video recording, the video and audio tracks are, of course, laid down onto your tape. A control track is also recorded, but this cannot be seen or heard by us. It is used instead by the machine to make sure that your tapes are replayed at exactly the same speed at which they were recorded and to keep the individual picture frames in sync. You probably know that if you have a tape where one recording ends and another begins you see a lot of disturbance and noise on your TV screen. This is because the control track has been omitted in the blank bit of tape, or has been resumed out of step with that of the first recording.

When it comes to editing a tape you actually have two options – assemble edit or insert edit. When you use assemble edit, everything is transferred from your slave machine's tape – the video, audio and control track. When you use insert edit, only the video and audio signals are transferred and synchronized to the master tape's control track, which remains undisturbed. The join between what was originally on the master tape – up until you made your edit – and the new recording added to it will be undisturbed and free of noise.

Imagine a tape that has been edited using the assemble edit mode. At every edit point the control track will suddenly change, and there will be a disturbance. This will show on the screen as a flash of light and the picture may well jump and be unstable for several seconds until the recorder locks onto the new control track.

Now imagine a tape that has been edited using the insert mode. Although the pictures and sound will change at the edit points, the control track is continuous so there will be no picture instability at the edit points. To use insert edit successfully you have to lay down a control track first. This operation is called 'blacking' the tape, and involves no more than recording a tape with no camera or other video input connected. What you are doing, in effect, is making a recording that has no picture or sound, but does have a control track.

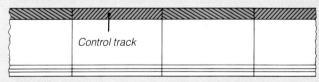

Control track

Assemble editing *lays down a new control track for each section of tape that is recorded – which can cause picture break-up.*

Control track

Insert editing *uses a previously recorded control track which is unbroken by the new sections of recordings. No picture break-up is caused.*

HOME EDITING – TECHNICAL PREPARATIONS

Having decided on your edit order, the next stage is to connect up the system and get everything ready to make the first edit. What follows, concentrates purely on the visual aspects of editing – dubbing on a new soundtrack is dealt with on page 130 – although you have the option of transferring the picture with the corresponding original sound, or just transferring the picture. The latter may be important if you have a shot with dialogue and want to insert a new shot in the middle of it without disturbing the sound track.

The picture on the right shows a typical editing set-up. Here, a portable is being used as the **slave** to take the material previously shot. If you have two TVs, linking one into this recorder via the RF out socket is very useful, although not essential, to preview the material going onto the master tape. The slave recorder is linked directly via the video and audio sockets to the second – **master** – recorder, which should be fitted with an insert edit function. The master recorder has to be connected up to a TV – preferably via direct audio and video lines if the TV has suitable inputs. Your video camera is also linked into the system via the camera socket on the slave recorder. The camera can be used for captions, still photographs or other special effects which will be described later.

Because the editing process involves a lot of button-pressing, try and lay all the equipment out on a table, so that the TVs are roughly at eye-level with the recorder controls in front of you, and the camera close to hand. If you are using a special effects console this should also be nearby. See page 139 for more details.

The set-up described here can be used with any pair of recorders, provided that the master is fitted with insert edit. Some manufacturers (notably Sony, Canon and Panasonic) market special edit controllers. These devices have to be used with particular recorder models but do offer a number of advantages over the basic set-up. They are computer-operated remote control units which coordinate the operation of both recorders at the push of a single

Connecting up the equipment

▶ Connect the video and audio outputs of the slave recorder to the video and audio inputs of the master machine.
▶ Connect the aerial socket of the slave (preview) TV to the RF out socket of the slave recorder and tune to the recorder's output in the usual way (see page 21).
▶ Connect the master TV to the master recorder. If this TV has direct audio and video inputs, you can connect these to the master recorder's audio and video outputs for better quality.
▶ Connect the caption camera to the camera input on the slave recorder. You can then either record new material on the slave, which can be played back and edited into the master tape, or you can feed the image from the camera directly to the master recorder to be edited 'live'. With the slave recorder in stop mode, the camera's signal wil be fed to the slave's audio and video outputs. You may find when recording onto the slave from the camera, that the picture may disappear from the slave TV. This is because some recorders shut off the output to the RF socket when recording. You will still be able to see the pictures on the master TV though, as the signals from the camera will still be coming out of the slave's audio and video outputs and passing into the master recorder.

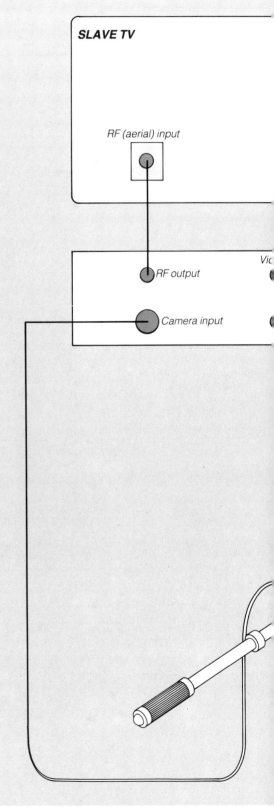

SLAVE TV

RF (aerial) input

RF output

Vid

Camera input

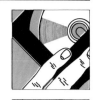

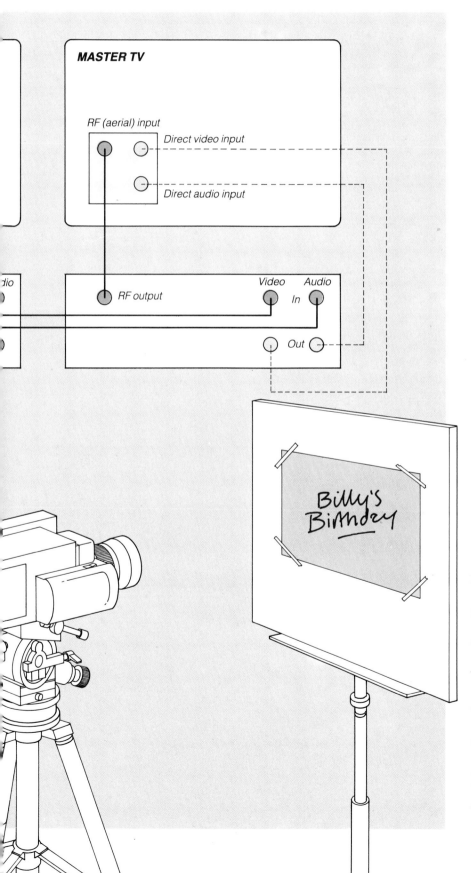

MASTER TV

RF (aerial) input

Direct video input

Direct audio input

RF output

Video   Audio

In

Out

Billy's Birthday

button. To use them, you simply find the end of the last sequence you have recorded on the master tape and program this into the controller. Then you find the start of the new sequence to be added from the slave and program this in. At the press of just one button, the controller starts both machines running at exactly the right time to carry out the edit. Some controllers (notably the Sony unit for the Video 8 system) can remember several such edit points and will let you preview a whole sequence before carrying out the edit.

Editing words

Assemble edit: Copying sections from one tape onto a master tape one-by-one. The control tracks from each of these sections are also transferred, so there is image interference at the start of each new section.

Back-space editing: A facility on some recorders which rolls the tape back when the record button is pressed. This is done to ensure an interference-free join between the old recording and the new one. It also means that the last few seconds of the old recording are lost – and is one of the reasons for always recording several extra seconds onto the end of each shot.

Blacked tape: Recording a zero level picture and sound signal onto a blank tape. This lays down a continuous control signal which means that picture and sound edits can be made in the insert edit mode.

Control track: A series of signals recorded onto the tape that the playback recorder locks onto, to maintain a stable picture.

Flying erase head: The erase head on most video recorders is mounted in a fixed position. This simply erases the tape some way in front of the recording head. Accurate editing requires that you erase as little of the signal in front of the new material as possible. This is achieved by mounting the erase head on the head drum – much closer to the recording heads. This is known as a flying erase head.

Frame: A complete TV picture. There are 25 frames every second in the PAL and SECAM systems and 30 for NTSC.

Insert edit: Transfers audio and video signals of each sequence onto a previously blacked tape. The control track is not transferred. The blacked tape's control track is undisturbed, so there is no picture interference at the edit points.

EDITING IN PRACTICE

When you get to this stage you will have been through copies of all the material you've shot and made a careful note of exactly which takes – or sections of takes – you are going to use. You will have decided on how much rostrum camera material you're going to include (see page 136) and assembled that separately. This will include titles and other graphics, unless you've decided to record them live. You will also have recorded all your computer-generated sequences, if you're using computer graphics (see page 144), and will have processed the images you are going to use as special effects (see page 140).

You will also have to decide at this stage which images you are going to transfer complete with sound track and which you are going to transfer without sound. This is important if you want to retain some original dialogue while editing in new pictures. Although you should know by now exactly what you are going to put onto the soundtrack, the initial editing stages are rather more concerned with assembling the images. The sound dub is the next stage and is described on page 130.

Video editing is a slow process unfortunately, and care and patience are needed if you are going to get exactly what you want. It is worth taking time and trouble over each edit as you can't go back and change something six or seven edit points back, without having to re-edit everything that follows.

Having said this, it is in some ways advantageous to edit your video in blocks and then assemble those blocks in order. The only drawback here, is that you are making copies of copies, with the attendant problem of loss of quality. The material in each block will be a copy of the original (a first generation copy), and the assembled blocks will be copies of this (second generation copies). If you then make another copy of this completed set, so that you can dub on a sound track complete with sound effects and music, you're creating a third generation copy. This is as far as you can go without unacceptable quality loss with domestic video, and you would have to use a professional format from the start, if you want to process the pictures any further.

At each stage it is always a good idea to copy your completed edit, so that if you do lose or ruin any cassettes, you won't have lost the complete edit. These 'safety copies' are a rule of thumb in professional video making – and there's no reason to think that your material is any less valuable than theirs.

The professional editing suite

The professional editing suite is different from our home set-up in two ways. First of all it transfers material by insert edit as a matter of course. Secondly, you can fade between shots and dissolve one into the other. You also have much more precise control over the selection of the edit points – it can be accurate to the exact frame at which you want to make the cut.

Editing in a professional suite happens something like this. After transferring the first sequence, you find the start of the second. This can be done by moving the tape forwards and backwards very slowly or even frame by frame until you find the exact point. The elapsed time and frame coordinates are entered into an edit computer. You then go to the master tape and locate the precise point where the first sequence ends and enter those co-ordinates. To perform the edit, the 'execute' button is

pressed. The computer rolls master and slave recorders back to a point just before the edit point. It then starts both recorders running and at precisely the right point, records the sequence from the slave onto the master recorder. The equipment also lets you preview the edit. This means that you watch the edit as it would appear if the material was transferred, without actually carrying out the process.

If, after a preview, you don't like what you see, you can change the edit point co-ordinates and preview the edit again. Some systems will allow you to store all the edit coordinates for a complete segment or even a whole program. The suite will then assemble the entire tape from its instructions.

If you decide to use a professional set-up, there are many small local companies in existence which would be most suitably equipped to deal with home video. Depending on the company, they may allow you unsupervised use of their equipment or provide a technician.

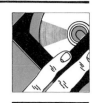

Editing step-by-step

1 Insert a freshly blacked cassette into the master recorder.

2 Insert the cassette that contains the first sequence in your edit order into the slave recorder.

3 Zero the counter on the master recorder.

4 Run the master recorder in fast forward mode until the counter reads around 0200.

5 Rewind the master recorder. This operation is to make sure that the tape will run smoothly.

6 Find the start of your sequence in the slave recorder and zero the counter. Select the memory function to rewind to the exact point.

7 Run the master recorder in play mode for around 10 seconds. This is so that the start of your edit sequence is not at the very start of the tape, which gets worn the most.

8 Run through the first sequence several times until you are sure where you want it to finish.

9 Rewind the tape in the slave recorder back to the start of the first sequence and engage play and pause.

10 Select picture transfer with or without sound.

11 Put the master recorder into insert edit mode with the pause control engaged. Consult your recorder's instruction book if you're not sure how to do this.

12 Release the pause on the slave and then quickly release the pause on the master. The material is now being transferred.

13 When the material from the slave has passed the end of the sequence you want to transfer, push the counter to zero on the master

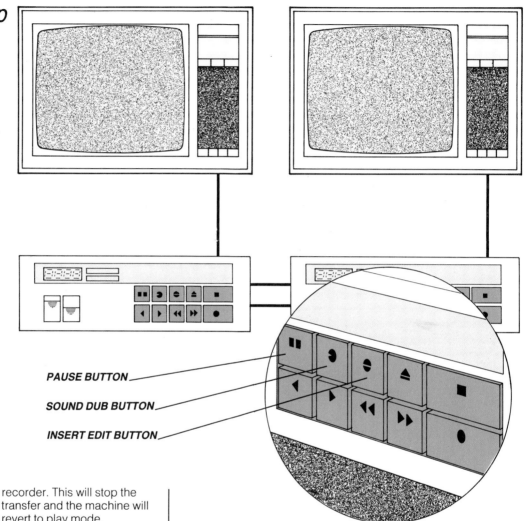

PAUSE BUTTON

SOUND DUB BUTTON

INSERT EDIT BUTTON

recorder. This will stop the transfer and the machine will revert to play mode.

14 Stop the master and slave recorders.

15 Find the next sequence to be added to the master tape.

16 Run the master tape back to the point at which you want the first sequence to end and zero the counter.

17 Having found the exact end of the first sequence on the master tape, engage pause and insert edit.

18 Run the slave tape back to just before the start of the next sequence and, when you're sure of everything, put the slave recorder into play mode.

19 At the exact moment the slave recorder reaches the start of the next sequence, disengage pause on the master recorder and the transfer will begin.

20 After the slave tape has passed the end of the sequence, press the counter zero button on the master. The master recorder will then change from insert edit to play mode, and the transfer will have finished.

21 Stop the master and slave recorders.

22 Find the next sequence to be added and go back to step 16.

This process is repeated from step 16 for each edit until you have reached the end of your edit order. The important thing to remember is that you use the counter zero to end the transfer onto the master recorder, not the stop button. This keeps the master recorder in insert edit mode. This means that you must always ensure that the counter reading is not approaching zero at the point on the master tape where you want to start the transfer. Otherwise the machine will switch off when zero is reached.

SOURCES OF SOUND

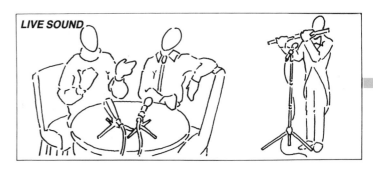

LIVE SOUND

The primary source of sound for your finished video tape will be the sound you recorded live when you recorded your shots with the camera. This, however, is just one of a number of options that you can choose from when building up the final soundtrack. Live dialogue is important, but you may well have a number of shots where there isn't any dialogue – in a holiday film, for example – which leaves you free to incorporate all manner of new sounds into the finished tape.

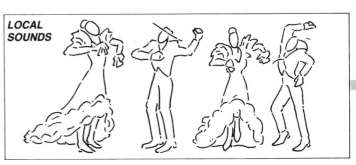

LOCAL SOUNDS

Music is the first alternative choice most people turn to. A well-chosen theme tune and incidental music can do a lot to lift an otherwise mundane and, dare we say it, boring, video. If your tape is good to start with, music can add the final polish. But do be careful of copyright here. Although you shouldn't have any problems if your video is purely for personal use and pleasure, as soon as you put it to commercial use you may well run into legal difficulties. Look at page 148 for more details. If you have friends who can put together an original score and record it for you, so much the better.

Separate recording

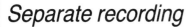

There are, however, many other sources of sound. The most obvious will be new dialogue or commentary recorded separately to the original shots and dubbed onto the final tape – perhaps mixed with background music or other sound effects. Your holiday video, for example, will probably work much better if there is a narrative linking your shots together. Don't forget that you can use the sound already on the tape mixed with the new sound and commentary (see page 132).

Local sound is also important. This is made up of the background sounds of the people and the environment where your shots were taken. It may be recorded onto the video tape as you're recording the pictures or recorded separately with an audio recorder. The more local sound you have the better, as it will give you a greater variety of material to play with. But don't forget to record it in continuous stretches of at least 10 minutes, so that it can cover the longest of edited sequences.

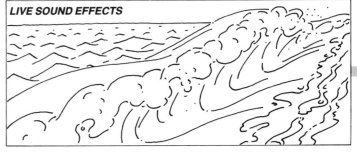

LIVE SOUND EFFECTS

Finally, there are specific sound effects. These can be anything from a car door slamming to an explosion. You can put these at any point on the soundtrack you think relevant. Sound effects can either be recorded live by yourself or taken from records. Live recording can be great fun and a challenge to the imagination of the recordist. There are some suggestions for specific effects on page 72, but some further reading is recommended. The records of professionally recorded effects can solve many problems if you can't create them yourself. Fortunately, most of them are copyright-cleared for amateur use.

The actual process of taking all the elements of sound and combining them into a completed soundtrack is detailed on the following pages.

Creative use of sound

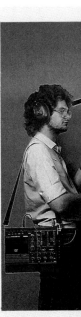

Film and TV soundtracks make up a powerful element of the complete program. Although there is a natural sound to accompany any visual shot, sound can be used as creatively as the pictures to help tell the story – whether that story is your cousin's wedding, or an intensely dramatic play. There are three elements to sound – dialogue, other noise and music.

Taking dialogue first, the main rule is don't let your subjects ramble on ad nauseam – spoken contributions to your videos should be short and to the point. Remember, a picture is worth a thousand words. Video is a visual medium, so use it.

The use of noise and sound effects can be very interesting and creative. Any kind of action is accompanied by a noise. If you want to indicate a passing train or a gunshot for instance, you need not actually show pictures

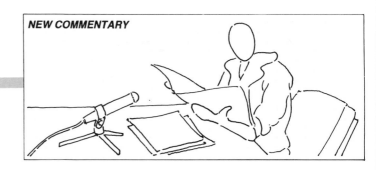
NEW COMMENTARY

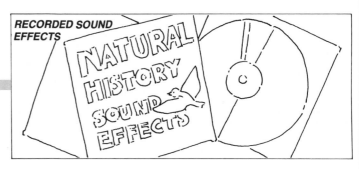
RECORDED SOUND EFFECTS

NATURAL HISTORY SOUND EFFECTS

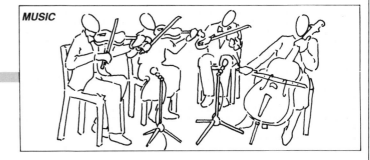
MUSIC

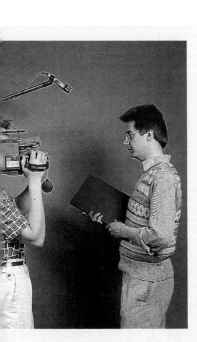

of these things – the sound will do the job just as well.

As an example, consider this situation. The bride and groom are sitting in a room. You hear the sound of mumbled speech, then applause, then speech, then perhaps cheers. You can conclude from this that they are in a waiting room at the registry office, waiting for the previous couple to leave. Because of the length and ferocity of the noise, you also conclude that the previous party is probably runnng late and is making the couple more nervous. All this additional information has been revealed while you are concentrating on their actual dialogue and so has taken up no extra time.

Sounds can also serve to identify places – the sound of boats and seagulls means that the setting is obviously by the sea.

Another important function of noise is

connection. Although the visual elements in a film or TV program are assembled as a series of shots, the sound remains continuous. In real life we can turn our heads and eyes to look at many different things but our ears will always hear the same constant sound. Using a continuous soundtrack binds the whole program together. A tip to remember is not to cut from subject to subject at the end of a line of dialogue, but just before it. This makes sure that a flow is maintained and allows you to see more of the responding person's reactions.

Background and theme music provides another element that can add to the atmosphere of a video. Ideally, the music should be so suited to the tape that the viewer is not immediately aware of its existence. However, the gap in the soundtrack would soon be noticed if there was no music.

Sound words

Live sound: Sound that is recorded at the same time as the pictures. This will be mainly dialogue with some background sounds.

Local sound: The background and ambient sounds of the location, plus any special sounds that could not be recorded with pictures. This may be recorded either separately or on the video soundtrack.

Live sound effects: Sound effects that you record specifically for your own video.

New commentary: Spoken dialogue recorded separately to the pictures and dubbed on in post-production.

Recorded sound effects: Sound effects taken from commercially produced records and dubbed into the final soundtrack.

Music: Music from records or that written and recorded especially for your video. This can be a theme tune and/or incidental music.

SOUND DUBBING

Sound dubbing is the name given to the process of adding elements to the video soundtrack. This may involve replacing the existing soundtrack altogether, or selectively adding elements to it. The new track may contain several elements that have been mixed together. You may, for example, have background music underneath a commentary (ideal for that holiday video), or ambient sound which has been recorded separately, mixed in with a voice-over

Virtually all video recorders have an **audio dub** facility. This allows you to replace the existing audio track while leaving the pictures intact. On some stereo recorders you can audio dub on one channel while leaving the other undisturbed. This is very useful should you find you've made a mistake and want the original back. Alternatively, you can have one channel of 'live' dialogue and use the other to record sound effects, music etc.

Whatever you are going to dub onto your existing video should be prepared on tape – standard audio cassettes are perfectly acceptable, although some purists prefer to use reel-to-reel machines. You can, of course, use records, compact discs, or any other sound source – including the soundtracks from other video cassettes – in making up your final sound tape. It is also possible to mix the sync sound already on a video cassette with extra sound

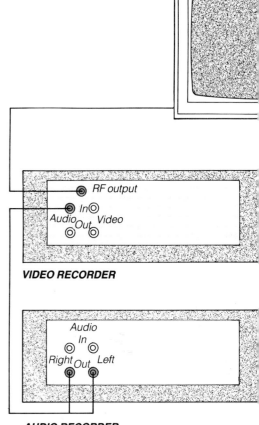

VIDEO RECORDER

AUDIO RECORDER

Direct sound dubbing step-by-step

Assume for the moment that your new soundtrack has been recorded onto a standard audio cassette and is timed exactly to the visual images. If you want to fade the sound up or down at any point you have three options. First, you might already have incorporated the fades into the sound tape; secondly you can connect a **mixer** between the output of the audio recorder and the audio input of the video recorder; or lastly you can use a hi-fi video recorder which has manual recording level adjustment. Watch the

images from the video tape on the TV monitor to find out exactly when to start the audio dub. You can hear the sound going onto the video tape on the TV's loudspeaker, or you can monitor it on headphones.

Proceed as follows:

1 Roll the video tape back to the point where you want the sound dub to begin and familiarize yourself with it.

2 If you are using a video recorder with manual audio level control, make sure that this is set properly.

3 Find the exact point on the audio tape where the material to be dubbed begins, remove the cassette from the recorder and manually wind the tape back around half-an-inch. Replace the tape and put the recorder into the play/pause mode (play and pause both selected).

4 Run the video tape back to around 1 second before the point where you want the sound dub to begin and engage the audio dub and pause modes. Check your instruction book for details.

5 Release the pause on the video recorder and, fractionally before the point where the audio dub is meant to begin, release the pause on the audio recorder. This may need several attempts to get it exactly right, although with practice you'll soon be able to judge the exact point at which to start the audio recorder.

6 When the video tape reaches the point where the audio dub is due to finish, engage pause on the audio recorder then pause on the

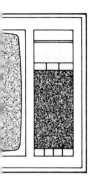

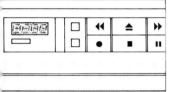

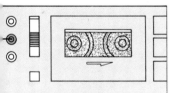

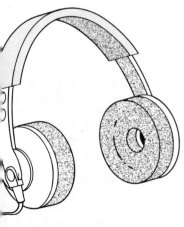

effects, although this does involve copying the visual elements on the tape at the same time, with the subsequent loss in quality. Full instructions for the compilation of sound mixes are given on page 132.

Before you start any practical work on sound dubbing, it is essential to work out exactly what you are going to do in advance and write it down – preferably in the form of a dubbing chart. This will then allow you to work methodically through the program, and you're far less likely to miss anything out or make a mistake. As with video editing, if you don't notice a mistake until you're well into the video, it may mean redubbing the whole of the tape from that mistake point, just to correct it.

Preparation

Like everything else in video production, preparation is vital before you start the sound dubbing. Otherwise you might end up wasting time redubbing material simply because you forgot to put in a particular effect, or suddenly had a bright idea for the beginning when you'd got to the end. If you make a mistake or change your mind about something, you may well have to go back and re-dub the entire tape.

You should think about the sound at the same time as you look through the original takes to decide on the picture edit order. There may, for example, be occasions where the pictures should fit the sound, instead of it being the other (usual) way round.

It is unusual to complete the picture editing first, and then consider the soundtrack in detail. Your first choice is whether to replace

the whole soundtrack with something new or combine new elements with it. If you decide to replace all of it, then you have to decide whether to pre-record the whole of the soundtrack and dub it on in one go, or to pre-record one element (say the background music of a holiday video) and live dub another (a commentary, for instance). Live dub means actually recording the sound directly onto the video tape while watching the images.

If you are going to combine an existing soundtrack with a new one, the new track has to be prepared in advance. Don't forget that in the video editing stage you should have decided which bits of live sound were going to be transferred with the pictures and which weren't.

Whatever dubbing method you choose, you'll no doubt find it essential to prepare a sound dubbing chart, like the one shown below. This lists all your shots, complete with accurate timings, and gives space for you to note the precise places at which all the different elements of sound are to be added. A chart should be used right from the start of soundtrack preparation, so that you can time each individual element precisely and match it exactly to the pictures.

video recorder. Stop the audio recorder and stop the video recorder.

7 Wind the video recorder back and listen to the dub you have just carried out to make sure that it has transferred as you wanted.

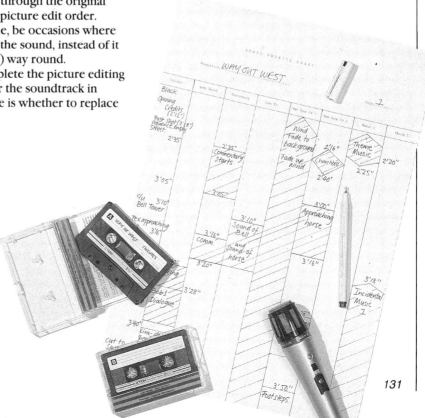

THE MIX DUB

You may come across occasions when you want to combine the soundtrack already on the tape with new sounds – either background music, sound effects, a new dialogue track, or a combination of all of these. To do this, you need to carry out a **mix dub**. This involves taking the edited video tape with the original soundtrack and copying it onto another video tape. The video signal is transferred direct, but the audio signal is routed through an audio mixer where it is mixed with the new material. The output of the mixer is then fed into the second video recorder to be recorded alongside the video signal. This is the only way you can combine an existing audio track with new material without using professional equipment which can synchronize separate audio and video tapes.

To prevent any loss in picture quality, the newly mixed sound can be put back onto the arranged tape when you are satisfied with it. This can be done by using the audio dub facility and starting both recordings at exactly the same frame. The fact that both tapes have the same control pulses means that they will keep in sync with each other when played continuously.

If, on the other hand, there is no sync sound on the original tape, the second video recorder could be replaced by an audio recorder and the TV monitor plugged into the slave video. The resulting audio tape could then be redubbed back onto the video cassette in the manner described on page 130. This way, you preserve picture quality, but at the same time have a perfectly-timed audio track. This is very useful when you're producing a video with a commentary that is mixed with natural sound and perhaps some music, but which doesn't have any dialogue or other sync sound.

You can add in a 'live' commentary while mix dubbing if the mixer you are using has a microphone input. There are two sorts of input to a mixer: line and mic. The line input matches the output of audio and video recorders, radio tuners, CD players and other

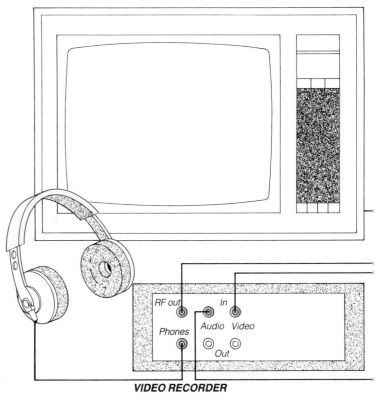

VIDEO RECORDER

audio gear with a standard line output. The mic input is much more sensitive but even that comes in two types – high impedance and low impedance. Check the type of mic you are using. Try to get hold of a low-impedance type if at all possible, as these are compatible with most video recorders.

The mix dub step-by-step

1 Line up the tape in the slave recorder to just before the start of the sequence to which you're adding the new material.

2 Line up the tape in the audio recorder to just before the new (recorded) material to be added.

3 If using the microphone, check with the speaker that he knows exactly where he is and what he is doing. Rehearse several times while playing back the visual sequence if necessary.

4 Run through the segment without operating the master recorder, setting the mixer's various input levels as required for each sound source and effect used.

5 Wind the audio and video cassettes back to just before the start of the sequence to be transferred. The video should be 10 seconds before the sequence, and the audio tape as close as possible to it.

6 Proceed as if you are insert editing (see page 127), except that you have to start the audio cassette recorder as well as the video cassette recorder at the right time. It is also possible to fade any of the input sources up and down – something not possible with a straight insert edit transfer.

7 If you're using live dialogue, the speaker should see the TV monitor and should be cued just before speaking (see page 134).

8 At the end of the segment, press the counter reset on the master recorder. This will make the machine drop into the play mode and the recorder can then be stopped.

9 The slave video and audio recorders can be stopped, and everything wound back if there is going to be a retake.

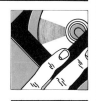

If you want to add sound in from records, it is usually far preferable to first transfer it to tape, and then dub. If you can't do this, remember that the output from most pick-up cartridges is unsuitable for direct input into a mixer. You should feed the cartridge's output into a hi-fi amplifier and then connect the tape output into the mixer.

As a final point remember that the soundtrack on your original recordings will be in mono unless your camera and portable recorder are stereo-compatible. An audio tape deck on the other hand will almost invariably be stereo. The inputs to the mixer can be mono or stereo depending on the model, while the recorders you use may well be stereo. You will probably need to have many spare recording leads to hand, and have your wits about you when connecting all the equipment up. The basic connections are shown in the diagram below.

Adding a record input

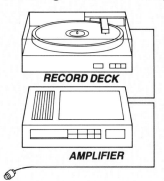

RECORD DECK

AMPLIFIER

Material from records should first be transferred to audio tape before dubbing onto video tape. Otherwise, the record deck can be played into the mixer by connecting its output into the phono input of a hi-fi amplifier and then plugging the tape output into one channel of the mixer. You will probably need a stereo-to-mono phono lead for this.

Composite track

There will be times when you want to combine several elements onto one audio cassette before mix dubbing onto video. If you don't have access to a multi-track recorder, the easiest way of doing this is to perform what is known as a **bounce mix**. This basically means starting with the first two elements of the mix and combining them via a mixer onto another audio recorder. This composite tape is then re-recorded, but mixed with another set of sounds. This new composite tape can then be re-recorded again, this time with another layer of sound effects, and so on.

The problem is that every time you add a new layer of material, the tape is copied, so the material which went onto the tape first has been copied the most. Ideally, you shouldn't need to bounce mix more than once, and you should record those elements that are least quality-oriented first – dialogue, followed by sound effects, followed by music.

Avoid bounce mixes if at all possible. It is much better to combine original material, sound effects and music, and commentary 'live'.

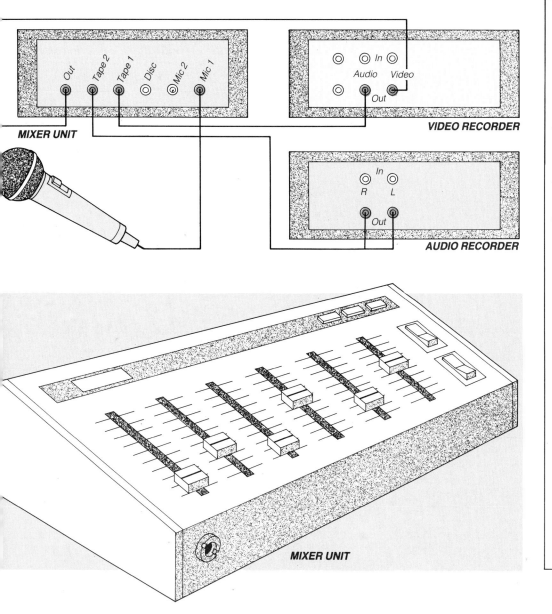

MIXER UNIT

VIDEO RECORDER

AUDIO RECORDER

MIXER UNIT

ADDING A COMMENTARY & VOICE-OVER

A commentary is one form of extra sound that needs a little more work in its creation. It usually consists of a spoken dialogue track that is written, recorded and dubbed onto the video, after the images have been edited. So the words fit the pictures – not the other way around.

A spoken commentary usually best fits a factual video like a record of a holiday or a family event. It can describe the events from a personal point of view and point out the interesting features to the audience.

As with most things to do with video, the first stage is preparation. The pictures are edited first, and of course these may nor may not have their own background sounds. The commentary is written when a final edit is available and is precisely timed to that visual track. It is then dubbed onto the final video tape, together with the other soundtrack elements.

Commentary style

There are two fundamental points to bear in mind when writing commentary.

▶ **DO** make the commentary fit the picture.
▶ **DON'T** describe what you see in the picture.

Let's look at the second point. It may seem obvious, but video is a visual medium – nothing is worse than telling the viewers what they can already see in the picture. Instead, use the commentary to add information to the images. Do not say "The tourists are leaving the airplane on the tarmac", but "The shaken tourists arrive from England, having been delayed by bad weather". This tells us something about the flight, the airplane, its origin and so on.

Making the commentary fit the pictures boils down to the logistical problem of making sure that you can say everything that you want to while the relevant image is on the screen. So, you'll have to go through the pictures and make out a list with exact timings for each shot.

Then start to write your commentary. You will find that in spoken English you get between two and three words per second. An easy way to count words is to write on squared paper and set everything out in broad columns – perhaps six words across the page. Using a stop watch to time your words is not such a good idea, simply because you can't look at the words and the dial at the same time.

Each piece of writing that relates to one image or series of related images, is called a **cue**. The first words of the first cue should be no earlier than three seconds into the video. The reason for this is that, should you be copying the tape and get very close to the start, you may clip material off and lose the first few seconds.

With everything planned and counted, you can then prepare the final commentary. A typical version is shown on the right. The commentary is typed double-spaced on one side of the paper only and the whole lot is held together with a paper clip. The reason for this is that while recording, any rustling of paper will be picked up by the microphone. Turning over stapled sheets will inevitably make some noise, as will turning over individual sheets to follow the words onto the other side.

Arrange each cue as a separate paragraph. If it looks as if a cue is going to carry over from one sheet to the next, re-type the whole cue on the next page.

The exact start time is noted in the margin for each cue. If there is a point in the middle or end which also has to coincide with a particular timing, then this is also noted. Numbers and dates should be written out in full.

Keep the cues short, especially those leading up to vital timing points. In any event, if each cue is more than three or four sentences long, then its complexity will lose the viewers' attention.

Finally, don't cover all the available time with words. Silence can be just as effective in its way, and gives the audience time to think and reflect between cues.

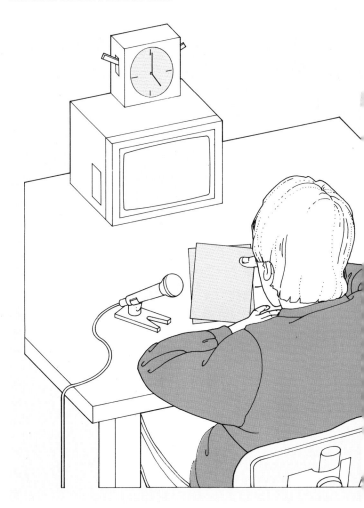

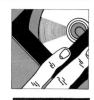

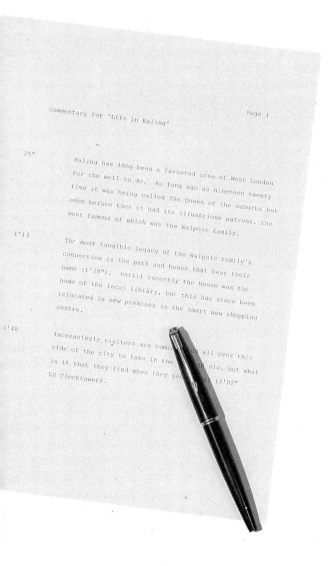

Commentary for 'Life in Ealing'   Page 1

25"
        Ealing has long been a favoured area of West London
    for the well to do. As long ago as nineteen twenty
    five it was being called The Queen of the suburbs but
    even before then it had its illustrious patrons, the
    most famous of which was the Walpole family.

1'13
        The most tangible legacy of the Walpole family's
    connection is the park and house that bear their
    name (1'28"). Until recently the house was the
    home of the local library, but this has since been
    relocated in new premises in the smart new shopping
    centre.

1'48
        Increasingly, visitors are comi...   all over this
    side of the city to take in the ...   nd old, but what
    is it that they find when they ge...   ...2 (2'02"
    LS Clocktower).

There are one or two obvious pitfalls to avoid.

▶ **Drop the meaningless.** Many phrases like "if you ask me", and "you have to admit" are used by people while they think of something to say. They are superfluous in a commentary.

▶ **Don't state the obvious.** Sentences like "There are many children in the school" or "The island of Lewis is isolated in the sea" tell you nothing at all.

▶ **Avoid jargon.** Whether it's RAMs and VLSIs in computers or OHCs in cars, stick to phrases everyone can understand.

▶ **Clichés.** Avoid them like the plague. No "sick as a parrot" or "over the moon" or "in this day and age." There's always a better way of saying things.

▶ **Keep it short.** Short sentences are better than long ones. Don't use long words where short ones will do. Use start instead of initiate, weather instead of meteorological conditions, delay instead of procrastinate, and so on.

▶ **Which and that.** Replace both of these words with a dash. For example "The opera house, which had long been the scene of his most memorable performances, was now closed", becomes: "The opera house – scene of his most memorable performances – was now closed."

Recording a commentary step-by-step

Sit the speaker at a table with a TV monitor and a stopclock in front of him. Connect a microphone to a separate audio recorder and mount this in a convenient position in front of the speaker – probably with a boom mic stand. Connect the TV to a video recorder loaded with the video requiring the commentary. The stopclock should be set to zero. Finally, bear in mind that the room should be as acoustically dead as possible (see page 34).

At the start of the tape, record an image of a clock face with a second hand counting from the 45-second mark up to the top (zero sound) mark, followed by about five seconds of black before the actual pictures begin. This gives you a precise point from which you can time the various images and write the script around them. This timing point should remain on the tape throughout the editing process but can be erased later. After the script is written and the speaker has had a couple of run-throughs, the recording proceeds as follows:

1 Run the video tape back to before the timing point and zero the clock.

2 Put the audio recorder into record/pause mode.

3 Ask the speaker to say a few lines as loudly as he will when actually recording and adjust the recording level on the recorder. The meters should just be peaking into the overload zones.

4 Put the video recorder into play/pause mode.

5 As soon as the speaker is ready and settled, call for silence, shout "tape running" and release the pause control on the audio recorder. It will now be recording.

6 Release the pause control on the video recorder.

7 When the hand on the recorded clock reaches the 12 o'clock zero point, rap smartly on the table and at the same time start the stopclock. This sound will give you a precise timing point on the audio tape which corresponds to the zero point on the video tape. It will allow you to match them up precisely when it comes to dubbing the commentary back onto the video tape.

8 When you get to the end of the pictures and commentary, it is vitally important that everyone in the room remains perfectly still and quiet until the audio recorder has been stopped. You can call "cut" (or some such word) to indicate the end of recording.

You can also live mix commentaries onto tape. The set up and procedure is exactly the same as that described on the previous pages, except that the microphone is connected into the correct channel on the audio mixer, and you will also have other sound sources to contend with as well as the voice-over. The job is made immeasurably easier if several people tackle the various tasks.

THE ROSTRUM CAMERA

The **rostrum camera** is the name given to any set-up that allows you to shoot the whole or part of any flat artwork in order to incorporate it into your finished program. 'Artwork' can be pictures, captions, photographs, printed material, books, maps, magazines, newspapers etc. You could, in fact, make an entire video using still material, carefully chosen with an appropriate commentary and soundtrack. One good idea is to compile a video family history (see page 106) from a collection of old family photographs, press cuttings, contemporary illustrations, magazines and books, and other memorabilia such as wedding invitations and birthday cards.

Two problems arise when you start improvising a rostrum camera set-up. The first is being able to get the camera close enough to the object being shot while still keeping it in focus; the second is lighting that object evenly. The best way to get in close is to attach a close-up lens to your camera. You could use the built-in macro facility but you have to be very close to the object (often less than 2-3cm, which causes lighting problems) and you also lose the ability to zoom in and out.

For even lighting you need two bright lamps, one on either side of the object being shot. You may well have to experiment with their position to obtain the best image, especially if the object is reflective. Focus is vitally important in these circumstances. So remember that the brighter the light, the greater the depth of field, which reduces the chances of anything being out of focus.

Some practical points

Assuming for one moment that all you have is the camera and recorder – and no editing facilities – you will first have to prepare a shooting script. This will match commentary and background sound with each individual image and give precise timings for each image. Don't forget that you can use any of the camera's facilities, such as fade in and fade out, image reversal, and so on, for special effects.

With the script complete you can begin. Set everything up as shown opposite and use a TV monitor to line up each shot exactly. Your camera viewfinder may not show all the picture area and, therefore, will cause you to miss things at the edges of the frame. So that you can synchronize sound and picture, record a clock counting from 45 seconds to zero (see page 135) and several seconds of black before you start to record the first image.

With everything set up, start the recorder and let it run for the planned duration of the shot. You will be using the start/stop button on the camera to operate the recorder, so be careful not to jog the camera or you'll get a shaky picture.

The tape is built up shot by shot until everything is recorded. With editing facilities, you can take your time in choosing and assembling images, but using a 'live' edit (as described above) by-passes problems of picture quality altogether.

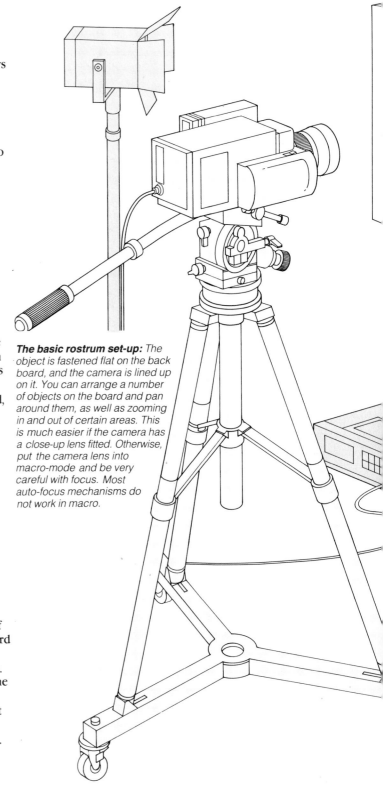

The basic rostrum set-up: The object is fastened flat on the back board, and the camera is lined up on it. You can arrange a number of objects on the board and pan around them, as well as zooming in and out of certain areas. This is much easier if the camera has a close-up lens fitted. Otherwise, put the camera lens into macro-mode and be very careful with focus. Most auto-focus mechanisms do not work in macro.

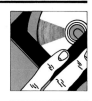

Maps and graphs

Any visual information like this should be presented as simply as possible. Maps should be redrawn with the minimum amount of information needed to do the job they have to do. Intricate details get lost on a TV screen and will just confuse the issue.

Graphs should also be kept very simple and clearly labeled, since fine detail will be lost on the screen. Graphs should be used to show trends rather than to convey detail.

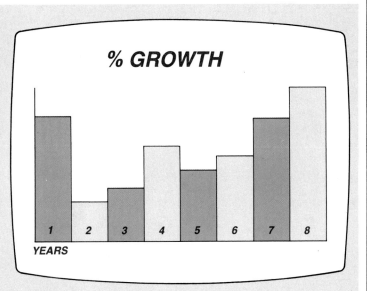

Press cuttings

A little tricky to shoot as they are rarely the right shape for the screen and have too many words to read clearly if they are overly long. Highlighting particular sections of text or focusing on headlines provides shots that are easy to read, while in some cases retyping a particular quote may solve a reading problem.

> A little tricky to shoot as they are rarely the right shape for the screen and have too many words to read clearly if they are too long. Highlighting particular sections of text or focusing on headlines provides shots that are easy to read, while in some cases retyping a particular quote may solve a reading problem.

Slides and color negative film

You can incorporate slides into a video sequence by using one of the adaptors sold by most video camera manufacturers. This screws onto the front of the camera lens which is set to macro mode.

If you have a negative image facility on your camera, you can put color photo negatives in the slide holder and turn them into positive images. This is preferable to shooting from prints as you will get brighter and more life-like colors.

Otherwise, slides should be back-projected onto a bright screen. The camera is then aimed at the projected image and can move around it and zoom in and out in the usual way. For best results the projected image should be as small and as bright as possible.

Lighting: *The lights are arranged so that the whole of the area you are going to shoot is as brightly and evenly lit as possible,. You can use colored filters over the lamps to give tinted effects if needed. Sunlight is another possible source of illumination if you have a workbench near a large sunny window.*

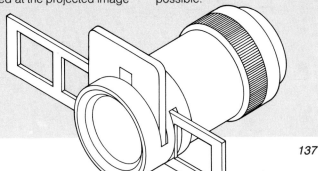

TITLE SEQUENCE

No video is really complete without a title or title sequence to tell the viewers what it is called, and perhaps the names of some of the people in it. You may also choose to add some credits at the end, giving more information on the production. Titles can be created in a variety of techniques and styles – from a simple succession of handwritten cards to a complex special effects sequence.

Fixed titles are created individually on cards which are then shot using a rostrum camera. To create 'rolling' titles you have to put all of the captions in place on a continuous roll of paper, which is unwound in front of the camera.

Combining title graphics and material already shot is rather more difficult. Without using a professional editing suite, the only way of doing this is to use a home video production console, like the one made by Panasonic described on the right.

Another source of captioning is computer-based. Many cameras have their own built-in caption generators which allow you to create title sequences with various colors and sizes of lettering. Look at the panel below right for more details. An even more exciting method is to use a home computer with suitable graphics software. This enables you to create quite complex titles and image sequences which can be recorded from the computer's RF out socket.

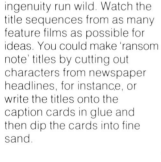

Creative: This is where you let your imagination and ingenuity run wild. Watch the title sequences from as many feature films as possible for ideas. You could make 'ransom note' titles by cutting out characters from newspaper headlines, for instance, or write the titles onto the caption cards in glue and then dip the cards into fine sand.

Rub-down lettering: This is by far the easiest way of producing good-looking caption cards. Rub-down lettering can be obtained in a wide variety of sizes and styles. You should choose a size of lettering that is easy to work with. Your caption cards can be as big as you like. But not so large that you're going to use a lot of sheets of lettering which are expensive. A4 size is a good choice.

Your imagination can really come into play with titling. Instead of using cards with words neatly written on them, you create your captions in other ways. Here are some examples.

The wipe: This involves creating a special image sequence which flashes to bright white at periodic intervals. The titles are superimposed using the home production console. Each time there is a bright white flash, the caption card is changed. If the lettering is black on a white background, the change is not noticed and appears to have been 'wiped' by the flash.

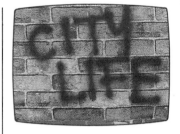

Graffiti: Create a wall from brick wallpaper and write your credits all over the 'wall' using spray paint. Make it as big as you can. You can then shoot the titles as a continuous sequence, panning from credit to credit.

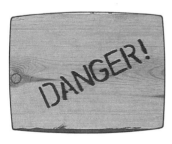

Stencil: You can buy stencils with all sorts of designs and sizes. Your choice will depend on the individual production. Generally speaking, the bigger the stencil, the better.

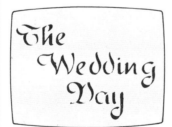

Handwritten: Potentially the most difficult. If you can find someone who has a particularly beautiful handwriting style, then this will be ideal. Otherwise it is far better to find an alternative way of creating titles. Why spoil the whole production for the want of decent credits?

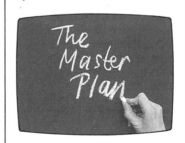

Blackboard: Write your titles on a blackboard, or piece of black paper, with some chalk. Colored chalk can be used for variety. Actually shooting a hand writing the titles, with each one being rubbed off ready for the next could give an interesting angle.

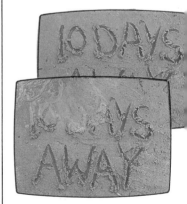

Seashore credits: Each title is written in the wet sand of the beach. Shoot the title for several seconds and, with the camera still running, you can obliterate it using water from a bucket to simulate a wave on the beach.

The home production console and titles

The home production console is basically a 'vision mixer' that, as well as mixing together your shots when editing, allows you to 'mix' captions with material that you have already recorded. It also has inputs for one or more color video cameras which give even more possibilities for combining images. A basic audio mixer is part of the package too.

Superimposition: This allows you to combine a simple caption with material either already on tape, or coming live from a camera. By separating two elements of the caption in this way you can vary one element – the names, say – while keeping the other – the background – constant. The caption cards should be made in black and white. The lettering can be artificially colored by the production console.

Coloring titles and graphics: A black and white title or graphic can be electronically transformed by the home production console into color on a white background or white on a colored background. There are seven colors to choose from: white, red, yellow, green, cyan, blue and magenta. Preparing a white title on a black background gives the choice of colored caption on black background or black caption on colored background.

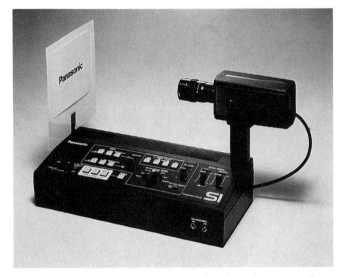

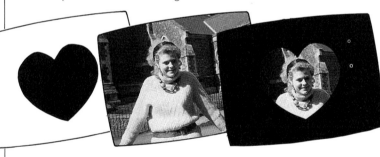

Key effects: By using a drawn shape in front of the black and white camera attached to the home production console, instead of a caption, you can create a number of cut-out effects. The shape can be reproduced in solid color,

superimposed on the image coming from the tape or live camera, or else it can appear as a cut-out with the image from tape or live camera within it. The black and white camera is called a **key camera** when it is used in this way. Those production consoles that have two color camera inputs, in addition to the key cameras, allow you to put one image in the background area, and another in the foreground. The key camera and the graphic/shape defines the areas where the image from each camera will fall within the frame.

Fade in/out: You can gradually fade in the image from the key camera so that your titles come and go smoothly rather than just appearing on the screen. It is also possible to fade the live camera in and out and crossfade or dissolve between the two color cameras (if you are using a production console with two color camera inputs). However, currently available machines don't allow you to fade the video recorder picture input onto which you're superimposing titles.

Built-in caption generators

If you've just bought a fairly advanced video camera, the chances are that it will have a caption generator built in, or available as an extra (see page 18). The caption generator's facilities will vary from model to model. A basic specification will give you all the capital characters of the alphabet, numerals and simple punctuation. There may well

be two sizes of type and a choice of positions where you can place your titles on the screen. You can certainly have white characters and you may have other colors. More advanced machines also give lower-case characters, a choice of more colors, sizes, movements and positions and may have the facility to store up to around eight different

caption 'pages' in memory.
You can superimpose titles while actually shooting or add them later – either superimposed or on a black background – depending on the camera's facilities.
The character generator will also give you a stopwatch facility which can be recorded live on the screen, as well as other time and date indicators.

These can be useful to mark and identify particular tapes.
The character generator's biggest drawback is the fact that the captions look like computer script. This may be fine for some videos and is OK for labeling material, but it is very limited for most caption sequences.

POST-PRODUCTION SPECIAL EFFECTS

Although there is much you can do with your pictures while shooting, there are also certain visual effects which you can add during post-production. Images from the slave recorder can be transferred in slow or fast motion and you can re-record those images using a video camera set up in front of a TV screen. Although you do get some loss in picture definition by not recording directly, this is an entirely appropriate method to use in certain cases. You are able to use facilities such as fade in and out and picture reversal, which are fitted to the camera, as well as being able to concentrate on part of the image instead of the whole of it. At extreme magnifications you will pick up the individual phosphor bars on the TV screen which may be an attractive effect.

A practical home set-up is demonstrated below. The TV set is connected to one video recorder which contains material to be copied. The camera is connected to another recorder which contains a blank tape. (At this point you could connect your camera into the editing set-up described on page 124 and 'live mix' the effect into your final edit.) It is also a good idea to have a second TV connected into the camera's recorder so you can check that the effect being recorded is close to what you're trying to achieve.

Make sure that there is no direct light falling onto the TV screen – working in a darkened room is the best idea – and set the camera up so that the image from the screen is just too big for the viewfinder. Set up a predominantly white picture on the screen – a previous recording of a piece of white card would be ideal – select the daylight position on the camera's filter selector and set the white balance. Finally, you can select the sections of tape you want to copy, and when you are sure that everything is set up as you want it, start the camera's recorder running in record mode, and then start the playback recorder.

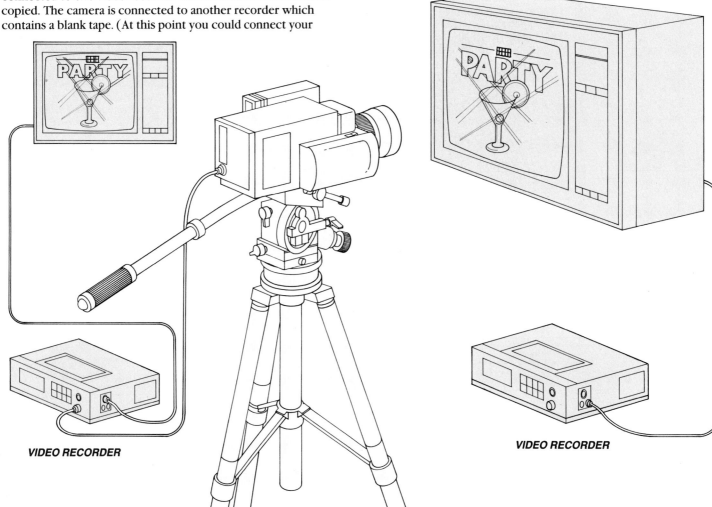

VIDEO RECORDER

VIDEO RECORDER

Solarization

This is an effect caused by massive overexposure of the image in the camera. Try and use shots which have plenty of bright but contrasting images. Converting to black and white can help here. Turn up the brightness and contrast of the TV rather higher than you would have it normally, and keep the camera close to the screen. The amount and extent of the solarization can be controlled using either the white-balance control or the manual tint adjustment. You can try even more effects by fixing colored filters onto the front of the camera lens (see page 66).

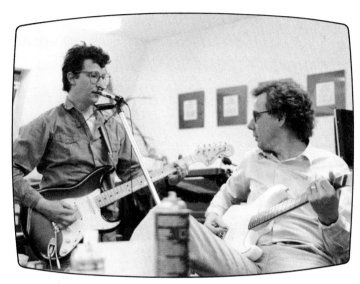

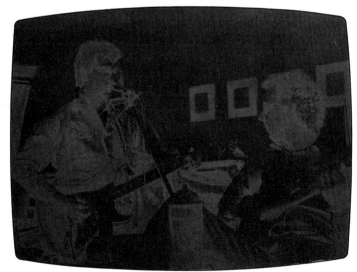

Slow/fast motion

Very simply this involves playing back the image to be re-recorded in slow motion, fast motion or even still frame instead of normal playback speed – a slow motion sequence at a rate of around six pictures per second is particularly effective. This can either be done on the slave recorder as part of the normal editing procedure, or as part of the off-screen copying process. The actual quality of these 'trick frame' images depends very much on the recorder that is being used to play them back. Some models, for example, give massive noise bars – thick lines across the screen – when put into slow motion. Other machines, usually top-of-the-range models, give almost perfect interference-free images. These effects can be combined with any of the others described here.

Fade and picture reverse

If there's a particular part of the video or shot you would prefer to fade out rather than cut, and if the picture quality is good, and the shot is short, then it may be worth re-recording it off-screen with a fade at the end – assuming, of course, that your camera is fitted with this facility. Re-recording a shot with image reversal can give an interesting effect too. Any loss in picture quality is not really noticeable because of the strangeness of the image. Fades and reversal can also be incorporated into any of the other effects described here.

Black and white

There are occasions when a sequence in black and white fits very well into a video's story-line, and this can be achieved in two ways. If you look at the back of your AC video recorder, or the tuner/timer if you're using a portable set-up, you'll find a small slide switch labeled Color/Black and White. This is really intended to match broadcast signals to the VCR's recording circuitry. The switch is usually left in the color position, but

can make black and white films a little sharper and without color fringing when you put it to the other setting. If you simply want a straight switch from color to black and white images without other picture modification, then flip over this switch to the black and white position when recording.

Combining black and white images with a solarization effect and perhaps even slow motion can give a particularly

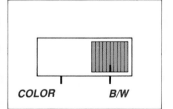

COLOR   B/W

eerie feel to a section of your tape, but any combination of effects is possible. Monitoring the final image on a second TV connected to the camera's recorder is almost essential in order to judge what the finished picture actually looks like.

HOME SPECIAL EFFECTS SUMMARY

Special effects for the home video user fall into four main categories and can be achieved at various different points in the production process. These are: in-camera effects; optical effects; lighting effects; and post-production effects.

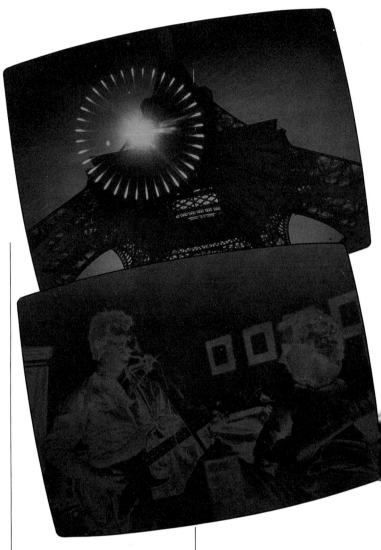

Lighting

Low lighting – makes a character look evil and dominating.

High lighting – makes a character look weak and dominated, makes a scene look drab, accentuates signs of age.

Side lighting – brings out contours on one side of face and, if sides are lit alternately, can cause some startling change effects.

Flag – a piece of metal or board used to control light spill and flare entering camera lens. Can be used very effectively to light just a small portion of a scene – for example, the eyes – leaving the rest in relative darkness.

Gauze – similar to a flag except that it reduces the light falling into a particular area rather than stopping it altogether. The edges of the lamp beam are softened and judiciously placed gauzes can help soften the contours or shape of a face.

Gobo – a perforated metal sheet placed in front of a lamp that causes it to cast a particular pattern according to the design of the holes.

In-camera

Fade in/out – using the built-in fade mechanism to achieve fade up and down from black or white. Must be included as part of each shot for which it is needed. It can also be used in post-production copying.

Image reversal – creates a negative image of the one coming into the camera. Must be included as part of each shot for which it is intended. It can also be used in post-production copying.

Solarization – massive over-exposure causing intense white and deep shadow. Fringes can be tinted red or blue by pushing the white balance right out of adjustment.

Optical

All of these take the form of filters that screw onto the front of the lens.

Colored filters – put an overall color cast over the entire image.

Graduated color – intense color at the top weakening down to clear at the bottom. Useful for dramatic skies or intense foregrounds.

Diffusion – softens the edges of the image and gives a 'soft-focus' quality.

Fog – gives a misty whitish cast to the image.

Dream – gives several spots of blur or distortion.

Center spot – can be combined with any of the above and leaves a portion in the centre of the image unmodified while the surround takes on the quality of whatever the rest of the filter imparts.

Star – causes bright point sources of light to give off points or rays.

Diffraction – causes point light sources to give off brightly-colored fringes.

Multi-image – splits the image into a main image surrounded by a number of smaller ones.

Vignette – a cut-out shape through which the image can be seen. This may also be created using an electronic production console with a key camera.

Post-production

Any or all of these processes may be combined and also used with any of the in-camera and optical effects described above.

TV to camera (off-screen) copying – a process of playing back recorded images onto a TV screen. These are then picked up by a camera and re-recorded. This allows the addition of all the in-camera effects to shots as well as providing a measure of image manipulation – you can, for example, zoom into a specific area of the shot and change its composition.

Black and white conversion – a color image can be converted to black and white as it is being transferred in the editing process. This can also be carried out by off-screen copying.

Slow and fast motion – running the slave recorder at speeds other than normal during the edit process. The quality of the resulting slow/fast motion image depends on the recorder from which it is being played. Sound will not be transferred under these circumstances.

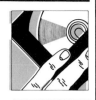

PROFESSIONAL SPECIAL EFFECTS

Virtually all image manipulation systems and video special effects are computer-based, and the sudden widening of possibilities and facilities available to the video director has followed the rapid growth in computer technology.

One of the pioneers in this field is Quantel. Their equipment was initially designed to manipulate real images, either from tape or live from camera. By storing each picture in the form of a computer code, their machines are able to make that picture any size, to stretch it, squash it, roll it into a cylinder, place in anywhere in the TV frame, or cause it to spin, flip or move in any number of ways.

This is possible because the shapes into which the image fits can be described very simply in computer terms, the movement of those shapes can also be defined very precisely, and the contents of those frames – the image – is also in computer code. To the computer, everything is just a set of numbers and co-ordinates to be manipulated according to its instructions. The only factor that has slowed down the introduction of the Quantel system is the fact that each image frame takes up a lot of computer memory space, and has to be processed at high speed. It has taken recent developments in low cost, high-density memory and ultra-fast, high capacity computer processors, to make these systems as comprehensive as they are today.

The video paintbox was a logical development of this form of image manipulation, which allows you to combine real images and computer-based information. The paintbox system works in two parts. It is possible to 'color-in' a specific area of a shot by simply delineating the area on one still frame. The computer follows that area for as long as the shot lasts and maintains the same color throughout. It is also possible to draw images on top of existing ones, combining live action and computer graphics. The latest paintbox systems offer a complete graphics package – finely detailed drawings can be created completely within the computer, and they can then be animated on their own or combined with live action.

Other professional image manipulation techniques include pixilation and mosaic. Although similar, they involve differences in scale and size. A pixilated image is one which has been converted into a pattern of fine dots. These are similar to the dots you might find on a printed color poster and of course are much bigger than the phosphor dots that are used to build up the picture on the TV screen. The end effect is a bit like a pointillist painting. Mosaic, as the name suggests, converts the picture into a number of coloured squares. The size of the squares can be varied, but they are always recognizable as such and are far bigger than the individual **pixels** (picture elements) of a pixilation effect.

The field of computer graphics is very wide, and it is now possible to produce very high quality animated video images. Inevitably, some of this technology will rub off onto the amateur market – the use of home computers in amateur video production being one viable proposition.

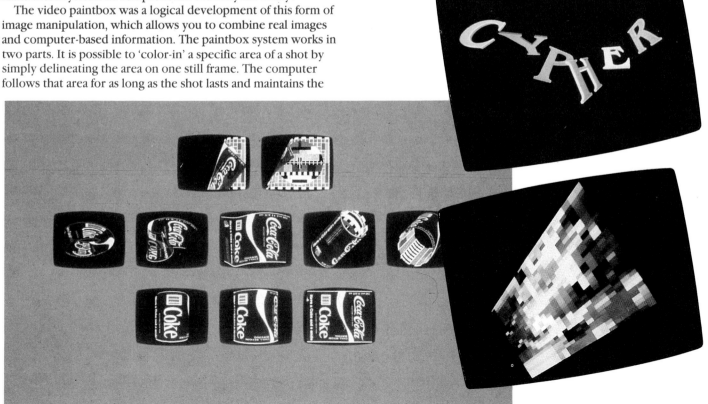

THE HOME COMPUTER

We've touched on the applications of computers to TV and video, both for editing and special effects, but so far these applications have been more in the realm of the professional than the amateur video maker. However, home microcomputers can be used to provide yet another source of images which you can use to enhance your productions, and add that extra polish and originality.

Anyone familiar with a home computer will know that it is capable of producing a wide variety of images – both in terms of text and also pictures or graphics. These images can be generated one by one and recorded as a set of still pictures or generated in a sequence and animated.

Obviously, a computer will not produce anything on screen without a program, so your first task is to find a program that will generate the images you want to use. Here you have three options. You can either write your own program; write one into the computer line by line from a book; or buy a ready-made graphics package which you simply load into the computer. The best option is going to be the graphics package, simply because this will have been written by experts in machine code (not a high-level language such as BASIC), and so will be able to exploit the capabilities of the computer to the full while operating very quickly – essential for animated graphics.

If you want a complex set of pictures but don't have a graphics package, you may well be able to 'borrow' something from another program – such as a computer game. A word of caution, however. Computer programs of all kinds are now covered by copyright legislation, so the same rules apply to taking parts of an existing program as to copying any other material. It is just about acceptable to reproduce copyright material without clearance, provided it is for your own personal pleasure and use. Any other use is definitely not on – see page 148 for more details.

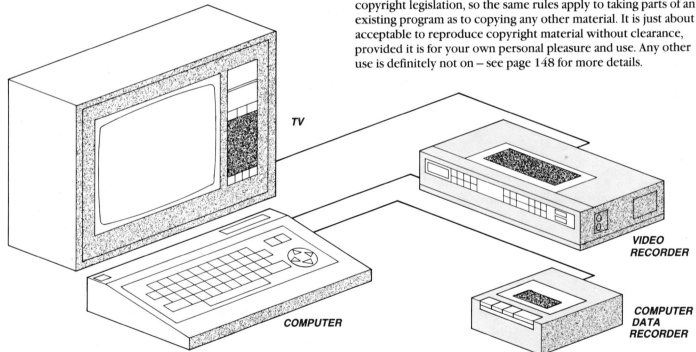

TV

VIDEO RECORDER

COMPUTER

COMPUTER DATA RECORDER

Graphics recording step-by-step

1 Having loaded the graphics program with your sequence(s) on it into the computer, its RF output socket should be connected to the RF (aerial) input socket of the recorder.

2 A TV monitor is connected either to the RF output socket, or direct video and audio sockets if fitted.

3 Switch on the TV and select the channel that is tuned to the video recorder.

4 Select a spare channel on the tuner in the recorder, run the graphics program and tune that channel until the images and sound (if sound is being generated) come up on the TV.

5 Reset the computer, load the video recorder with a blank tape and select record/ pause mode.

6 Disengage pause and let the recorder run for about 10 seconds with no input signal. This is to leave you with some space before the actual graphics sequence which will help in the editing process later on. Re-engage pause.

7 Get the computer ready, disengage pause and let the computer program run.

8 When the sequence has finished, leave the recorder running for a further 15 seconds before re-engaging pause.

9 If you have another graphics sequence to record, set this up and go back to step 6. Otherwise press the stop button, rewind and view the material that you've just recorded to make sure that everything is satisfactory.

Computer generated special effects

Titles: The scope for different sizes and styles of computer-generated titles is literally limitless – in theory – but in the end the software determines just how fancy or sophisticated you can be. Another limiting factor is the TV itself. Any computer image is built up of tiny picture elements (**pixels**). The size of these pixels determines how much detail you can pack into the computer image. The smaller the pixel, the more detailed the image will be. Unfortunately, a standard TV set can only accommodate a certain maximum number of pixels, but to get around this, some computers come with special high-resolution monitors. However, working with video means that you are stuck with the standard TV screen, and so your graphics resolution *will* be limited by what you can get onto that screen.

So, you should keep your titles big, with as few colors on screen at any one time as possible. Steer clear of any type styles that have lots of curves – these will end up looking like a series of little blocks.

If you have a series of titles, then the method by which they change can follow one of several different options. The easiest is a simple change of screen – the equivalent of cutting from one shot to another. This is rather abrupt and not really recommended. Far better is some form of dissolve. This can be very simple, or you could have a sort of picture explosion depending on your graphics software. The next credit can be built up line by line or simply appear, or could be assembled in the visual reverse of an explosion. Titles can be stylised to the theme of the

video program or even combined with images.

If you are thinking of buying a software package, make sure first of all that you know exactly what you want out of it and that it will run on the equipment you have – or are prepared to buy. Secondly, make sure that you have a proper demonstration and see that the package will give you what you want.

Pictures: You have theoretically limitless possibilities here, but in practice you are limited by the TV and the software. Computer-generated graphics can be used in two ways – either as pictures to complement the rest of the tape or as useful illustrations of specific points.

In the first category, you might include pictures as part of a title sequence, or even drop them in to parallel something in the action. You might, for example, be making a drama about a bank robbery. You could then include a computer graphics sequence to show how the robbers were getting closer and closer to the safe.

On the other hand, you might be making a documentary on the local church. You could use computer graphics to draw a graph showing how much the different costs in maintaining the church have risen over the years. This could be animated to show different conditions – a "what if?" situation. Many business programs have a graphics package. The main program calculates business forecasts and so on, and the graphics part automatically draws a graph from the results. If you change the data going into the business part, the graphs are automatically redrawn.

Superimposition

Superimposition of any two sets of images is difficult in the domestic situation. This is because the sync signals for the two video images you are trying to combine have to be exactly in step. The home production console allows you to combine material from tape with images from a title camera, it allows you to mix images from the title camera and an outside color camera to be re-recorded onto tape, and it allows you to mix images from two color cameras – provided one is equipped with a **gen lock** output. It also allows you to mix images from one color camera and another video recorder – provided the camera is again fitted with gen lock. You cannot mix images from two recorders.

Similarly, you cannot mix the images from a computer and a recorder directly. But there are two ways round this. First of all you can use the set-up described on page 140 in conjunction with the home production console. The computer images are played back onto the TV screen, the camera picks them up and this camera signal can then be combined with whatever material is coming in from another video recorder. You do lose some picture quality, but because the computer images are bright and sharply defined, the loss is usually acceptable.

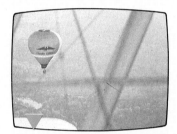

Another, potentially more exciting, method is to use a computer manufactured by the same company as the video equipment, plus a video interface. With the acceptance of the MSX standard by virtually all the major video manufacturers, we are now seeing the integration of the MSX computer into a total video/audio/computing/ communications concept. In other words, a TV, hi-fi, video, computer, video camera, musical keyboard, and so on, made by one manufacturer, will all be compatible and capable of interconnection.

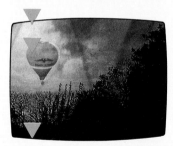

As far as creative video is concerned, it means that the computer will be able to be used to control video editing. This includes the automatic integration of video and computer images. You can then drop computer graphics, games sequences and charts into real video images, both live

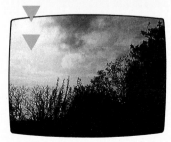

and recorded. Inevitably, the scope and sophistication of the system will vary from manufacturer, but the capability is there.

FILM AND VIDEO

Throughout this book we have been careful not to use the word 'film' when we mean capturing an image using a video camera and recorder. Film and video are two quite separate ways of permanently preserving visual images – each one having its own advantages and disadvantages, its own image quality and 'feel'. If you need any convincing, just watch a program that has been recorded on video tape, then watch a movie that has been made on film.

Although you will see the differences yourself, it is worth listing the more obvious here. The color intensity of the film image is much deeper and there is a subjective 'quality' feel about something made on film. It looks and feels expensive – one reason why virtually all of the most prestigious TV series, both American and British, are made on film and not video tape.

On the other hand, manipulating a film image is very costly and the possibilities are relatively limited. You can't, for example, use any of the effects that are quite commonplace with video systems such as Quantel, without considerable laboratory work. So virtually all pop promos and advertising that depend on trick effects are either made on video tape, or originated on film and then transferred to video for post-production.

But where does this leave the amateur in relation to film? At the very least, you can transfer your old home movie footage to video very simply and have the convenience of being able to view the material on TV rather than having to set up a screen and projector. Many photographic shops offer this transfer service – and they will even add titles and incidental music.

Incorporating film footage into a video program causes few problems. Once you've transferred the material to video – the process is called **telecine** – it can be edited into a final program like anything else. The film material may be old family footage – you may want to incorporate it into a family history video – or you may want to film new material for a variety of reasons and then incorporate this into your program.

There are several special effects that are easily achieved with film but are difficult to carry out well on video – such as slow motion and animation – and these are detailed opposite. At this point we will assume that if you want to use film, you know how to operate a film camera. Film is probably best used as a contrast to video because of its difference in look and 'feel'. Either you can film real people doing real things, and drop them into your video program as an alternative to events captured on video, or you can use film to record abstract images which can then be further processed while still on film or on video later.

Home telecine

The simplest way of transferring film material to video is to project the film to form a small, bright image and then shoot that image with a video camera.

Many home video manufacturers sell a telecine rig as part of their accessories range. Using one of these, the projected film image lands on a ground-glass screen. Behind this is a mirror which turns the image through 90 degrees so that the video camera can record it the right way round. Because of the relatively small size of the image, it is often necessary to fit a close-up lens to the camera, and this is usually supplied as part of the kit. In each case, the projector's sound output (if any) is fed directly to the recorder's audio input socket.

For normal film footage the projector is run at the same speed at which the film was exposed (usually 18 or 24 frames per second). There is no reason, however, why you shouldn't use a different speed for special effects. Try experimenting – video tape costs very little. You must be careful to watch the image that the camera is recording on a monitor TV, though, as you may get interference lines at some speeds.

Don't forget that you can zoom in on any area of a projected film image and move around it in much the same way as you can with a rostrum camera (see page 136).

As an original touch, you could try projecting two images, one on top of the other, from two separate projectors and then record the result. This method of superimposing images gives all sorts of new possibilities and is something that is quite impossible to achieve with a basic home video set-up.

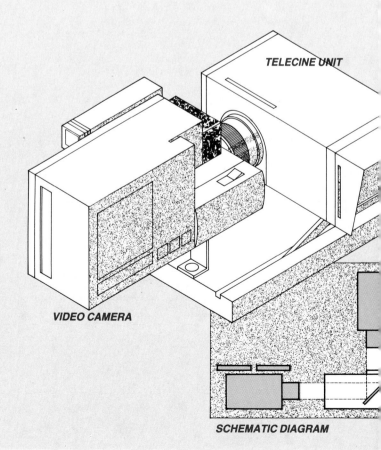

TELECINE UNIT

VIDEO CAMERA

SCHEMATIC DIAGRAM

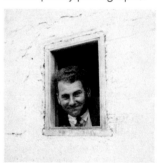

Film special effects

There are two areas where it is possible to create certain special effects with film, which are quite impossible to achieve with home video. One is in the area of slow motion photography, the other in animation.

Slow motion

Although it is possible to achieve passable slow motion video effects in the editing process, this relies on the fact that your slave recorder can give noise-free pictures, and even this isn't entirely satisfactory. When you record material on video you record 30 (or 25 if you're using PAL equipment) frames (complete images) every second. Completely smooth and jerk-free reproduction of any movement depends on there being at least around 15 pictures every second. Any less and the human eye starts to detect the separate images. The more frames there are, the more natural the effect.

When you slow video tape down, you slow down the frame rate and very slow motion looks like a set of fast-changing single images, rather than a continuous movement.

Slow motion movie photography works differently. Say you wanted to show something happening at half the normal speed. If the normal frame rate for your film is 24 frames per second, then you would first shoot the action at 48 frames per second. When you play this back at 24 frames per second, it will appear to be moving at half normal speed, but because the frame rate is still normal, the slowed down movement will still seem perfectly smooth. The slower you want the final result to be, the higher the frame rate you use to shoot it. The reason you can't change the video frame rate is simply that it is part of the basic overall specification of the TV system in use.

Animation

Animation comes in two forms – cartoon and stop motion. Both involve the shooting of a succession of still images – the illusion of life and movement is created by the fact that the object has been moved slightly between each shot. Most home movie cameras have the facility to shoot single images, and the ability to produce animated sequences to drop into a video program can be a valuable option to have 'up your sleeve'.

Cartoon animation is two-dimensional – it is the bringing to life of drawings. Backgrounds are usually created as flat artwork. On top of these go the characters to be animated. Each character is created on clear plastic film and each of the features that move – eyes, hands, legs, etc. – is drawn on a separate sheet of plastic. Each of these sheets is called a cel. Those elements of the picture that don't move between frames are not redrawn. But the cels that show moving objects are replaced frame by frame with new ones in which the new movements have been incorporated.

Stop motion animation is three-dimensional. This involves the creation of a model or puppet whose features have sufficient freedom of movement to allow them to be repositioned between frames. The models can be very intricate figures, or simply blobs of modeling clay.

Old movie footage

A family history: Insert the film to break up and illustrate still pictures of the family and contemporary photographs.

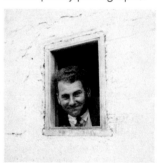

Weddings: Include a short history of the bride and groom including film of them both as children.

Local history: Contrast the same locations now with those portrayed on the film – you could even try putting the same people from the film in the modern setting.

Tapes about the children: Include film of when you or your mother or even grandmother were children. Contrasting Christmas and summer holidays is a good idea.

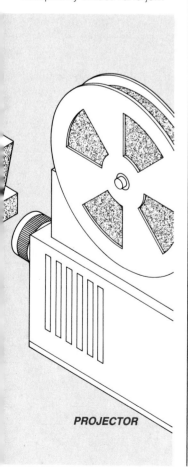

PROJECTOR

YOU & THE LAW

There are three areas of law with which the video maker is likely to come into contact. At the very least, he should be aware of their implications for, as the saying goes: 'Ignorance is no excuse'. By far the most important is the law of copyright, although the legal implications of trespass and also of customs and excise regulations are also important. We can only give brief guidelines here – specific points of law vary from country to country – but it is the video user's duty to be fully acquainted with the legal implications of what he or she is doing.

Copyright

Imagine you had just written a novel – you had spent months, even years doing it perhaps – and then somebody calmly came along, read it through, copied it out and passed it off as their own, making a vast fortune in the process. You would feel robbed – something that was yours had been stolen!

It was to protect these very rights that the laws of copyright evolved, and although the details vary from country to country they are pretty similar in their scope.

Very simply, when someone creates a work and records it in some material form, the laws of copyright give him certain rights over that work. The definitions of a 'work' are quite extensive, but fall into four categories: literary, dramatic, musical and artistic. Copyright also exists in the following subject matters: sound recordings, cinematographic films, television and radio broadcasts, cable programs, and published editions of literary, dramatic and musical works. Outside these areas, the 'creation' does not have copyright protection – although it may have some other form of protection such as being a registered design – and don't forget that there is no copyright in ideas. A work does not acquire protection until it is in some material form.

It is here that the video user starts to wander into a minefield of regulations. Let's start with TV broadcasts. It is permissible to make a video recording of a TV broadcast for private and domestic use. If, however, there is anything in that broadcast which is also covered by copyright, then it will be a breach of copyright to record it, since the exception for domestic use only applies to the broadcast itself. So, for example, it is OK to record a sports program or news bulletin, as sporting events or live TV are not in themselves 'works' which are covered by copyright. If, however, you record a film or concert then you are infringing the copyright law as films and music are works which are copyrighted.

Let's be quite clear – it is an offense to record copyrighted material off-air for whatever reason without permission. Similarly, it is an offense to copy records onto audio cassettes. However, it is tacitly accepted that these practices do go on in the home and a prosecution for such infringements would be very unusual.

This also extends to literary works. An adaptation or recording of, say, a book, or a play without permission is also an offense – and this applies as much to an amateur dramatic production as a full-fledged professional show. Again, a prosecution of someone who points a camera at a school play would be extremely unusual, but not impossible.

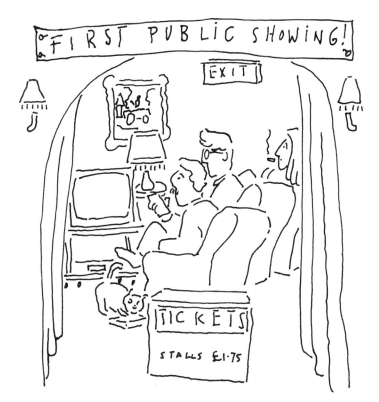

Public performance

Copyright also applies to performance. Every time a film, record, play or whatever is 'performed' or shown or played in public, permission is needed. Video and audio cassettes, records and other recordings are sold with the implicit restriction that they will only be used for private and domestic uses. If they are played to a non-private audience – and the definition of 'private' is not clearly defined – then an additional licence is required. It is generally accepted that 'non-private' means outside the domestic situation. Whether the audience pays or not is irrelevant. When performing a play, the appropriate permission is required from the publisher.

All of this may sound daunting to the amateur video maker but the laws exist to protect the livelihood of those creative people who take the personal risks to produce such material. Although the provisions of the law are quite clear, it would be very unusual to see a prosecution of someone who creates a video film purely for his own fun and pleasure, with no intent to show the program to more than a small circle of personal friends, even if he has infringed copyright in certain areas. What the amateur must be aware of is that the moment he steps out of this tightly-defined area, the law is unlikely to be sympathetic.

The only other way around this is to avoid copyright material altogether. If you create your own script – or shoot natural or live events – then these will not be copyrighted. If you arrange to have original music, then this will not be copyrighted. If you record your own sound effects or use records that are specifically copyright-cleared for amateur use, then you will not be infringing copyright.

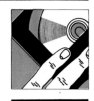

Trespass and permission

This is really just a reminder of what we've already discussed on page 77. Again the laws of privacy and trespass will vary from country to country but there are certain principles.

First of all, it must be remembered that the law of trespass is **civil** not **criminal** law. This means that the trespasser must be sued in the civil courts rather than prosecuted by the police. There are certain exceptions to this, notably for defense installations.

Technically, a person is trespassing the moment he steps off public land. The word 'public' is not well defined but can be taken to mean public road or common land. Whatever you can see and photograph is not private if it can be seen and photographed from public land, although there are some exceptions to this ruling –

again especially defense establishments.

However, this does not give you the right to set up a full crew in the middle of the road and start shooting passing pedestrians. You are still subject to any local by-laws and other laws, such as obstruction and breach of the peace. In practice, you have to obtain permission to shoot virtually anywhere except on your own property and this will include notifying the local police and highway officials.

Customs and excise

If ever you are thinking of taking your equipment abroad – on holiday perhaps – then you must be aware of customs regulations concerning the temporary export of goods. This stems from the fact that certain items manufactured abroad are subject to import duty when they are brought into the country. Although the classes of items vary from

country to country, luxury goods, such as video recorders, are usually among them.

If, therefore, you have bought your recorder and camera quite normally, and then taken it out of the country, you won't want to pay a hefty import tax just to bring it back again. Regulations vary, but at the very least you should take your receipts for the equipment with you, so that you can prove that you bought the equipment in your home country and have simply taken it on holiday with you. Some countries may require you to fill in a customs declaration form.

Don't forget that, just because your home country doesn't require a temporary export certificate, it may not mean the country you're visiting doesn't require an import one. You can check the detailed requirements with your travel agent, the tourist bureau for the countries concerned or your local chamber of commerce. Don't forget that if you're touring through several countries, you have to comply with customs regulations for every country you enter and leave.

If you are working professionally, certain other regulations are required. You must produce a document which lists every single item of equipment you are carrying. This is checked thoroughly at all customs points and must be correct, otherwise you will end up having to pay duty, and then go through the involved procedure of reclaiming the money.

Exactly what constitutes 'professional' is not clear. If you are an amateur but working with a lot of equipment then this appellation may well cover you. Check with your local chamber of commerce if you are at all unsure.

Your questions answered

Q. What rights does the copyright holder have?

He is able to prevent others from doing certain specified acts which are laid down in the copyright laws of the country concerned. In practice, this means that others may not reproduce, publish, perform in public, broadcast, make an adaptation of, include in any broadcast program or generally have any dealing with, any part of the copyright material, without consent from the copyright holder.

Q. Who is the copyright holder?

The original creator of the work, except if it is created under contract for some organization, then the organization has copyright.

Q. Where does the copyright apply?

Initially, in the country of origin. There are, however, two major international treaties whereby a copyright holder from one country automatically enjoys protection in all the signatory countries. The two treaties are the Berne Convention and the Universal Copyright Convention (UCC).

Q. How long does protection last?

This varies according to which treaty your country operates under, but is usually to death of the author plus either 50 years (Berne signatories) or 25 years (UCC signatories, notably the USA). These terms do vary from category to category and work to work.

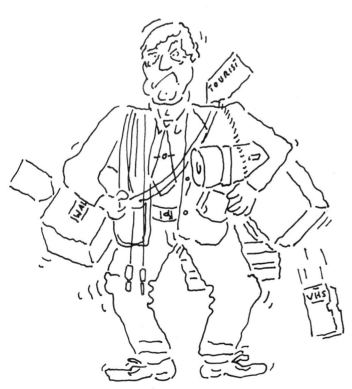

GLOSSARY

A

Alternating current (AC):
Electricity where the voltage
switches between a positive and
negative value many times a
second.

Audio frequency (AF):
Frequency of sound that we can
actually hear. This is usually in the
range 5Hz to 15kHz.

AFM sound: See hi-fi video.

Automatic gain control (AGC):
Electronic circuit which adjusts a
recorder's input sensitivity to suit
the signal being recorded.

Ambient sound: Sound of an
environment without additional
sounds such as speech.

Amp: Unit of electrical current.

Aperture: Hole in the lens
through which light passes.
Adjustable by means of an iris.

Aspect ratio: The ratio of the
width to the height of a screen.
In TV it's 4:3, on most cinema
screens it's 3:2 and widescreen is
2.55:1.

Audial design: Creating timed
sound tracks for use with image
sequences.

Assemble edit: Copying
sections onto a master tape one
by one. The control tracks from
each one are also transferred, so
there can be picture interference
at the start of each section.

ASA: Short for American
Standards Association, the ASA
number gives the speed – or
sensitivity to light – of
photographic film. The higher the
speed, the higher the sensitivity.

Attenuator: A device that
reduces the strength of an
electrical signal.

Audio frequency response: The
range of 'notes' that an audio
recorder is capable of recording,
measured in Hertz (Hz). The
human ear can hear 5Hz to
15kHz. A good hi-fi system (and
hi-fi video recorder) can
reproduce 20Hz to 20kHz but
most video recorders can only
give 100Hz to 8kHz.

Azimuth angle: The angle
between the tape head and
recording tape. Must be exactly
right or the play head will not pick
up the original recorded signal.

B

Backlight: Light directed
towards the camera onto the
subject, in order to give depth to
the picture.

Back-space edit: A facility on
some video recorders which rolls
the tape back when the record
button is pressed to ensure an
interference-free join between the
old recording and the new one.
The last few seconds of the
previous recording are lost.

Barn doors: Hinged flaps
mounted on a lamp. They can be
opened or closed independently
to control the size and shape of
the light beam.

Bass: Those 'notes' or
frequencies at the lower end of
the audio frequency band.

Big close-up (BCU): A shot
framing only a small part of the
subject – the section between
forehead and chin of a face for
example.

Betamax: Half-inch video
cassette format developed by
Sony from their U-Matic system.
Launched in 1975.

Black burst: Another name for
sync pulse.

Blacked tape: Tape with a zero
picture and sound signal
recorded on it. (A black image
and silence on the sound track).
This is necessary before the tape
can be used in insert editing.

Blonde: Trade name that has
become general term for a
particular form of 2kW **Quartz
Halogen** movie lamp.

BNC: Form of connector
commonly used for video signals.

Boom: Arm or pole on which the
microphone is mounted.

Boom operator: Person in the
video crew who holds and
manipulates the mic boom.

C

Cameraman: Person who looks
after the camera, sets it up and
operates it during each take.

Camera script: Script marked up
with all the details regarding
camera position, shot size, and
so on.

Captions: Titles, drawings,
lettering and other graphic work
placed in front of the camera and
used as an alternative to live
action.

Cardioid: A particular
microphone pick-up pattern that
is heart-shaped.

Cel: Transparent plastic sheet
used as a base onto which
animated drawings are traced
and painted.

Chrominance: Part of the video
signal that conveys the
information on the picture's color
content.

Crossing the line: A continuity
problem. A shot of a person
walking along a path must not be
mixed with shots taken from the
other side of the path. The reason
for this is that shots taken from
one side of the path may show
the person walking from left to
right across the screen. If you
move your point of view to the
other side of the path then the
person will then appear to walk
from right to left, confusing the
viewer and breaking continuity.

Clapper board: Used to both
identify the shot and to provide a
reference point for matching
sound to picture. The project,
shot and take number are
chalked on the board, and the
hinged flap is brought down
smartly on the rest of the board
(clapped) to give a visual and
sound sync point.

Close-up: Shot which looks
'close' to the subject. In the case
of a human subject a close-up
would be a shot of the face or a
detail of the hands.

Color balance: Matching the
camera to the ambient light so
that whites look white and all the
other colors are accurate (see
color temperature).

Color cast: False hues in the
color of the image caused by the
subject being placed very close
to an object which is brightly
colored.

Color conversion filters: Placed
over the camera or specific lights
to raise or lower the color
temperature of the light. A subject
that was primarily lit by daylight
would have an odd mixture of
flesh tone colors if additional
artificial lighting with a lower color
temperature was used.

Color shift: Deliberately putting
the camera's white-balance
system out of adjustment.

Color temperature: Light that the
eye perceives as white in fact
varies between very blue and
very yellow. The eye automatically
compensates for these variations,
a video camera can't and so has
to be adjusted. The color
temperature is a measure of how
hot an object would have to be to
emit light of a certain color.

Continuity: Making sure that all
details in shots that are meant to
follow each other are identical.

Continuity person: Member of a
video crew who makes detailed
notes after each take so that the
scene can be reproduced exactly
at some future date.

Control track: Signal recorded
on the tape which tells the
playback recorder where the start
of each picture is and keeps the
images in step.

Crane shot: Shot made using a
camera mounted on the end of a
long boom, allowing it to move
freely up and down and from side
to side.

Crossfade: Fading out one
picture as another is faded in.

Cathode ray tube (CRT): Part of
the TV set which actually displays
the picture.

Cut: Direct transition between
one shot and the next. Different
from a dissolve or crossfade
which involves fading one image
into the next.

Cutaway: Camera shot out of the
continuity of the main scene.

Cyan: Complementary color to
the primary red, cyan is a mixture
of blue and green.

D

DC: Short for direct current. This is the form of electricity that you will get from a battery. The current stays at a constant level and does not fluctuate as it would with an **AC** supply.

Decibel (dB): Logarithmic measure for sound levels and voltage ratios.

Depth of field: Range of distances from a lens, in which all the objects are in focus. This varies with the aperture of the lens – the smaller the aperture, the greater the depth of field.

Dichroic filter: Alternative name for a filter used to raise the effective color temperature of movie lamps.

Diffusion filter: Optical material that softens the edges of an image. This can either screw onto the front of the camera or can be used to soften the edges of a beam coming from a lamp.

Director: Member of the production team with general artistic control over the project.

Dissolve: Shot transition in which one image fades as the other gradually appears.

Distortion: Measure of how much original audio signal is changed or modified by the recording and playback process. Can be expressed as percentage total harmonic distortion. The best audio cassette decks can manage 0.01%, a standard video recorder is between 5 and 10%.

Dolby: The Dolby noise reduction system reduces tape hiss and noise and comes in two types: Dolby B which gives around 5 – 10dB improvement in audio signal-to-noise ratio; and Dolby C which gives a 15 – 20dB improvement.

Dolly: A set of wheels on which the camera tripod is mounted. It can also be used to describe the form of movement a camera will make when actually mounted on a dolly.

Dream filter: Optical material that screws onto the camera lens and blurs the image at certain points within the frame.

Drop-out: Interference in the picture, usually in the form of white flashes or lines caused by the oxide particles on the video tape actually falling off the plastic backing.

Dubbing: Mixing of sounds from various sources to form a finished soundtrack.

Dubbing mixer: The person who looks after putting both sync sound and new sounds onto the tape after the material has been shot.

Dynamic mic: A microphone that works on the reverse principle of a loudspeaker. These give good performance at a reasonable price, and can be used with long cable runs. They work with virtually all recorders and mixers.

Dynamic range: Range between the quietest and loudest sounds that equipment can handle without distortion. Measured in dB. Varies between 90dB for a compact disc player, through 65-70dB for audio cassette recorders to around 40dB for standard video recorders.

E

Editing: Process of assembling a complete video program from a set of shots, rostrum material, computer-generated images and special effects.

Editor: Person who controls the editing process.

Electret condenser mic: Modified version of the condenser mic. These combine the qualities of a condenser mic without the need to have a separate power source.

ENG: Short for electronic news gathering. Refers to a news crew that uses video to gather its pictures and sound.

Establishing shot: Shot that appears first in a sequence. Used to give the viewer an idea where the action is taking place.

Eyeline: Direction in which a person is looking across the image.

Equalizer: Glorified tone control unit that lets you cut or boost sounds at different frequencies. A graphic equalizer is so called because the pattern of the setting knobs actually resembles the tailored frequency modification that you have set.

Erase head: The head on either a video or audio recorder that removes signals already recorded.

F

Fade: Gradual increase or decrease in either volume of sound or brightness of picture.

Feedback: Fierce, high-pitched, high-volume sound produced when a microphone picks up sound from a loudspeaker connected to the same circuit. May easily happen if recording with a video camera that is connected to a TV in the same room. The TV sound must be turned off.

Field: Half a TV image frame.

Fill light: Light source to one side of the subject to fill in shadows cast by **key light**. Any shadows cast by the fill light are not visible from the camera position.

Filter: Transparent material which changes the nature of light passing through it. Usually colored, but it may modify the light in other ways such as blocking out ultraviolet rays.

Flag: Wood or card which may be mounted on a stand, and is used to stop stray light falling into the camera lens, or in front of a lamp to cut off part of the light beam.

Flare: A sudden bright patch or lines in the picture caused by light shining directly into the camera.

Flutter: Rapid variations in tape speed. Usually expressed as percentage variation. Most video recorders will give a figure of 0.005%, a good audio cassette recorder gives up to 0.01%.

Flying erase head: The erase head on most VCRs is mounted in a fixed position. This simply erases the tape some distance before the recording head. Accurate editing requires that as little of the signal in front of the new material as possible is erased. This is achieved by mounting the erase head on the head drum – a flying erase head.

Focal length: The distance from the center of a lens to the point behind it where a distant image can be focused. In practice the focal length of a lens is used as a guide to its type. A short focal length lens has a wide-angle of view and is referred to as a wide-angle lens. A lens with a long focal length magnifies the image and is referred to as a telephoto lens. A zoom lens is one in which the focal length can be altered.

Fog filter: Similar to a diffusion filter but imparts thick white mist all over the image.

Focus: An image is in focus when all the points in the image are sharp without blurring. In some circumstances it is impossible to have all points in the image in focus and this can be used to emphasise certain elements in the image (see depth of field).

Focus puller: Member of video crew who keeps camera in focus in complex moving shots.

Format: The particular type of video cassette and its associated video system. Current formats are VHS, Betamax, V2000 and Video 8.

Frame: Complete single image. In film it would be the individual pictures from which the film is constructed. In video it is comprised of two fields – two interlocking electronic images that make up the final frame.

Fresnel lamp: Form of lamp that has a fresnel lens fitted. This gives an even, widespread, diffuse beam.

Fringing: Colored fringes around images in a video picture.

G

Gaffer: Title used for the lighting electrician in a film or video crew.

Gen lock: If you use more than one video camera (in, say, a vision mixer) all their sync systems must be in step. The easiest way to achieve this is to use one camera to generate the pulses and lock the rest onto that. This facility is known as gen lock.

Gobo: Metal lamp attachment with a pattern punched in it. Can be used to throw variegated pattern of light onto the set or for some specific effect such as moon or clouds.

Graduated filter: Optical material fitted onto the camera lens. Has intense coloring at the top gradually getting weaker towards the bottom.

Grip: Person responsible for all the camera hardware, such as tripods, tracks and dollies.

H

Hard light: Quality of light which casts hard, sharply defined edges to shadows.

Head room: Space on the image between the top of the performer's head and the upper edge of the screen.

Helical scan: System of video recording where the heads are mounted on a rotating head drum and lay down a series of diagonal stripes on the tape.

Hertz (Hz): Unit in which frequency is measured. 1Hz is one vibration or cycle per second.

Hi-fi video: Sound recorded using a pair of heads mounted on the revolving head drum. The high writing speed of the heads increases the quality. The sound signals are recorded along with the video signals. They are buried deep in the tape and the video signals are recorded on the top 'layer'. Because the recording of **azimuth angles** are vastly different there is no interference between the sound and vision signals.

Horizontal resolution: Test of how much detail a video camera and recorder can capture. It is measured in lines – the higher the figure the better. A good domestic camera can manage up to 350 lines, professional cameras over 500.

I

Image reversal: Turning a positive image into a negative. Many video cameras have a built-in image reverse feature.

Impedance: Measure of electrical resistance of microphones, loudspeakers etc.

Insert shot: Another name for the cutaway shot.

Insert edit: Editing process which transfers audio and video signals of each sequence in the edit order onto a previously blacked tape. The control track is not disturbed, so there is no picture disturbance at the edit points.

Introductory shot: Shot that introduces the content of the video, unlike an establishing shot which establishes place. A video report on a local butcher might feature an introductory shot of sides of meat.

Iris: Mechanical part of a lens which controls the amount of light passing through to the image tube or pick-up. The size of this 'hole' (**aperture**) varies according to the brightness of the image. Automatically controlled in all home video cameras although some cameras have a manual override.

J

Jack: Connector, usually used for audio signals. There are two types in common use – the 3.5mm and quarter-inch jacks.

Jump cut: Two shots cut together which are obviously of the same time and place, but with a section missing that causes the image to jar or jump. These jumps are usually disguised with a **cutaway** shot.

K

Kelvin: The unit in which **color temperature** is expressed.

Key light: The principle source of illumination when lighting a subject giving it shape and form.

L

Lens: Complex arrangement of shaped optical glass elements, that enable an image to be focused on the video camera's pick-up tube.

Lip-sync: Sound synchronized to images of a person speaking.

Location: A place where you are recording that is not usually used for making a video.

Lux: Measure of light intensity. Also found in camera specifications where it tells the user the minimum illumination needed for satisfactory video pictures. Sunlight can be many thousand lux, ordinary room lighting is around 50 lux, candlelight 10 lux.

Luminance: Part of the video signal which carries the information that indicates how bright all the various parts of the image are.

M

Macro: Feature of camera lens that allows extreme close-ups.

Magenta: Complementary color to primary green. Magenta is a mixture of red and blue.

Master shot: Shot of a whole sequence of the video that captures all the action in one take. If anything is missed in the close-up or other shots, there is always something in the master shot which can be used in the final edit.

Medium close-up (MCU): Shot that shows the head and shoulders of a subject.

Microphone (mic): Device that turns sound waves into electrical signals.

Mixer: Piece of electronic equipment used to combine several sound sources and give one composite output. A vision mixer will do the same thing for several video sources.

Medium long shot (MLS): Shot that shows the subject from around the knees upwards.

Monitor: TV set used during shooting to see exactly what is recorded on tape.

Monochrome: 'Black and white', when applied to video equipment.

Monopod: Single collapsible leg used to add additional support to a handheld camera.

Motivated sound: Sound which could be expected to be heard in a scene. For example, traffic noise with a shot of a street scene.

Medium shot (MS): Shot that shows the subject from the waist upwards.

Multi-image filter: Add-on lens (screws onto existing camera lens) that splits the scene into several kaleidoscopic images.

Multi-tracking: Method of sound recording which allows you to lay down a number of tracks and then mix them into one stereo or mono soundtrack.

Mute shot: Shot that only captures the visual aspect of the subject. Sound is either not recorded or discarded in editing.

N

Noise: Any unwanted part of a signal. In an audio recording noise is actually heard – tape hiss, circuit hum, whistles and pops. In a video recording, the noise is seen as 'snow' and graininess in the picture as well as flashes and diluted colors.

NTSC: National Television Standards Committee: Color TV system developed in the USA. Also used in Japan and parts of Central and South America and the Far East.

O

Omnidirectional: Pick-up pattern of a microphone that 'hears' everything around it.

Oxide: Magnetically sensitive material bonded to the plastic backing of a recording tape. The most common oxide is a ferric (iron) type but chrome oxides are often used.

P

PAL: Phase Alternate Line. Color TV system used in most parts of Europe and British-influenced countries.

Pan: Moving shot that consists of the camera swinging about its vertical axis.

Photoflood: Lamp used primarily in still photography. The photoflood bulb is similar to the domestic light bulb except that it is 'driven' a lot harder. It gives maximum brightness at the expense of shorter life.

Polarization: Light is an electromagnetic radiation that renders things visible. As a radiation it can be thought of as a wave motion, vibrating in all directions. Polarization causes light to vibrate only in one direction.

Polarizing filter: Used to polarize light entering the camera lens. By doing so reflections can be reduced and skys can be made to appear darker.

Polar response (pick-up) pattern: Diagram showing the area around a microphone in which it will pick up sound. There are three patterns – **omnidirectional, unidirectional and cardioid**.

Post-dub: To add sound after shooting has taken place, usually in the editing stage.

Post-sync dubbing: Adding **lip-sync** sound in the editing stage after the visual images have been recorded.

Point of view (POV): The camera may take a particular character's point of view for a shot.

Producer: Person who oversees a whole video or film project, finding locations, arranging everything and generally making sure that the production runs smoothly.

Production assistant: General assistant who carries out any and all jobs that aren't specifically assigned to others.

Q

QH: Short for Quartz Halogen – a particular form of light source that gives out an intensely bright light for a physically small size of bulb.

R

Racking focus: Technique where there are two objects in the image. Initially one is in focus, the other is not. Racking focus means changing the focus of the lens so that the first object goes out of focus and the other comes into focus.

Radio mic: Microphone with an integral radio transmitter. Allows a subject to be miked up to the recorder without the need for trailing cables.

Reaction shot: A shot which shows a subject's reaction to action.

Redhead: Trade name that has acquired a general meaning for a particular form of 850W QH movie light.

Refractive filter: Attaches to the camera lens and causes bright point sources of light to give off brightly colored fringes.

Reverberation: Multiple short echoes. They are not heard as distinct sounds but give a room an impression of being 'live'. Reverb can be added electronically to a sound either in the studio or in the editing stage. For this reason most recordings are made with as little original reverb as possible.

RGB: Red, Green, Blue – the primary colors of TV. In TV systems the image is broken down into these three colors and the three signals are known as the RGB signals. When connecting together video equipment it is sometimes possible to link the separate RGB signals before they are turned into a single composite video signal, thus avoiding a certain loss in quality.

Roller caption: Lettering on a long strip of material which is wound in front of the camera on parallel rollers, so that the words are seen to move across the screen horizontally or vertically.

Rostrum camera: Camera set-up used to record still images – captions, maps, diagrams, flat artwork, etc.

S

Scouting: A detailed survey of a shooting location to note such things as lighting, access (including looking at potential shooting positions), permission, power sources and sources of noise interference.

Shot: A shot is the name given to a complete uninterrupted sequence between starting the camera and stopping it again. The shot may include movement such as a pan or zoom or it may be completely stationary.

SECAM: Sequence Avec Memoire – TV system developed by the French and used in many parts of Eastern Europe, the USSR and some Middle Eastern countries.

Sensitivity: Measure of how well a piece of equipment will respond.

Sibilance: Sound fault where hissy sounds, especially S sounds, are given undue prominence.

Signal-to-noise ratio: Proportion of wanted signal to unwanted or **noise** signal. Signal-to-noise (s/n) ratios are measured in dB. Can be applied to audio or video signals. A good domestic video camera will give around 45dB video s/n although you would expect 55 to 60dB from a professional camera. A domestic video recorder will give around 40dB as the audio s/n ratio although this rises to over 60dB for hi-fi recorders.

Soft focus: Image with softened edges, usually using a soft focus or diffusion filter.

Solarization: Massive overexposure of the image causing artificially bright areas of pure white and intense shadows with color fringing.

Sound editor: Person in a video crew responsible for assembling the soundtrack from both sync sound and separate sound sources such as effects and music.

Snoot: Conical lamp attachment which confines the light beam to a very small area.

Star filter: Attaches to the camera lens and causes bright point sources of light to give off rays, the number of which is determined by the design of the filter.

Still frame: A feature of a video recorder which allows you to display one frame of the recording on the screen.

Storyboard: Visual description of the video program made before shooting. It shows a series of thumbnail drawings, each one giving a visual representation of a shot, with accompanying notes and directions.

Super 8: Cine film gauge originally intended for the amateur market, but also used by specialist and independent film makers. Can provide a means of generating certain images that are impossible using video.

Swish pan: Another name for **whip pan**.

Sync: Short for synchronous or synchronized.

Sync sound: Sound that must exactly match images on the screen. **Lip-sync** is the most obvious example. The sound of someone speaking must match exactly the movement of their lips, if the lips are in shot.

Sync pulse: Part of the video signal that tells the TV set where on the video signal the start of each frame comes. If the sync pulse is missing the pictures will not be stable or may not appear at all. If you are using a vision mixer, all the cameras feeding into that mixer must be in sync. This can be achieved if one of the cameras has a **gen lock** facility which will lock all the cameras together, or by feeding all the cameras from one external sync source. The same applies to video recorders used in a professional edit suite, although in their case the video signals coming from them are modified using a **time base corrector**.

T

Take: Each attempt at getting a shot right is called a take.

Telecine: Equipment used to transfer cine film to television. Can be very complicated or simply the process of projecting an image on a wall and recording it with a camera.

Tilt: Camera movement in a vertical plane. The camera is tilted about its horizontal axis.

Time base corrector: Device that can compensate for the differences in the video signal control tracks coming from different recorders. With corrected signals it is possible to connect two recorders to a vision mixer, so that **fades** and **dissolves** can be carried out.

Tracking: This has two completely different meanings. In the video recorder, the tracking mechanism ensures that the replay head always picks up the whole of the video signal including the sync signals. Adjustment can be made to compensate for the differences between recorders. In camera shots, a tracking shot occurs when the camera and its mount are physically moved from one spot to another. For complete stability and smoothness the camera and tripod can be mounted on a wheeled platform which then runs along specially laid tracks. Unlike a **dolly shot** where wheels are attached to the bottom of the tripod, which is then wheeled across the floor.

Transient: Literally the word means 'short-lived', but is often used to refer to a very short-lived fluctuation or sudden surge in any cable carrying an electrical current.

Treble: Those frequencies or 'notes' that occur at the high end of the audio frequency band.

Tripod: Sturdy three-legged stand upon which the camera is mounted. The actual camera platform or head can move from side to side (**pan**) or up and down (**tilt**). This head is damped so that the movements are smooth and jerk-free. The head may be damped either by fluid or friction.

Tungsten: Material from which most lamp filaments are made. Tungsten has a **color temperature** of 3200K, to which all cameras working under these lights are balanced.

Two shot: Shot that involves two persons.

U

U-Matic: A semi-professional video format using ¾-inch tape. Devised by Sony, from which was developed Betamax.

Unidirectional: Pick-up pattern of a microphone which picks up sounds from only one direction.

V

VCR: Adopted as a standard abbreviation for video cassette recorder. Also the trade name of the first domestic video cassette format.

VHS: Video cassette format using ½-inch tape. Now dominant in most of the world.

VHS-C: A compact variation of VHS developed for use in all-in-one camcorders. This is a cassette the size of a packet of cigarettes containing 30 minutes worth of VHS tape. When put in a special adaptor it can be played on any standard VHS-format recorder.

V2000: Cassette format developed by Philips to replace VCR. Has several advantages over VHS and Beta – it can be used on both sides like an audio cassette and the machines employ 'Dynamic Track Following' which gives interference-free slow motion and still frame. Format is now confined to West Germany and a small number of other European countries.

Video 8: Latest video cassette format to be launched. Developed by Sony and has widescale backing. The cassette itself is a little smaller than an audio cassette and uses evaporated metal tape. Other features include hi-fi sound as standard and twin speed recording.

Vignette: Shot which consists of the main image seen through a shaped cut-out, such as a key hole or binocular shape.

Voice-over: Commentary or other recorded voice which is dubbed onto a video tape.

W

Walking and looking room: If you have a shot in which the subject is either walking across the frame or looking across it, then there must be space on that side of the frame into which the subject is looking. This means that if a subject is looking to the left of the frame then the subject must be in the right-hand side of the frame with room for him to 'look' on the left-hand side. Similarly if the subject is walking right to left then he should be followed so that the subject is kept in the right-hand side of the frame.

Wallpaper shot: General shot which is recorded 'ad-lib' at the time of shooting and inserted in editing as a filler.

Whip pan: Pan in which the camera is moved very quickly.

Wild track or sound: Soundtrack not synchronized to the pictures. May be sound that is recorded at the same time as the pictures or can be dubbed on at the editing stage.

Wipe: Process of moving from one shot to another where the changeover follows a pattern or patterned edge. You might see the new image grow out of a circle in the middle of the old one or the new image might have a straight or jagged edge which is swept across the screen.

Wow: Slow rate fluctuations in the tape playback speed. These can be heard as a rhythmic change in the pitch of the sound. Wow is expressed as a percentage and is often quoted with the **flutter** specification.

Writing speed: Relative tape-to-recording-head speed. The faster the writing speed, the more information can be put on the tape – so quality is better. Video recorders achieve a high writing speed as although the tape is moving very slowly through the machine it is wrapped around a drum which rotates at high speed, so the heads actually pass over the tape very quickly.

Z

Zoom lens: Lens with an adjustable focal length. Can be varied from wide-angle to telephoto. This variation can be carried out while the recorder is running (zooming) and most cameras have a motorized zoom mechanism to ensure a smooth transition between focal lengths.

READING & VIEWING

The books

Equipment:
Using Videotape – J.F. Robinson and P.H. Beards – Focal Press
On Camera – Harris Watts – BBC Publications
Sound Recording – David Tombs – David and Charles
The Work of the Motion Picture Cameraman – Freddie Young and Paul Petzold – Focal Press

Technique:
On Camera – Harris Watts – BBC Publications
The Work of the Film Director – A.J. Reynertson – Focal Press
Videotape Recording – Joseph F. Robinson – Focal Press
Basic Film Technique – Ken Daley – Focal Press
The Technique of Documentary Film Production – Hugh Baddeley – Focal Press
Independent Film Making – Lenny Lipton – Orbis Publishing

The Inspiration:
Grierson on Documentary – Forsyth Hardy (ed.) – Faber and Faber
Costume References 1 to 10 – Sichel – Batsford
Documentary, A History of the Non-Fiction Film – Erik Barnouw – OUP
The Art of Film – Ernest Lindgren – George, Allen and Unwin
The Technique of Screenplay Writing – Eugene Vale – Souvenir Press
Masters of Light: Conversations with Contemporary Cinematographers – Dennis Schaefer and Larry Salvato – University of California Press

Lorrimer also publish an extensive range of annotated film scripts including *Bonnie and Clyde, The Exterminating Angel, Jules et Jim, The Lady Vanishes* (Hitchcock version), *Battleship Potemkin, The Seven Samurai, The Third Man,* and *Metropolis.*

Post-Production:
The Technique of Film Editing – Karel Reisz – Focal Press
Sound Recording – David Tombs – David and Charles
The World of Animation – Raul de Silva – Eastman Kodak
A User's Guide to Copyright – Michael F. Flint – Butterworth

The films

This is a personal selection of films, all of which have something to teach the amateur director. It's not an exhaustive list and it must be said that you can learn something from critically watching any TV, video or film. We've chosen films rather than specific TV programs because films are available throughout the world, and are usually on video cassette.

The Tempest – directed by Derek Jarman – 1979
An example of how a lot can be achieved with small resources. This was shot within the half dozen or so rooms of a country house using just a few lamps for lighting. The play has been rewritten to work in the claustrophobic atmosphere of these few rooms. The lighting picks out those elements of the frame that are important, while consigning the fringes of the rooms to darkness – disguising their real shape and dimensions. *The Tempest* shows how you can create your own world with just a few lamps and some imagination.

Wetherby – directed by David Hare – 1985
A low-budget film that positively revels in its dark brooding atmosphere. Although there are some flashback scenes to the late 40s, most of *Wetherby* is set in modern times. There are no special sets or locations – they are the sort of places anyone might find – the back yard, the kitchen, the dining room. Lighting is sparse, again restricted to a few lamps and concentrates our attention on the actors. This film is an object lesson in powerful playing and attention to detail.

Kes – directed by Ken Loach – 1969
Any amateur director is going to be confronted with the problem of finding actors who can look good and sound convincing on screen. The star of *Kes* was an untrained 11 year-old local boy – the same material that any amateur could employ in his productions. Mention should also be made of the photography – an object lesson in how to create atmosphere by careful selection of views and angles.

Brief Encounter – directed by David Lean – 1945
There is far more than just an interesting stage-to-screen adaptation in *Brief Encounter*. Riveting performances from Celia Johnson and Trevor Howard show how film acting should be done – understated, economic with all the passion and power coming from within. Nor should we forget David Lean's excellent cinematography. No scene is wasted, and the attention to detail results in a vivid sense of style and period, which is just as strong 40 years on.

Look Back in Anger – directed by Tony Richardson – 1959
Another interesting example of how a stage play can be rewritten into a successful film script. The author and screenplay writer is John Osborne. The most powerful feature of this film version is Richard Burton's performance of the original 'angry young man', but the restructuring of the work is equally fascinating.

Amadeus – directed by Milos Forman – 1984
A play by Peter Shaffer, completely rewritten for the screen by him, with the result that it works extremely well as a film. This seems to confirm that to successfully adapt a dramatic form to a new medium you must re-think the approach – as Coward did in *Brief Encounter* or Osborne did in *Look Back in Anger.*

Koyaanisqatsi – directed by Godfrey Reggio – 1981
A film of images and abstract patterns, all of which come from nature and real life but are arranged and photographed in a totally novel manner. The range and diversity of imagery is too large to describe, but the effect on the home video director must be to encourage a fresh examination of everyday objects, to see how light falls on them, how they relate to other objects, and to find new ways of relating them to other objects.

Night Mail – directed by Harry Watt and Basil Wright, produced by John Grierson – 1936
This documentary shows how seemingly mundane subject matter – the mail train from London to Scotland – can spark off all sorts of interesting ideas, and can be used as a model for any number of amateur videos. By watching how Grierson tackled his subjects you can learn a lot to help make your video documentaries that much more interesting and stylish.

Company of Wolves – directed by Neil Jordan – 1986
Company of Wolves is a set of fairytales – for adults. Shot entirely on indoor sets, creating a world of nursery rhymes, myths and magic, leaning towards the unnerving world of legends. The film tells several different tales based on the short stories of Angela Carter. Although the sets are lavish and special effects equally spectacular there is much that the amateur director can learn from this film in terms of lighting, and the choice of camera angles, which turn a seemingly ordinary room into one that positively reeks of danger.

Television News and Sport
A sweeping topic perhaps but you can learn much about handling impromptu situations by seeing how a news camera crew capture a story. Notice which shots they chose in preference to others when trying to cover a fast-moving story such as a riot or natural disaster, how they frame up a political interview, using perhaps very limited lighting. Notice the edit order and how cutaways are used to hide breaks in the soundtrack.

Sports coverage is similar in that it is fast-moving, but different in that the rules of the game and the playing area are known before the game starts. Notice how fixed cameras are used to give an overall impression of the game and mobile cameras are used close to the action.

INDEX

ACKNOWLEDGEMENTS

Picture credits

Cover: Robert Gibb. **Page 6:** Mary Evans Picture Library. **Pages 6-7:** BBC Hulton Picture Library. **Page 7:** Sony (U.K.) Ltd, Mary Evans Picture Library, Topham Pictures. **Page 8:** Philips, Sony (U.K.) Ltd. **Pages 13-14:** Stuart Dollin. **Page 15:** Woodmansterne. **Page 16:** Stuart Dollin. **Page 19:** Tony Stone Photolibrary, Michael Little. **Page 22:** Macmillan Intek Ltd. **Page 25:** Sony (U.K.) Ltd, Panasonic U.K. Ltd, JVC U.K. Ltd. **Page 26:** Michael Little, TDK U.K. Ltd, Philips. **Page 39:** Michael Little. **Page 45:** Michael Little, Stuart Dollin. **Pages 46-49:** Stuart Dollin. **Page 49:** SYGMA. **Page 50:** Michael Little, Pictor International. **Page 52:** Tony Stone Photolibrary. **Pages 54-55:** Tony Stone Photolibrary, The Kobal Collection. **Page 58:** The Kobal Collection. **Pages 60-61:** Stuart Dollin, Pictor International. **Page 63:** The Kobal Collection. **Page 64:** Leichner. **Page 65:** Stuart Dollin. **Page 66:** Hoya Filters/Introphoto, Jean Coquin/Cokin Filter System (sepia effect). **Page 67:** Hoya Filters/Introphoto. **Page 68:** Hoya Filters/Introphoto (starburst), Jean Coquin/Cokin Filter System. **Page 71:** Michael Little. **Pages 72-73:** Thames Television Ltd. **Page 74:** Tony Stone Photolibrary. **Page 75:** Stuart Dollin. **Pages 75-76:** Michael Little. **Pages 78-79:** Stuart Dollin. **Page 82:** Stuart Dollin. **Page 84:** The Kobal Collection, Rex Features Ltd. **Pages 84-85:** The Kobal Collection. **Page 85:** M.G.M., The Kobal Collection. **Page 94:** Tony Stone Photolibrary. **Pages 94-95:** Michael Little. **Page 96:** Tony Stone Photolibrary, Michael Little, Anna Fox. **Page 97:** Michael Little, Tony Stone Photolibrary. **Page 98:** Michael Little, Jon Lambert, Tony Stone Photolibrary, Pictor International. **Page 99:** Michael Little, Sony U.K. Ltd. **Pages 100-101:** Redgrave Theatre Farnham, Stuart Dollin. **Pages 102-103:** Redgrave Theatre Farnham. **Page 104:** Stuart Dollin, The Kobal Collection. **Pages 104-105:** The Kobal Collection, The Raymond Mander and Joe Mitcheson Theatre Collection. **Pages 106-107:** Michael Little. **Page 108:** Sally Anne Thompson Animal Photography, Tony Stone Photolibrary. **Page 109:** Chessington Zoo, Tony Stone Photolibrary, A.J. Wood. **Page 112:** Dunlop Slazenger, S & G Press Agency. **Page 113:** Dunlop Slazenger, All Sport. **Page 114:** Michael Little, Tony Stone Photolibrary. **Page 115:** Redgrave Theatre Farnham, Dee Conway, Michael Little. **Pages 116-117:** Tony Stone Photolibrary. **Page 118:** Redgrave Theatre Farnham, Rex Features Ltd. **Page 119:** Zoe Dominic, Danjaq S.A. **Pages 120-122:** Michael Little. **Page 126:** Thames Television Ltd. **Pages 128-129, 131, 135:** Michael Little. **Page 138:** Anna Wood. **Page 139:** Panasonic U.K. Ltd. **Page 142:** Hoya Filters/Introphoto, Jean Coquin/Cokin Filter System. **Page 143:** Quantel Ltd. **Page 147:** Shootsey Animation Ltd/Foote Cone & Belding/Young and Rubicam.

Especial thanks to JVC U.K. Ltd for loaning equipment used in the preparation of this book, also to the Grayling Company/Sony U.K. Ltd for providing photographs and information.

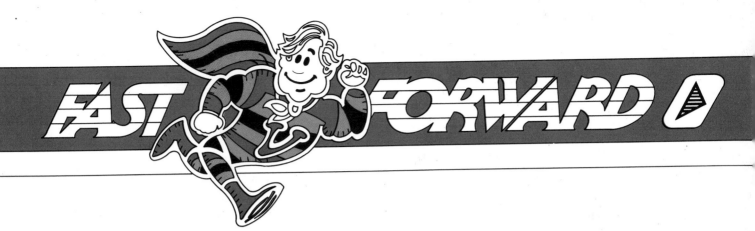

FAST FORWARD

FINAL EDITION

By Doug Fraser

This issue of Fast Forward completes this series of videophile newsletters from "Scotch" Brand videocassettes.

Since its inception, Fast Forward has gathered a loyal and ever increasing following of videophiles who are eager to learn more about the exciting medium of video.

One of the most popular features of Fast Forward has been 'Ask Video Phil', which gave readers the opportunity to get expert answers to their technical questions.

And Fast Forward gave readers the chance to share their often very good ideas with fellow videophiles in the 'Why didn't I think of that?' section. Fast Forward also gave 3M the opportunity to explain some of the more technical aspects regarding the history, manufacture and care of videotape. 3M is proud of the role it has played in the development of videorecording. Since 1956, when network television first used 3M videotape to delay broadcast of a national news program, "Scotch" Brand videotape has become the choice of professional broadcasters, as well as videophiles.

In recognition of its pioneering efforts in the development of videotape, "Scotch" was awarded an "Emmy" by the National Academy of Television Arts & Sciences in September, 1983.

The eight issue series of Fast Forward newsletters have been part of that history. But now, it's time for Video Phil to bid farewell to his readers. Regrettably, issues of Fast Forward have been in such demand that there are no longer any back issues available.

On behalf of Video Phil and "Scotch" Brand videocassettes, 3M Canada Inc., Home Entertainment Products, says thank-you for the interest and support you have shown for Fast Forward.

Scotch™ Brand Videotape Designated Official Videotape of the Olympic Games

3M Scotch Brand videotape has been selected as the "Official" videotape of the 1988 Olympic Games as part of the company's sponsorship of the Winter Games in Calgary and the Summer Games in Seoul.

As a "Worldwide Sponsor" of the Olympic Games, 3M will be allowed to promote "Scotch" Brand videotape and several other products as "Official Products" in most world markets.

3M will provide magnetic recording media to Olympic committees and set up technical centres at the Winter and Summer Olympic Games to provide service support for broadcasters at the Games.

The company will also provide various other products including: "Thinsulate" thermal insulation for the uniforms worn by more than 6,000 officials and many athletes at the Winter Games and; reflective sheeting for outdoor signs.

John Myser, President of 3M Canada calls 3M's association with the Olympics "a natural" because it links a competitive global company with the premier global sports competition.

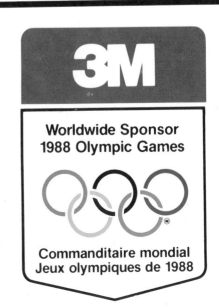

3M

**Worldwide Sponsor
1988 Olympic Games**

**Commanditaire mondial
Jeux olympiques de 1988**

(M) Official Mark of the Canadian Olympic Association
Marque officielle Association olympique canadienne

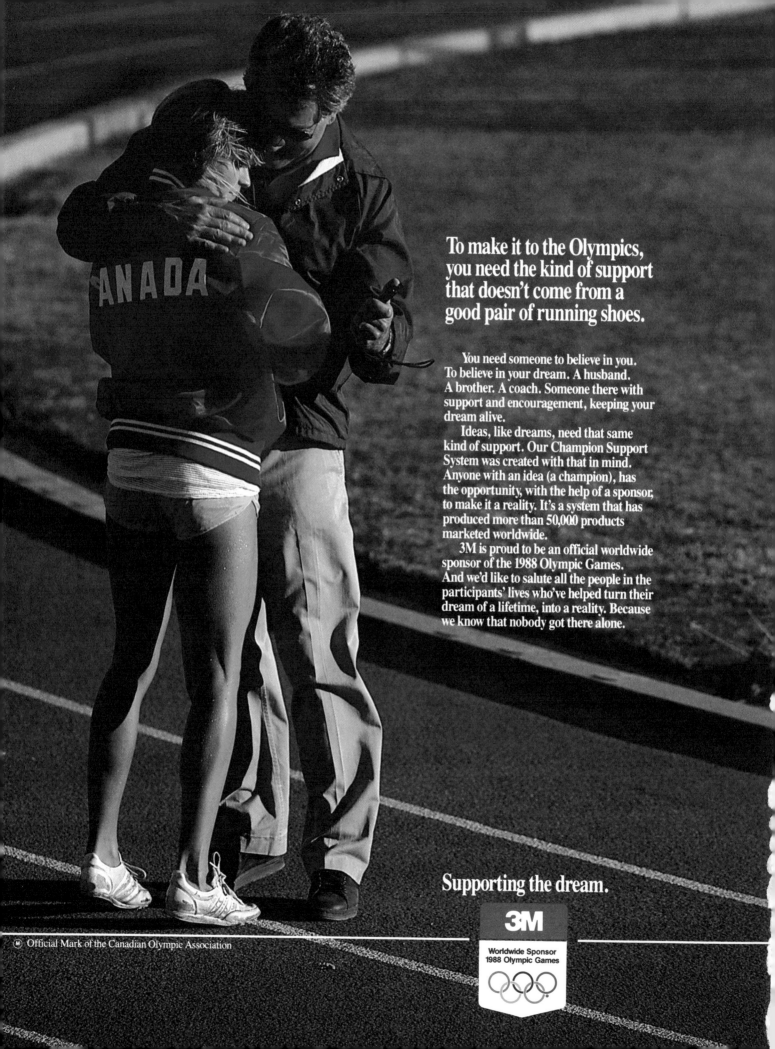

TECHNICALLY SPEAKING

by George Pucula

The home video market is a fast changing industry. New formats are continually being introduced and help confuse the consumer wishing to purchase his/her first or second machine. In this last technical article we will provide an overview of some of the new formats and leave a few words of wisdom to help you get the most out of your video recording.

The major formats available are Beta, VHS and 8 mm. Beta was the first commercially successful home video recorder introduced in 1975 by SONY. In 1976, JVC introduced the VHS format to compete with Beta. Super Beta was introduced in 1985 and offered improved picture signal. VHS HQ was then introduced and also improved video picture quality. The VHS-C compact format was introduced by JVC in 1981. The VHS-C offers a much smaller cassette for portable applications and with the use of an adapter offers compatibility with the standard VHS format. In 1983, the 8 mm format specifications were approved by 122 video equipment and software manufacturers around the world.

New formats currently on the horizon are 4 mm and S-VHS. The 4 mm system uses tape designed for the R-DAT system and records video on it. This was shown at the January 1987 Consumer Electronics Show. There is a lot of speculation about the S-VHS format thought to be introduced at the June Consumer Electronics Show 1987. The format is expected to offer much increased video performance.

Now, for a few words of wisdom:

Hi-Fi VCRs offer excellent stereo sound because the audio information is mixed with the video information and recorded at a much faster speed. However, not all stereo machines or tapes have Hi-Fi sound. Before purchasing a machine or tape, make sure it is the type you want i.e. stereo or stereo Hi-Fi.

When purchasing a machine, the first thing that should be done, is to list features you want. The last thing you want to do is to start thinking about features when facing many different VCRs. Many magazines offer annual or semi-annual guides discussing the types of features available. An unprepared shopper may be overwhelmed by the number of options available and purchase a machine that may or may not satisfy their needs.

A VCR is a complicated piece of equipment. Proper care and handling of the VCR and tape is a **must** for trouble-free use of the equipment. No-name or bargain brands of tape should be avoided. They offer an immediate dollar savings, but over the longer term, may induce severe machine damage, loss of recording or damage to other tapes. The short-term bargain is quickly forgotten when a $200 head replacement is required.

The following points are general guidelines that should be followed to increase the performance of tapes:

- **Don't leave video cassettes in direct sun or other hot places.**
- **Don't subject video cassettes to high humidity.**
- **Don't allow the tapes to get dusty or dirty.**
- **Don't store tapes near a magnetic field such as speakers, motors, or transformers.**
- **Store the tapes in an upright position.**
- **Don't leave tapes partially rewound. Rewind completely for storage.**
- **Leave splicing a broken tape to professionals.**
- **Have a periodic service check performed on the VCR by an authorized repair centre.**

Remember, after this article, that video is a dynamic field and its very nature is to make the home entertainment experience exciting. Don't be concerned that there are new formats that are difficult to understand. The field is open to people who buy a machine and simply rent movies to the videophile who reads magazines and books to continually keep up with the new technology. The bottom line is "have fun."

Why didn't I think of that? — Lots of you did...

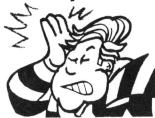

Security

A videotape of personal possessions is accepted by many insurance companies for claims. Walk around your house inside and out taking all possessions into view. Keep the tape in a safety deposit box.

Keep Organized

Program descriptions clipped from the newspaper or TV Guide can be attached to videocassette boxes or 3" x 5" cards as helpful, informative labels.

Kid Stuff

Your child's TV viewing can be upgraded by taping PBS and children's specials to be shown on rainy days or when he/she is home sick.

Audio Dub

Avoid voice-over announcements on closing credits by dubbing in music. Music can also be taped into the blank areas between recordings.

Connections

Hook up your VCR to more than one television with simple antenna splitters.

Labels

"Scotch" Brand Re-Label Tape makes it easy to change titles and has an easy to write on surface.

Tension

Fast forward a new tape before using and then rewind for a more uniform tension.

Sound Effects

Need a police siren, waterfall or fireworks for your audio dubbing? Then visit your local library where LP records are available for loan.

Start Right

Push PAUSE, then PLAY and RECORD. Then release PAUSE when you're ready to record. You'll start fast and clean.

paths around the magnetic core. At the gap, some of the lines spread outside the core to form a "fringing field."

When magnetic tape passes through this fringing field above the gap during recording, the tape is magnetized. This happens because the tape's oxide provides an easier path for the flux than does the non-magnetic gap spacer material on the head.

The resulting magnetic imprints on the tape are an exact magnetic representation of the original images and sound.

The Playback Head

The process just described is reversed in playback.

A playback head detects the magnetic imprints stored on the tape and converts them into magnetic field lines. These are transferred into an electric current which recreates the original images and sounds when fed into a television monitor.

Dropouts and Headclogs

Dirt, dust or loose oxide particles that accumulate on the tape or recorder head create a rough spot that will bounce the tape away from the video head for an instant and cause a momentary loss of magnetic signal. This type of video dropout would appear as a white flash on the television monitor.

Diagram 2 shows the size relationship between dust and dirt particles, a one inch videotape and a video head. As indicated, a spacing loss of only 0.032 mils between the video head and tape will cause a colour dropout. That is about (fraction) the thickness of a sheet of typing paper.

If this dust and debris is allowed to accumulate in the small gap of a video head, the head will clog, impeding the signal from the tape to the head. This causes varying degrees of picture quality loss, from only a minor viewing annoyance to a complete loss of signal when both heads are clogged.

Diagram 3 shows what happens when a video head becomes increasingly clogged with dirt from the tape.

Incidentally, if the problem of clogged video heads is suspected, a video head-cleaning cassette should be used or the unit should be examined by a trained technician. Video heads can be damaged easily by an unskilled hand and they are expensive to replace.

Manufacturers go to great lengths to provide dropout free tape of consistently high quality. However, machine maintenance and clean tape storage are also important to ensure continued satisfaction.

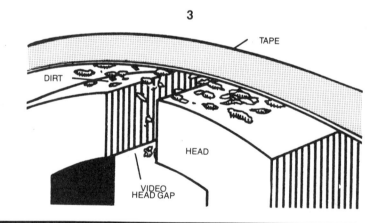

2   A Cross-Section of Debris

VIDEO HEAD

SPACING LOSS NECESSARY FOR COLOR DROPOUT 0.032 MILS

CIGARETTE ASH 0.3 MILS

COTTON FIBER 6 MILS

HUMAN HAIR 3 MILS

DUST 1.5 MILS

ALCOHOL RESIDUE 1.3 MILS

FINGERPRINT 0.62 MILS

OXIDE LAYER 0.23 MILS

1" VIDEO TAPE TOTAL CALIPER 1.18 MILS

3

TAPE

DIRT

HEAD

VIDEO HEAD GAP

How to make your friends disappear.

When you're taping a scene with someone in it, hit the pause button. Then ask the person to leave. Then record again. Use the reverse technique to make someone "pop on" magically.

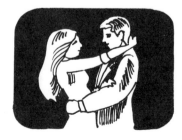
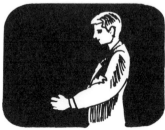

Taking the mystery out of video

This 'technical'' article should be of interest. It takes a straightforward look at how video recorders work, the basics of tape construction, and why minute particles of dirt in the wrong place cause so much trouble.

It starts with magnetism

All magnetic recorders, from the teenager's boom box to the television station's one-inch video equipment, operate on the same basic magnetic principles.

Magnetic recording, whether audio or video, changes images and/or sounds into electronic impulses. These in turn are converted into a magnetic pattern on a moving magnetic surface. Playback is essentially a reversal of the recording process.

Tape construction

Thin plastic tapes are used in all tape recorders (early audio equipment used wire or paper-backed tape). These tapes have a magnetic coating made up of very tiny particles (oxides). In tape manufacture, these particles are dispersed in a thermosetting resin or binder, and this mixture is spread evenly on the surface of the plastic backing as a viscous liquid, which hardens.

The important thing to remember is that each tape coating particle is a tiny permanent magnet embedded in resin so it cannot move.

The Recording Head

The electronic impulses which form the input signal from a camera, TV broadcast, another videocassette recorder or videotape recorder is transferred to magnetic tape by the magnetic recording head. While the actual appearance of magnetic heads differs widely, diagrams 1A and 1B show their basic form. This is the same whether looking at recording or playback heads, or a single head used for both functions.

As shown in the diagrams, heads are simply a coil of wire wound on a magnetic core, with a non-magnetic gap formed by cutting out a small section of the core. Ideally, the record gap should be as wide as possible (1-10 mils) to allow as much magnetic flux as possible across it. The reason should be clear in a moment.

When an electric current passes through the coil, magnet field lines corresponding to the current follow

1A

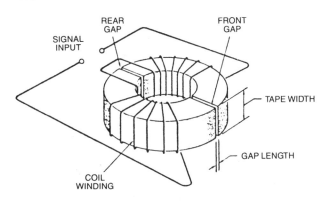

Construction of a recording head.

1B

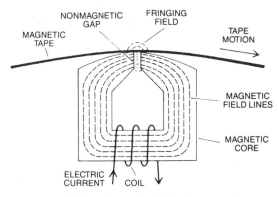

Schematic respresentation of a magnetic recording head.

World Television Standards

Have you ever received a tape from England or Australia and when you played it were disappointed by a blank screen?

The reason is that there are different systems used to broadcast TV signals. The three main systems are NTSC, PAL and SECAM and these systems are incompatible.

Canada operates on the NTSC system as does the U.S., Japan and most countries in the West. The PAL system is used in some parts of Europe, Africa and Australia. SECAM is a French system used in parts of Europe and Africa.

Sending a **blank** videocassette is not a problem as BETA and VHS formats have been standardized.

If you have a tape recorded on a different system it **is** possible to convert it to ours. There are services now available that perform this conversion.

The best of "Ask Video Phil"

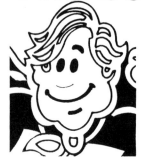

Should I unplug my VCR while I am on vacation?

It is not necessary to disconnect your VCR while on vacation. The power used to run the clock is miniscule, in fact, less than the power used by an "instant on" TV. Besides, if you have a multiday programmer, you may want to record programs while you're gone.

Today's electronic devices, VCR's included, are not affected by the usual voltage strikes caused by distant lightning. However, a direct hit to your television antenna would probably damage both your TV and VCR if connected though chances of lightning striking a TV antenna are rare.

Lots of readers asked how to eliminate the "snow" at the beginning and end of movies...

The simplest solution I have seen to the clean beginning and happy ending problem is to use the camera/TV switch.

When you want a blank section, put the machine in record and put the switch into the camera mode. Since there is no input, a blank signal will be recorded. Remember to put the machine into TV again after recording the blank portion.

Is it possible to connect an 8 mm sound movie camera to a VCR?

A video camera converts picture information to electrical information and feeds it to the VCR. A movie camera places picture information onto a piece of film which is later developed. The answer, therefore, is no, the systems are totally incompatible.

Some video stores now have the capability of converting your super 8 home movies to video.

How many times can you play and record on a tape before the quality of the picture is effected?

If the VCR is maintained properly, the tape will last forever. The same videocassette can be used over and over hundreds of times without any loss of quality or performance.

Why does a picture get grainy when duplicating tapes, ie. original copy to 1st duplicate copy?

There are two factors involved when considering loss of picture quality. There is video noise generated by the machine which makes the picture grainy and causes colour streaking and there is also the fact that you are copying defects that are already on the original tape, ie. dropouts and poor tuning.

8705RD1213E

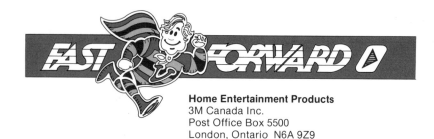

Home Entertainment Products
3M Canada Inc.
Post Office Box 5500
London, Ontario N6A 9Z9

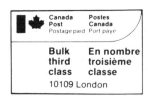

Canada Post	Postes Canada
Postage paid	Port payé

Bulk third class — **En nombre troisième classe**
10109 London

```
ID#3424
Ms. S. Leet
601-2515 Bathurst St.
Toronto, ON    M6B 2Z1
```